THE FUTURE INFORMATION REVOLUTION IN THE USSR

Edited by Richard F. Staar

CRANE RUSSAK & COMPANY
A Member of the Taylor & Francis Group
New York•Philadelphia•Washington, DC•London

USA Publishing Office:	Crane Russak & Company 3 East 44th St., New York, NY 10017
Sales Office:	Taylor & Francis · Philadelphia 242 Cherry St., Philadelphia, PA 19106-1906
UK	Taylor & Francis Ltd. 4 John St., London WC1N 2ET

The Future Information Revolution in the USSR

Copyright © 1988 Crane, Russak & Company

First published 1988
Printed in the United States of America

Library of Congress Cataloging in Publication Data

The Future information revolution in the USSR/Richard F. Staar,
  editor.
         p.   cm.
    Papers from a workshop sponsored by Hoover Institution on War,
Revolution, and Peace at Stanford University.
    Bibliography: p.
    Includes index.
    ISBN 0-8448-1557-8
    1. Electronic data processing--Soviet Union--Congresses.
2. Computers--Soviet Union--Congresses.   I. Staar, Richard F.
(Richard Felix), 1923-   II. Hoover Institution on War,
Revolution, and Peace.
QA76.F88   1988
004'.0947--dc19   88-10901
                                                                   CIP

Contents

1

INTRODUCTION

Richard F. Staar

In the words of U.S. Secretary of State George Shultz, communist leaders "face an agonizing choice: they can either open their societies to the freedoms necessary for the pursuit of technological advance, or they can risk falling even farther behind the West."[1] Why is the information revolution of vital importance to the USSR, and why might its development pose a threat to the regime?

Soviet economic productivity, and indeed its military capabilities, would be enhanced by the successful large-scale introduction of computers. On the other hand, widespread access to information technology, as well as automatic and ready transfer of data, have the potential for undermining the communist party's ability to rule in the way it has done over the past seven decades.

The USSR has shown itself able to adopt a variety of modern technologies while managing to resist the kind of change that usually emanates from their introduction. The regime maintains control over broadcasting, printing presses, and even copiers.[2] Hence, the impact of advanced data processing on the USSR is anything but self-evident. Perceptive analysts in the West have noted the computer's potential also for monitoring the performance of workers, recording who communicates with whom, noting who goes where, and so on. "The leaders of closed societies. . .are afraid that information technologies will undermine the state's control over its people—what they read, watch, hear, and aspire to."[3]

In other words, like all technology, modern data processing may be put to a variety of uses. Soviet government and industry already have priority, the highest being allocated to military production for computer-dependent hardware like that in the newest SA-12 surface-to-air anti-missile system. It is obvious that the USSR wants to bring other sectors of the economy up to world standards in science and technology.

The current five-year plan calls for 1.1 million personal computer units to be produced by the end of 1990, some one-half million to be made available for the eight million students in the ninth and tenth grades. However, the Soviet Union in 1987 numbered its personal computers in the tens of thousands, whereas more than 20 million were in use throughout the United States.[4] This comparison provides some idea of the difference between the two countries.

According to an unclassified U.S. intelligence report, the mid-1990s will be critical for the USSR in its attempts to close the information technology gap with the West. It is suggested that the Soviet leadership will attempt to exert tight political control over economic decentralization. If this prediction holds true, one can expect the year for catching up with the West to recede even further into the future.[5]

Finally, the potential future widespread availability of VCRs and personal computers will not necessarily lead to more freedom in the Soviet Union. Although an estimated 300,000 foreign-made VCRs reportedly exist in the country, they are used primarily by the urban elite for entertainment purposes. Personal computers represent even less of a threat, due to their smaller numbers and lack of hard-disk storage capability. Modems are nonexistent and link-up with printers is rare.[6]

Outlook for Computers

The key to success in educating the current generation of Soviet youth involves the production of personal computers (PC). The first Agat PC intended for schools, produced in 1984, had to be withdrawn in early 1987 because of deficiences. Two new models, called Korvet and Kvant, by the end of that year had not entered mass production.[7] The net result is that only about 1,000 classrooms in the 60,000 secondary schools of the USSR are able to offer hands-on instruction with about 15,000 domestic BK-0010 computers. Another 40,000 PCs were slated for manufacture during 1987, most of them for schools.[8]

Even if one million personal computers could be produced through the end of 1990, the need is for 28 million, according to Boris M. Naumov, who directs the Inter-branch Scientific-Technical Complex (MNTK), Personal Computers. Dr. Naumov, in the same interview, suggested as a solution joint ventures with capitalist companies that would provide access to advanced technology.[9]

The Soviet Union already relies upon its East European client states for computer aid. Under an existing division of labor, Bulgaria exports disks and electronic components; Czechoslovakia specializes in peripherals and components; East Germany produces microcircuits and magnetic tape units; Hungary makes minicomputers, terminals, and computer software; Poland manufactures microcomputers, licensed printers, ferrite main memories, and tape casettes—all for the USSR. Romania alone barely satisfies its own domestic market.[10]

The USSR also has difficulty in completing the introduction of computer-based automated enterprise management systems (ASUPs) which, after two decades, operate in fewer than 8.4 percent of the 44,000 Soviet industrial enterprises. If the present rate is maintained at introducing some 200 to 300 ASUPs per year, only 25 percent of the plants will have them by the end of the twentieth century.[11] Nevertheless the USSR has been successful with automated control systems for technological processes, for example, to run steam generators at power plants.

The centralized system in the Soviet Union represents an obstacle to innovation and industrial experimentation. A symposium of NATO experts, held at Brussels, concluded that lack of incentive is not conducive to creative and enthusiastic work under Soviet conditions.[12] Furthermore, a pervasive atmosphere of secrecy within the USSR restricts dissemination of data and isolates most of the indigenous computer scientists from their Western counterparts. Not only are regime limitations imposed on international exchanges, but they also extend to scientific and technical literature, which is difficult to obtain because of small publication runs. A further impediment is the regulation that all computers must be institutionally based and, thus, tightly controlled. Soviet leaders may not recognize the costs they are paying for such a policy.[13]

Future of the Information Revolution

It would appear that USSR decision-makers will not loosen control over the system to the extent of risking that computers may be used for potentially "counterrevolutionary" purposes. Without relaxation, how can the Soviets expect to narrow the lag in microcomputer hardware? The CMEA "comprehensive program of scientific and technological progress to the year 2000" covers production of mainframes, minicomputers, and PCs. If the USSR does not meet its target of 1.1 million microcomputers by the end of 1990, under the current five-year economic plan, the short-fall could be made up in part through imports from Japan and/or the West. This will require hard currency, which represents another problem. In the field of turnkey operations, that is, construction of complete plants, a spokesman for Hewlett-Packard[14] suggests that American firms will be unwilling to become involved.

On the other hand, the development of a Soviet supercomputer already had been mentioned several years ago. The PS-2000 (one model of several PS-X00 machines), for example, had the goal to achieve 200 million operations per second[15] for vector processing in applications such as seismic analysis in the petroleum industry. It was not until April 1985 that a 155-member task force began work on a multiorganizational project, and after two years reportedly produced the MARS-M miniprocessor with a claimed speed of 20 million operations per second[16] as well as the Kronos processor, both part of a fifth-generation machine. The fastest Japanese (SX-2) and American (Cray Y-MP) supercomputer each performs over one billion mathematical calculations per second.[17] This competition obviously will continue, with almost 300 supercomputers already installed by five companies in the United States and Japan. See Table 1.1 for USSR developments.

Conference at Stanford

A workshop was sponsored in 1987 by the Hoover Institution on War, Revolution and Peace at Stanford University.* Professor Seymour E. Goodman presents the first paper (Chapter 2), which is based on his model of a Soviet-style information society. Elements include centrally formulated goals, driving forces, systemic conditions, development and application of command/control. The author suggests USSR commonalities with the United States regarding time pressure, more rapid communications, and politico-economic applications.[18]

Drs. Richard W. Judy and Jane M. Lommel continue their earlier research about the origins of educational computing in the USSR in Chapter

---

*We wish to thank the John M. Olin program on Soviet and East European studies for its generous support, which made the conference sessions possible. All but two of the scholars represented in this book were able to attend the weekend of meetings.

Table 1.1

Soviet Computers by Generation

I. First Generation:
   1951–58, U.S.
   Vacuum tubes used in electronic circuits
   Slow speed
   Limited main-storage capacity
   Magnetic drum used for internal storage
   Soviet examples: BESM-2, Strela, M-3, Minsk-1, Ural-1, the Ural-2, and
      the M-20
   U.S. examples: IBM 650, UNIVAC I

II. Second Generation:
   1959–64, U.S.
   Increased speed
   Differentiated applications
   High level program languages such as COBOL and FORTRAN
   Magnetic core internal storage
   Faster input/output
   Soviet examples: Minsk-2, Razdan-2, Razdan-3, M-220, BESM-4,
      BESM-6, MIR, NAIRI, Minsk-22, Minsk-32, and the Ural 14
   U.S. examples: IBM 1401, Honeywell 200, CDC 1604

III. Third Generation:
   1965–71, U.S.
   Integrated circuits
   Magnetic core and solid state storage
   Disk-oriented
   Minicomputers introduced
   Time-sharing
   Operating system programs that control functions previously requiring
      human operators
   Soviet examples: YeS EVM series (unified series), SM EVM series (small
      system series), ASVT-M, KTS LIUS, AVK
   First year of production in Soviet Union: 1972
   U.S. examples: IBM System/360, NCR 395, Burroughs B6500

IV. Fourth Generation:
   1971–present, U.S.
   Large-scale integrated circuits
   Modular design
   Compatibility between hardware from different manufacturers
   Microprocessors and microcomputers
   Greater versatility, sophistication
   Soviet examples: YeS-1077 under development since 1982
   U.S. examples: IBM 3033, Burroughs B7700, HP 3000

V. Fifth Generation:
   (research underway)
   Artificial intelligence

Table 1.1
continued

Capable of learning
Capable of conversing in natural language
Soviet examples: Research begun on the MARS (modular asynchronous
    expandable system) in 1985

Sources: Articles in the Soviet press from which table was prepared by *USSR Technology Update* (April 23, 1986), p. 3.

3. Instruction began in middle schools as of fall 1986, with labs comprising between 12 and 13 computers networked to a teacher's workstation. Because of the lack of educational software and the emphasis on programming, students in grades eight and nine learn an algorithmic approach to computing.[19] Judy and Lommel also focus on the dynamics of introducing computers into classrooms: the rush of teacher training, the push to buy and build appropriate computers for education, and the philosophical differences among educators about the emphasis on algorithms versus computer-assisted instruction and word processing. The chapter ends with some predictions about the directions that the Soviets may take with educational computing.

Dr. Richard B. Dobson deals with the impact of computers on higher education, concentrating on the new specialized institutes for "informatics," a term that means information technology (Chapter 4). The importance attached by the Soviet government to this field can be seen from the appointment in October 1986 of G. I. Marchuk, a mathematician and computer specialist, to become president of the USSR Academy of Sciences. He will presumably watch over developments in his own area of expertise.[20]

Ross A. Stapleton and S. E. Goodman elaborate on the likely Soviet response to the revolution in personal computers in Chapter 5. They mention the purchase of 10,000 PC compatible machines from Japan, which were suitable for unsophisticated games. Personal computing in the USSR is examined through four stages of the technology, from design to incorporation of systems into the economy. A comparison is also made of the pervasiveness of personal computing in the Soviet Union with the levels achieved in the West.[21] Many of the initial attempts to develop PCs for mass production have failed, and it remains to be seen whether USSR industry can coordinate all of the necessary components, from technological innovation to service, which would make the PC a useful tool in the economy. Eastern Europe and the West itself may play an increasingly important role in helping the Soviet Union to overcome its deficiencies.

An integral component of the information revolution is the rapid exchange of data via computer networks. Professor William K. McHenry (Chapter 6) considers the full spectrum of networking activities in the USSR, ranging from management applications on a macroeconomic level to connections between robots[22] and machine tools as a part of factory automation. He concludes that networking applications represent a stage of sophistication in computing that the Soviets for the most part have not reached. He examines the prospects for growth in demand for computing in light of Gorbachev's round of economic reforms.

The computer's role in restructuring the economy is discussed by Professor Thomas H. Naylor, who deals with computer simulation models (which had been done several years before Gorbachev), gaming, and the future of Soviet management education (Chapter 7). He also outlines the ten specific strategies for implementing the current radical economic reform.

Computer-integrated manufacturing (CIM) is looked upon by the USSR as the key to improved productivity and efficiency in the machine building industry. Dr. Richard W. Judy (Chapter 8) quotes the Soviet leader as stating that "microelectronics, computer technology, instrument making and the entire informatics industry are the catalyst of progress." He suggests that the hierarchy in Moscow may look upon CIM as a technological fix and perhaps underestimate the difficulties of implementing the system throughout industry.

The presentation by Dr. John R. Thomas on scientific-technical performance (Chapter 9) also goes into the relationship of that performance to Soviet military output. He suggests that even now, ahead of the information revolution in the USSR, the science and technology community is unable to meet both civilian and military requirements.[23] This is largely due to the traditional Soviet problem of translating the results of research and development (R&D) into manufacturing production. Until this basic problem has been solved, the USSR cannot significantly enter the information age. Gorbachev's *perestroika* is an effort in part to solve that problem. However, he cannot succeed without basic political reform which he is yet to undertake. Should he do so, he could suffer the fate of Khrushchev who galvanized the government bureaucracy and the Party apparatus which led to his downfall.

The policy implications for the USSR and the United States are discussed in Chapter 10 by Dr. John P. Hardt and Jean F. Boone, who conclude that both countries may be drawn into expanded interaction for different reasons. The coauthors suggest that agreement must first take place on several primary issues before the foregoing development can take place.

Notes

1. George Shultz, "The Shape, Scope, and Consequences of the Age of Information," *Current Policy,* no. 811 (Washington, DC: U.S. Department of State, 1986), p. 3.

2. Inventories of typewriters and duplicating equipment are maintained, with the latter "strictly licensed and housed separately from basic offices." Ambassador Diana Lady Dougan's lecture at The Fletcher School of Law and Diplomacy on February 6, 1986, entitled "The Era of International Communications," p. 10 of transcript.

3. Shultz, "Shape, Scope, and Consequences."

4. William K. McHenry quoted in the *Mercury News* (October 25, 1987), p. 8B; San Jose, CA.

5. Central Intelligence Agency, *The USSR Confronts the Information Revolution* (Washington, DC: Directorate of Intelligence, May 1987), SOV 87-10029, p. 15.

6. Richard B. Dobson, "Communications and Control in the USSR," *Research Memorandum* (Washington, DC: USIA Office of Research, November 24, 1986), p. 9.

7. Interview with V. M. Naumov in *Pravda* (August 20, 1987), p. 2; L. Semenev article about Korvet in *Pravda* (August 26, 1987), p. 2; announcement "S markoi 'Kvant'," in *Pravda* (October 26, 1987), p. 2.

8. *Radio,* no. 6 (June 1987), pp. 6–7; cited by Viktor Yasmann, "Personal Computers in the USSR," *Radio Liberty Research,* Munich (September 23, 1987), RL 338/87, pp. 2–5. The CPSU Central Committee discussed mass production of computers for secondary schools, according to Moscow radio (October 23, 1987), in *Foreign Broadcast Information Service* (October 26, 1987), SOV-87-206, pp. 30–31; henceforth, cited as FBIS.

9. Interview in *Pravda* (August 20, 1987), p. 2. Note that the USSR has amended rules covering joint ventures, although no contracts had been signed with U.S. companies as of Victoria Pope's article in the *Wall Street Journal* (October 27, 1987), p. 31.

10. Seymour E. Goodman, "The Partial Integration of the CEMA Computer Industries," in U.S. Congress, Joint Economic Committee, *East European Economies: Slow Growth in the 1980's* (Washington, DC: U.S. Government Printing Office, 1986), pp. 337–340; *Neues Deutschland* (October 3 and 4, 1987), p. 1; *Die Landwirtschaft des Ostblocks,* 25, no. 10/11 (March 24, 1987), 10; Budapest radio (June 17, 1987), in FBIS (June 19, 1987), EEU, p. 10; *Przeglad*

obrony cywilnej, no. 1 (January 1987), p. 48; and Bucharest radio (September 23, 1987), in FBIS (September 28, 1987), EEU, p. 34.

11. Central Intelligence Agency, *Enterprise-Level Computing in the Soviet Economy* (Washington, DC: Directorate of Intelligence, August 1987), SOV C 87-10043, p. 3. For figures on ASU production from 1971 through 1986, see *Narodnoe khoziaistvo SSSR za 70 let* (Moscow: Finansy i statistika, 1987), p. 86.

12. Craig Sinclair, "Civil Science in the Soviet Union—Report of NATO Symposium," *NATO Review,* 35, no. 1 (February 1987), pp. 20–25.

13. Nicholas Wade, "The Soviet Science Gap," *New York Times* (August 11, 1987), p. A-18; *USSR Confronts the Information Revolution.*

14. Tom Christiansen, manager of international trade relations for Hewlett-Packard, quoted in "Behind the News," *Datamation* (March 15, 1987), p. 56.

15. "Sovetskii superkompiuter," *Argumenty i fakty* (December 25, 1984), p. 6; Moscow.

16. "The Start of VNTK," *USSR Technology Update* (December 2, 1987), pp. 5, 8; Delphic Associates, Falls Church, VA.

17. "Japan's Computer Coup," *Early Warning* (January 1987), pp. 1–2, Mid-Atlantic Research Associates, Washington, DC; "Cray Unveils Powerful Super-computer," *Wall Street Journal* (February 10, 1988), p. 2. The National Aeronautics and Space Administration system can perform up to 1.72 billion computations per second. John Noble Wilford, "Advanced Supercomputer Begins Operation," *New York Times* (March 10, 1987), p. 14.

18. See also Goodman, who elaborates on all four points of his model in "The Information Technologies and Soviet Society: Problems and Prospects," *IEEE Transactions on Systems, Man, and Cybernetics,* SMC-17, no. 4 (July-August 1987), pp. 529–52.

19. G. Chogovadze, "Na svidanie s kompiuterem," *Pravda* (22 January 1988), p. 2.

20. Note his statement over Moscow radio (April 10, 1987); FBIS (April 14, 1987), p. U-9.

21. See also Goodman, "Partial Integration," pp. 329–53; published as a Joint Economic Committee print of the 99th U.S. Congress, 2nd session.

22. Leonid Pisanov, "Robot moloka ne prosit," *Pravda* (October 27, 1987), p. 2.

23. See also John R. Thomas, "Militarization of the Soviet Academy of Sciences," *Survey,* 29, no. 1 (Spring 1985), pp. 29–58; London.

2

INFORMATION SOCIETIES

Seymour E. Goodman

The "national presence" of the information technologies in the USSR differs, both quantitatively and qualitatively, from that in the United States and other large, industrialized Western countries. In this chapter we attempt, explicitly and compactly, to characterize that presence and compare it to its Western counterpart. To this end we start with a brief perspective on the information technologies in the West.

Western-Style Information Societies

There is no universally accepted definition or vision of a Western-style information society, and there probably never will be. Even the term "West" needs to be augmented to keep up with rapidly changing developments in technology and international business. There is now a significant membership from the Far East where several countries have important places as producers and consumers.

Although it is clearly beyond our scope to provide a comprehensive discussion, some loosely defined characteristics of Western-style information societies should prove useful. We consider two basic trends: (1) the pervasive application of the information technologies, and (2) the expanded access to information.

The common denominator of all portraits of Western-style information societies is that a broad spectrum of the information technologies will become part of a large number of products and processes that will be

11

widely distributed throughout all of the major organizational components
of advanced societies: offices, factories, farms, schools, government institutions, and the home. It can be argued that virtually all pervasive, or
potentially pervasive, technologies pass through five roughly defined evolutionary stages:[1]

1. An experimental rarity, often an entrepreneurial or laboratory discovery.
2. An exotic tool or toy used by a small group of experts.
3. Products that are well known and manufactured in modest quantity,
   but direct use is limited to a small fraction of industrial or other
   institutional environments.
4. Widespread production and availability, with direct use requiring
   little or modest training in a broad domain by a sizeable minority
   of the population.
5. The technology has become part of the fabric and infrastructure of
   daily life, and its absence is often more noticeable than its presence.

These five stages involve technology and infrastructure in more general
terms than those often associated with narrow technical developments.
For example, the presence of television at the fifth stage is dependent on
an infrastructure and technology that includes the large and varied number
of network and cable television stations, program listings and reviews in
the printed media, commercialized celebrities, repair services, and the
like. There is also some domain dependence to those definitions. For
example, by its nature computer-aided manufacturing will never attain
household pervasiveness, but it might reach stage four or five pervasiveness in a broad industrial domain.

The second frequently defined feature is the opportunity for much increased access and choice with regard to the range, volume, and time-
liness of information. This feature is often brought up in the context of
greater democratization and decentralization, but this need not necessarily
be so from a purely technical standpoint.

For both trends, three general forms of qualitative advancement in applications might be distinguished. In the first, products or systems do the
same things that people did previously, but faster and more accurately,
for example, hand-held calculators. In the second, they allow new or
much enhanced applications to be developed, for example, the solution
of some previously unapproachable scientific problems or the ability to
control processes in environments where humans cannot work. The third

form brings previously unthinkable or exotic applications; for example, when data, text, voice, and image processing are all integrated, computing and communications (C&C) technologies may serve as greatly augmented senses for humans. A more troublesome form of application is the kind that replaces, rather than augments, human beings.

Other often-cited characteristics are those generally associated with "postindustrial societies," such as the redistribution of the population away from agriculture and toward the service industries, near universal literacy, access to advanced education, and so on. The information technologies are increasingly contributing to the definition and achievement of these characteristics.[2]

A summary of the principal features, systemic conditions, and constraints that characterize our model of a Western-style information society is shown on the left side of Table 2.1.

A Soviet-Style Information Society

Roughly speaking, our model of a Western-style information society is described by general, intensive, somewhat unconstrained and chaotic, and broadly debated and determined progress in many directions and with many essentially independent actors. The Western-style information society is, therefore, best characterized in terms of rapidly emerging major *trends* as outlined above. The trends are a result of driving forces that operate within the constraints and possibilities determined by systematic conditions.

Similarly, our model of a "Soviet-style information society" considers the driving forces, systemic conditions, and constraints that are influencing the evolution of C&C applications in the USSR. The combination of both main Western trends is clearly excluded under these circumstances; so a different compact characterization is necessary. We believe that what is merging in the USSR is best characterized by goals rather than trends. Our analyses of the most important past and current Soviet efforts and sensitivities identify the following four primary goals:[3]

1. To attain real gains in productivity and to modernize the industrial base.
2. To improve the economic planning and control mechanism.
3. To support both military and internal security needs.

4. To present the image of a progressive society both to the people of
the USSR and to the outside world.

We emphasize the importance of all four. They form an irreducible set
in two senses: (1) other goals, such as keeping up with the West or providing selected improvements in education or the standard of living, may
be understood entirely within the context of these four, and (2) none of
the four may be understood entirely within the context of the other three
unless one is prepared to believe (which we do not) that the military
dominates the entire polity. Since the mid-1960s these goals have not
been determined in a simple Stalinist dictatorial fashion, but rather through
a fairly long and multifaceted process involving the participation of a
growing technocratic elite.

We have also identified the most important driving forces, systemic
conditions, and development and applications areas for the Soviet Union.
This enables us to construct a model similar to the one we have for the
West. Both are summarized in Table 2.1.

In our view, the contrast between trends and goals as principal relative
Western-Soviet features is the most pointed short statement that can be
made to illustrate what is happening and how things are happening to the
two kinds of societies. Western progress is chaotic, rapid, highly pluralistic, and relatively unplanned and unconstrained. A mish-mash of a
large number of independent, interrelated, or conflicting goals emerges
in some gross sense in the form of major trends. The trends may themselves be considered overall goals, but they also have the stronger status
of established trends, and so we prefer that term. Soviet progress must
await the cautious consideration and approval of the central authorities,
and suffers from relatively backward production and distribution capacities and options. Soviet goals are comparatively less complex and more
easily enumerated. Soviet trends are comparatively underdeveloped, and
prospects have to be assessed in terms of past performance and goals.

The second most pointed American-Soviet contrast is in the pervasiveness of applications. Each succeeding stage of pervasiveness as defined for the Western-style model is roughly an order of magnitude advance over its predecessor. Many of the information technologies explicitly
or implicitly considered in this book have attained stage four to five pervasiveness in the United States, with many others reaching stages two to
three. Much of this has occurred since 1970. In almost all areas, Soviet
levels are one to two stages lower. Television and radio broadcasting may

Table 2.1
Western/Soviet Information Society Models

Western-Style Information Society

Best characterized by emerging trends:
  pervasive application of the C&C technologies;
  expanded access to information.
Driving forces:
  opportunities for innovations inherent in the C&C technologies;
  large and diversified push-pull markets;
  fierce domestic and international competition.
Systemic conditions:
  little national-level control of social change;
  organizational flexibility;
  relatively weak controls on access to and dissemination of information;
  supports the broad dissemination of controls for economic efficiency, private
  activities, and for more communications of all kinds.
Development and application of the C&C technologies:
  interest in all technology areas;
  technological strength in all areas;
  interest in all applications areas;
  near-universal user community.

Soviet-Style Information Society

Best characterized by centrally formulated goals, to:
  improve industrial productivity and modernize the industrial base;
  improve the economic planning and control mechanism;
  support both military and internal security needs;
  present the image of a progressive society to the people of the USSR and
  the outside world.
Driving forces:
  national-level political processes;
  western achievements.
Systemic conditions:
  powerful national-level controls on social change;
  organizational rigidities;
  strong controls on access to and dissemination of information and lower
  level controls;
  centralized planning and control;
  leadership that distrusts the general population.
Development and application of the C&C technologies:
  interest in most technology areas;
  modest technological capabilities in most areas;
  interest in a relatively small number of applications areas narrowly related to
  goals;
  restricted, semi-isolated, relatively small user communities.

Source: Seymour E. Goodman, "The Information Technologies and Soviet Society: Problems and Prospects," *IEEE Transactions on Systems, Man, and Cybernetics*, vol., SMC-17, no. 4, July-August 1987.

be the one stage five Soviet achievement in the information technologies. Even so, it is a weaker form of stage five than its U.S. counterpart by almost all measures, the most notable exception being the strength and pervasiveness of censorship.

A note on terminology: the term "Soviet-style information society" appears to be an oxymoron since it excludes so much of the Western-style model and since the strict control of information has generally and historically been a strong characteristic of Soviet society. Unfortunately, none of the many other terms used in the West seem more appropriate. The Soviets themselves do not use such a technology-specific term to describe their whole society, although the terms "informatics" and "scientific-technological revolution" are commonly used, but their scope seems more limited than what is covered here. So, by default, we use "Soviet-style information society" and invite the Soviets to supply us with a better term.

Control

A common element that emerges from any serious discussion of broad Western developments of the information technologies is the need and desire to cope with and control increased complexity and opportunities, often under circumstances of intensified time pressure. This is a key factor for which the information technologies offer a wide spectrum of applications. Taken together with other economic and demographic trends, everything in our discussion implies more control possibilities and a more rapid pace of life. The Western systemic environment encourages the broad dissemination of controls for increased economic efficiency, for personal activities, and for greater communications. It may be argued that this has been a historical trend that predates the modern electronic C&C era by many decades.

However, the information technologies themselves also generate additional complexity and opportunities and shortened time scales, sometimes to the point of making human capabilities inadequate. Players who do not keep up with this fast and more-or-less uncontrollable treadmill of technological improvement fall behind in an increasingly competitive world. With more powerful C&C systems, there are often more difficulties integrating them into the surrounding environment. Technology-related pressures and opportunities increasingly dictate how that environment has to be changed.

Moreover, the most important common thread that emerges from our models of both Western- and Soviet-style information societies is the need and desire to improve control over increased complexity and reduced time scales. Even fantasy and entertainment applications may be viewed as a quest for greater control, in this case for building private worlds and of having the control to occasionally escape from the rest of society. Both societies see the information technologies as an increasingly necessary means for the quantitative and qualitative control of demand, production, and distribution. Both see these technologies as means for the control of the dissemination of noneconomic (e.g., political or entertainment) information, for the control of the military and intelligence activities, for increasing the volume and efficiency of communications, and so on. For both societies, there is a strong control element in all these applications, but the emphases and subgoals are often very different. Most of the differences, for example, those that govern access to and the dissemination of noneconomic information, are deeply rooted in the ways that Western and Soviet societies have functioned for many decades.

Nevertheless, it should be noted that both are seeking to use the information technologies for both greater concentration and greater distribution of control, but, of course, in vastly different proportions. The trends in the model of a Western-style information society promote the broad dissemination of controls for increased economic efficiency, for personal activities, and for more communications of all kinds. They also exhibit greater mixed centralization and decentralization of controls in such areas as military command and control and corporate management. Prospective Soviet dissemination of controls is much more limited and focused. There is also a far more important element of political control in Soviet applications. However, there is an increasing realization that more distributed hierarchial control along with limited forms of decentralization, in contrast to the heavy centralization of the past, are necessary and desirable. For example, the Soviets are likely to significantly modify some aspects of their detailed, pervasive, and highly centralized economic planning system.

Clearly, almost all the Soviet goals are subsumed under the Western trends (the most notable exceptions are concerned with state ownership and national centralized planning under goal two), but with differing emphases and different approaches to their achievement.

Notes

1. Modified from J. S. Birnbaum, "Toward the Domestication of Computers," in J. F. Traub (ed.), *Cohabiting with Computers* (Los Altos, CA: William Kaufmann, 1985), pp. 77–95.

2. Y. Masuda, *The Information Society (as Post-Industrial Society)* (Tokyo: Institute for the Information Society, 1980).

3. S. E. Goodman and W. K. McHenry, "Computing in the USSR: Recent Progress and Policies," *Soviet Economy,* 2, no. 4 (1986), pp. 327–54.

3

COMPUTER EDUCATION: AN INTERIM REPORT

Richard W. Judy and Jane M. Lommel*†

Until 1985, not quite a decade after the beginning of the microcomputer revolution, computers were scarce in the Soviet secondary school system. A few elite schools had taught programming since the 1960s, but the vast majority of children remained ignorant about computers. The same was true of their teachers. Few were prepared when the Ministry of Public Instruction announced early in 1985 that a new course entitled The Fundamentals of Informatics and Computer Technology would become obligatory for all middle schools beginning in September.

Several authors discussed the design and early experience of implementing the new computer course.[1] A double issue of a Soviet journal provided a large number of useful materials concerning it.[2] An American observer gave a first-hand impression of the new course in operation.[3] That the new *Informatika* course represents a bold and risky venture in Soviet education is a point that emerges clearly from this earlier literature. Two aspects of the program were identified as critical: (1) the quality and quantity of educational hardware and software available to schools, and

*Paper presented at the annual meeting of the American Association for the Advancement of Slavic Studies, November 5–8, 1987, Boston.
†The views expressed in this chapter are those of the authors alone, who express their gratitude to the National Council for Soviet and East European Research for its financial sponsorship of the research upon which this work is based.

(2) the objectives and curricular design of the new course. And it is with these two aspects that this chapter is concerned.

News from the Hardware Front

At its inception, the *Informatika* campaign found the USSR ill-prepared to provide the schools with enough appropriate computers. This insufficiency had both qualitative and quantitative dimensions. Existing computers were ill-suited for educational usage and, in any case, too few were available.

The qualitative shortcomings of microcomputers for educational computing have created problems. Much of the reason for this involves the lag in developing personal computers (PCs). During the late 1970s, the Ministry of the Electronic Industry designed and began production of a wide assortment of microcomputers bearing the Elektronika trademark. Intended for military and technical civilian usages, these machines were software-compatible with the Soviet SM-3 and SM-4 minicomputers which, in turn, were modeled after the PDP-11 computers first marketed in 1970 by Digital Equipment Corporation.[4]

By early 1985 only one PC model was visible on the Soviet scene. That was the Agat, a clumsy clone of the Apple II.[5] Agat's advantages over the Elektronika were its relative ease of use and the huge library of Apple software obtainable from the West. Its weaknesses were manifest. First, it was obsolete. The Agat 8-bit design dated from the mid-1970s; it was slow and restricted in memory capacity.[6] Second, its shoddy quality has been a constant source of user frustration.[7]

Despite the unsuitability of Agat and Elektronika computers for educational use, several thousand of these machines have been delivered to schools since 1984. The option of importing PCs in massive numbers has been considered. That sparked an ardent if brief courtship of Soviet authorities by several Western and Japanese microcomputer manufacturers, including Apple, Tandy, and Commodore among the American firms. The chronic shortage of hard currency combined with Cocom restrictions and a "buy Soviet" sentiment to squelch the idea of massive computer imports. In the end, a few Japanese computers were imported; the USSR purchased some 4,000 Yamaha machines during 1985–86.[8] The advantages of the Yamaha PCs were their high quality and reliability; the disadvantage was that Soviet school children have been forced to communicate with them in English, the only language that the machines "understand."[9]

During the first two years of the Informatika campaign, this limited number of Yamaha PCs has been augmented in Soviet classrooms by an array of USSR and East European machines. The Agat and the Elektronika BK-0010 have comprised the majority of these.[10] The latter have been supplemented, at the margin, by a few Polish and other machines and by permitting students restricted access to academic or industrial computer centers via remote or local time-sharing terminals.[11]

The preferred arrangement for computers in Soviet schools is in laboratories (*kabinety*), which have from 10 to 13 machines. Students are seated at two-person workstations, and the systems are connected via a local area network to the teacher's desk. Each student workstation is equipped with a computer, a monitor (usually monochromatic), and a keyboard. However, it lacks local disk storage and printing capability. The teacher's workstation differs from the students' by having one or two floppy disk storage drives and a dot matrix printer.[12]

Estimating the numbers of computers operating in Soviet schools is made difficult because the data are scattered and incomplete. Nevertheless, some information is available. In September 1986, for example, some 200 computer laboratories were reported to be operating in Moscow, or in about one-sixth of all middle schools.[13] By the end of 1986, the number of such schools was said to have reached 350, with another 700 slated to be so equipped during 1987. A prominent official prophesied that by 1988 all Moscow schools would be so equipped.[14]

That the schoolchildren in other cities and towns fare usually worse than those in the capital city is evident from the fragmentary data available. Leningraders apparently do rather well; over half of the upper-class students there are said to "have the opportunity for regular interaction with computers."[15] The Sverdlovsk city party secretary reported an inventory of only 40 microcomputers and 1,200 hand calculators in the summer of 1986, although he anticipated the early arrival of 275 "high quality" PCs, enough to equip 27 school computer laboratories.[16] Penza, which is the site of a major computer manufacturing enterprise, does far better with half of its middle schools equipped with computer laboratories by June 1986. Very few rural schools are fortunate enough to have such facilities.[17]

The non-Slavic republics have reported particular difficulties in obtaining computers. To the usual problems of inadequate numbers is added the fact that national languages are seldom "spoken" by the available machines.[18] Armenia reported only 40 computer-equipped schools in late 1986, whereas 250 were required. The Armenians have attempted to remedy their acute shortage by routing an Ikarus bus loaded with 14 PC workstations to Erevan's many computer-deprived schools.[19] A similar initiative in Gagra was frustrated by a fuel shortage and fears of the damage that might be done to the bus and computers.[20] Sixteen laboratories had been organized in Alma Ata by mid-1986, reportedly without computers and even hand calculators; students were said to be computing on their fingers.[21]

The deficiency of computers in Soviet schools has seriously if unsurprisingly impeded the conduct of the new Informatika course. The Minister of Public Instruction, S. G. Shcherbakov, lamented that only 12 percent of all students in the new course were receiving any "hands-on" exposure to computers during the school year.[22] Not until the fourth quarter of 1987 were domestic producers slated to begin delivering the specially designed UKNTs and Korvet school computers (discussed below). Only 58,400 of these machines are scheduled to be received in 1988, enough for 4,500 laboratories. By the end of 1990, the target is for the computer industry to deliver some 400,000 PCs to the schools. By that time, about one-half of the 61,000 Soviet middle schools are to be equipped with computer laboratories.[23]

Pending delivery of the promised classroom computers, something that skeptics fear will not happen, the overwhelming majority of schoolchildren will pass through their Informatika computer literacy course with little or no hands-on experience. Some will learn to program on programmable calculators. Many will lack even those. Supplying computers to the schools remains the most critical challenge confronting those who wish to make the new Informatika course a success.

Acquiring a new, more appropriate computer for schools has proven to be no simple matter for the Soviet educational and industrial bureaucracies. A complicated acquisition process, reminiscent of that followed by the military when selecting a new weapons system, has included the following six steps:

1. Specification of performance characteristics.
2. Negotiation with the computer-producing ministries for the design and production of prototypes.
3. Performance testing of the prototypes.
4. Selection of preferred designs.
5. Organization of mass production.
6. Delivery of computers to the schools.

Many actors played a role in the specification step. Early in 1985 academician Andrei Ershov, the father of Soviet educational computing, published his ideas of how classroom computers ought to perform. At a minimum, he said, such a machine should have 64 Kb of memory, a color display, expandability, and the capability of being networked in a school computer laboratory. It should be highly reliable, basically maintenance free, with easily replaceable parts, and sell for about 1,000 rubles. It should be mass-produced in a highly automated environment under a regime of strict quality control. Finally, since the schools would have no technical staff, the infrastructure of a PC distribution and support system would have to be erected to bear the burden of technical support traditionally (although reluctantly) borne by the users of Soviet computers.[24]

Creating such an educational computer, said Ershov, would be a "tough nut" for the Soviet computer industry to crack. Indeed the design and production of some 400,000 educational PCs by the end of 1990, together with the development of the distribution and support system, is an enormous challenge to Soviet computer producers. One anxious teacher worried that all of this constitutes a grandiose experiment in the field of education, threatening to turn educators and students into "experimental rabbits."[25]

The final specifications for the educational computer bore close resemblance to those propounded by Ershov. Before becoming final, however, they passed over many bureaucratic desks. In early August 1986 the specifications were ratified by the Ministry of Public Instruction, the Ministry of Post Secondary Education, the Academy of Pedagogical Sciences, the Academy of Sciences, the State Committee on Science and Technology, and others.[26]

Publication of the specifications sparked considerable competition among would-be designers. A surprisingly large number of computer designs were proposed in 1985 and 1986. The journals, *Mikroprotsessornye sredstva i sistemy* and *Informatika i obrazovanie*, carried articles advertising the merits of several of them. By late 1986 the competition appeared to have narrowed to two designs, the Korvet and the Elektronika UK-NTs.

The Korvet is a classroom configuration of up to 12 PK-8010 student computer workstations networked together and also to one PK-8020 teacher's workstation. Both the PK-8010 and the PK-8020 are members of a new family of 8-bit computers based on a 2.5 megahertz Soviet imitation of the Intel 8080 microprocessor.[27] They are said to be capable of 625 operations per second of the register-to-register type. The PK-8010 student workstation is normally equipped with 64 Kb of RAM, 24 Kb of

ROM, 48 Kb of dedicated graphics memory, black-and-white monitor
(512 × 256 pixels), whereas the PK-8020 teacher's workstation supports
a monochromatic and/or color monitor, one or two 800 Kb floppy disk
drives, a dot matrix printer, and an audio cassette tape storage device.
Main memory is said to be expandable to 256 Kb. The detachable keyboard, which accepts input in both Cyrillic and Latin characters, is augmented by five programmable function keys and a numeric keypad that
doubles as cursor control. The Korvet's speed is said to be 625 thousand
operations (register-to-register) per second, or about 25 percent slower
than the IBM PC/XT.

The PK-20X0 operating system is MicroDOS, a Soviet clone of Digital
Research's CPM/80. In network mode, the Korvet's operating system
presumably will be a Soviet modification of MPM/80. Standard programming languages are said to include a Soviet version of Basic which
is compatible with Microsoft's MSX Basic, Pascal, and Rapir.[28]

Soviet authors credit the Korvet's design to Moscow State University's
Institute of Nuclear Physics and the Moscow Scientific Research Center
for Calculating Machines. The Korvet computers resemble a cross between Radio Shack's color computer and CPM machines of the early
1980s, such as those made by now-forgotten American companies like
North Star, Vector Graphics, and Osborne Computer Corporation.

Hopes that serial production of the Korvet would begin early in 1987
did not materialize. Soviet sources indicated that the Korvet passed its
required state acceptance tests in early 1987 and that, after necessary design modifications, its serial production was scheduled to begin during
the fourth quarter of the year, with Minradioprom as the manufacturer.

On the face of it, an 8-bit CPM machine would seem an unlikely choice
for the Soviets as one of their main educational computers. In the past,
they have placed heavy emphasis on the quantity and quality of software
that they could "borrow" when they were deciding which American computer designs to copy. But in this case very little Western educational
software will run under CPM. The Apple II, Commodore 64, and TRS-
80, all with proprietary operating systems, were the 8-bit computers of
choice for American schools during the early 1980s. In the pre-IBM PC
era, the CPM machines held sway only for business applications. Even
in that field, they were quickly eclipsed by PC-DOS/MS-DOS machines
after the IBM PC was announced in 1981. Why, then, the choice of an
8-bit CPM machine for Soviet schools?

The reason for choosing an 8080A clone as the processor for an educational computer is not difficult to establish. The KR580 series of chips is one that Minelektronprom has learned to produce well and in abundance. That is no minor consideration in a country where mass production of reliable integrated circuits is the exception rather than the rule. The result is that the KR580, despite its obsolete design, is used ubiquitously in the Soviet Union. But if the choice of the KR580 is explicable, why not emulate the TRS-80, which used the Zilog Z-80, itself an Intel 8080 workalike, and for which an abundance of educational software is available, rather than produce a machine that looks more like the Northstar Horizon? The conjectural answer here is that the Korvet is to be coproduced with the Soviet PK 8001, which is slated for professional use in noneducational areas and where the abundance of CPM software is a definite advantage.

The second new Soviet educational computer is the Elektronika UK-NTs.[29] To be manufactured by Minelektronprom, this machine represents a further evolutionary step in the class of Soviet computers that trace their ancestry to DEC's venerable PDP-11. The UK-NOs hosts two Soviet 16-bit K1801VM2 microprocessors, one responsible for central processing, the other for control of peripherals. Memory consists of 32 Kb in each of ROM and RAM.[30] An additional 96 Kb serves its bit-mapped display. The standard configuration includes controllers for up to four 400 Kb or 800 Kb floppy disks, 48 Kb audio tape cassette, parallel input-output, and sound generator. It also includes a local area network interface. Although the machine's operating system is not MS-DOS, it appears capable of writing and reading data files in Microsoft format.

The UK-NTs' bit-mapped screen driver generates 640 × 288 pixels and eight tones from a 32-color pallet. In standard text mode, it provides 24 lines of 80 characters (8 × 11 pixels) and in large character mode, it produces lines of 40, 20, or 10 characters. Both Latin and Cyrillic alphabets are supported.

Its specifications make the Elektronika UK-NTs seem an interesting computer. Its software will be compatible with members of the mini-microcomputer family used most widely in Soviet process control and other technical applications. That family includes the SM-4, Elektronika-60, Elektronika BK-0010, DVK-2M, and many others that trace their roots to the PDP-11. The UK-NTs is said to be considerably less expensive than its predecessors. It will be manufactured by Minelektronprom and was scheduled to enter serial production during the second half of 1987.

If and when the Korvet and the UK-NTs classroom configurations are mass-produced and distributed, Soviet schools will be in receipt of respectably powerful educational computers that are roughly comparable to the Apple II+ or TRS-80. If these machines operate reliably up to their specifications, they will undoubtedly meet the requirements of the new Informatika course. Their selection as classroom machines illustrates some maxims of Soviet computer technology strategy:

1. Use technology that has been tried. Components used in the Korvet and the UK-NTs are not only old technology by world standards, they are old by Soviet standards. But they have the advantage of being familiar, and, most importantly, domestic industry has mastered the art of producing them.
2. Use technology that is widely employed in Soviet industry. This factor naturally is correlated with the first. The USSR counts it a virtue that the first computers that schoolchildren will encounter are close relatives of those most widely employed in industrial production.
3. Improve technology incrementally. Following a pattern observed in other areas of technology, from military weapons systems to automobiles, the Soviets have abjured qualitative leaps in computing technology. They prefer instead to innovate gradually via marginal improvements in familiar designs.
4. Acquiesce in technological followership. By choosing the Korvet and the UK-NTs, the Soviets have selected computers for the 1990s that embody American technology of the 1970s.
5. Avoid risk. This is the common strategic thread that runs through all of the preceding points.

Longer Term Outlook for Soviet Educational Computers

The present deployment of computers to Soviet schools comprises the first of a three-step educational computing plan that will span the period 1986–2000. This plan was formulated in 1985 and early 1986 and its three quinquenia correspond to the 12th, 13th, and 14th Five-Year plans.[31]

As indicated above, during stage one (1986–1990), Soviet schools are supposed to receive some 400,000 PCs, or enough to equip 30-35,000 computer laboratories. Planners intend to increase the number of these laboratories to 100,000 by 1995, and to more than 120,000 five years later.

In the long-range plan, such "first-generation" classroom computer networks as Korvets and UK-NTs, as well as the earlier KUVT-86 together with individual machines such as the Agat and BK-0010 are called UVT-1 systems.[32] In addition to the basic network configurations, the Soviet computer industry is supposed to deliver an assortment of equipment to make computers more useful in subjects other than those in Informatika. Such equipment is to include enhanced storage devices, minirobots, interfaces to physics and other laboratory equipment, and modems.

During the 1991–95 time period, a new generation of 32-bit hardware (UVT-2) is supposed to appear as the production of UVT-1 equipment winds down. The head of Minpros' computer administration says that this second generation of Soviet classroom computers are slated to be: ". . . quite powerful professional distributed computing systems with powerful graphics capabilities and a wide assortment of peripheral devices. They will connect to regional computer networks and have high capacity external memory devices."[33]

No useful purpose would be served by speculating here about what the second generation of Soviet educational computers might look like. If the past is any guide to the future, domestic industry will be more than sufficiently challenged in trying to meet its quantitative assignment for first-generation machines.

To fulfill the 1990 targets, USSR industry will need to increase the production of PCs for school use by an average annual rate of more than 50 percent during the 12th Five-Year Plan. By 1990 the annual number of PCs delivered to the schools will need to be about 200,000. Assuming that Soviet school computers have useful lifetimes of five years, annual deliveries would need to increase gradually to about 270,000 by the end of the century to meet the targets for the next decade. Figure 3.1 displays a graph of the estimated numbers of school computers in place each year and numbers to be delivered annually, if the announced long-range plan is to be fulfilled.

Can they do it? To put the Soviet task into an American perspective, it is useful to note that Apple Computer Corporation will ship more than 500,000 Macintosh computers in 1987 alone.[34] To deliver half that number of educational PCs by 1990 would not seem to strain unduly the capacities of Minelektronprom and Minradioprom, even if the schools take only 40 percent of total Soviet PC output. On the other hand, the USSR

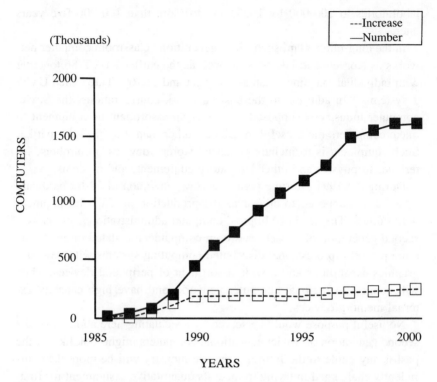

Figure 3.1. Planned Number of Computers in Soviet Schools. (Source: Estimate is computed from material in Uvarov, A., "EVM na puti v shkolu," *Informatika i obrazovanie,* 1986:1, pp. 13–17.)

record of mass producing highly reliable consumer electronic products is hardly encouraging.

A Paucity of Educational Software

Not much educational software is available in the Soviet Union. To be sure, most school computers support such beginner languages as Basic and Pascal. The new Korvet and UK-NTs are said also to provide Rapir. Beyond these languages and programs written locally, the most common software seems to be a myriad of computer games acquired from Japan and the West.[35]

As presently constituted, the Informatika course requires little software beyond an initial programming language. "Hands-on" experience for students is limited to writing and running these and other programs in Basic or Rapir.[36]

But the fact that the Informatika course requires only a programming language hardly means that the Soviets pay no educational price for their paucity of classroom software or even of general purpose packages such as word processors, spreadsheets, and data base managers. The software shortage means that the school computers are, in effect, special purpose instruments whose usefulness is limited to a single course. So long as that shortage persists, both students and teachers of other courses will find little reason to learn about computers and their potential contributions to learning.

The Soviet software industry is universally retarded, due to a general lack of incentives for developers. An underdeveloped system for protecting intellectual property rights, combined with impediments to private or cooperative software development, have stunted the USSR software industry for many years. Educational software development has suffered even more than management or industrial software, because there has been no market for it. The dilemma is familiar; no educational software is produced because no one wants it, and no one wants educational software because its paucity prevents people from developing a taste for it.

The Soviets have responded to the software shortage in typical fashion. They have created institutions. One of these is the new Institute of Programming at the Academy of Sciences. This body, organized in 1985 and headed by A. K. Ailamazian, is located in the ancient Russian town of Pereslavl'-Zalesskii. Among its charges is to develop software for Soviet schools.[37] Another newly created institution is the Scientific Technical Institute of Informatics and Computer Science at the USSR Academy of Pedagogical Sciences, oragnized in 1986 and headed by I. M. Bobko. It is located in the *Akademgorodok* (Academic City) at Novosibirsk and its scientific guru is none other than academician Andrei P. Ershov. Among its main tasks are those of developing educational software and of propagating good software developed in the schools.

The development of educational software is in its infancy in the USSR. The *Shkol'nitsa* (schoolgirl) package stands alone as an example of a piece of educational software that has achieved anything resembling nationwide acceptance.[38] That package includes the following components:

An interactive, screen-oriented text editor.
Robik and *Rapir*, two computer languages for beginners.
Shpaga, a graphics system.

Programmer's tools and utilities.

In addition, Shkol'nitsa contains "hooks" onto which may be hung educational programs applicable to various academic disciplines such as physics, chemistry, and others. Enveloping all the tools and programs is the Shkol'nitsa shell that purports to define an entire user environment.

The first version of Shkol'nitsa was developed in Novosibirsk during the period 1975–78. Its principal authors were A. P. Ershov and the late G. A. Zvenigorodskii, a brilliant junior member of Ershov's school of educational software developers at Novosibirsk, who acknowledge Shkol'nitsa's indebtedness to *Logo* and *Smalltalk*. The package was developed initially on the BESM-6, but its more recent improvements and implementations have been on the Agat, the Apple II, Riad, and newer classroom computers.

No evaluation of Shkol'nitsa is possible without some hands-on testing. Since the authors have not yet had an opportunity to do that, not much more can be said about the package other than to remark that it seems interesting and reports indicate that it is being used here and there in Soviet schools. Perhaps the most remarkable thing about Shkol'nitsa is that it remains so lonely on the USSR educational software scene.

Controversy About the Direction of Soviet Educational Computing

The earlier articles by Judy and Lommel (1986) and Kerr (1987) described the narrow focus of the new Informatika course on the logic of developing algorithms. This narrowness stands in sharp contrast to educational computing as it has developed in the United States. Kerr expressed it well in the following:

> There is little of the exploratory quality that characterizes most American courses in the subject; rather, there is a strong emphasis on learning how to think logically and how to make a computer do a very specific set of tasks that are seen as directly related to a student's future job. While Western enthusiasts extol the value of *Logo* as a way to learn logic without being taught logic explicitly, Soviet students will learn logic first—*without* computers—and then apply their learning in a very prescribed way to the use of computers as tools.[39]

This narrow focus of the Informatika course has become the subject of a major controversy in Soviet educational computing circles. The issue arose sharply in a public discussion surrounding a "program" for the course that was published as a guide for prospective authors hoping to enter the competition for designing a new textbook to replace the preliminary book edited by Ershov and Monakhov.[40] The new program preserves all the stress on algorithms and programming that characterizes the present version of the course.

The mounting cry from Soviet teachers and educators is that the narrow focus on algorithms and programming is harmful. It neglects the fact that most students will be users of computer software, not developers of it. Therefore, the argument continues that the goal of the Informatika course should be to teach students how to use packaged software such as word processors, spreadsheets, data base managers, and so on. At best, the critics claim, the present course is creating dilettante programmers. At worst, they say that the dry and abstract subject matter of the course is alienating students from computing, which is precisely the opposite of what is intended.

Ershov and other proponents of the algorithmic approach to educational computing respond that algorithms and programming are and should remain central features of the course. They fear that abandoning or diluting those features will rob the Soviet Informatika course of its rigor and turn it into the thin gruel that they perceive most American educational computing to be.

To foretell the outcome of this controversy is difficult, but we suspect that Ershov and his allies will eventually lose. The American experience is that educational computing initially was the preserve of mathematicians and computer scientists cut from the same cloth as Ershov. Early American school textbooks in computing effused no less algorithmic zeal than present Soviet ones.[41] As microcomputers began to filter into American schools, homes, and offices, most people quickly shifted their interests from learning to program (few ever had such an interest in the first place) to learning to use the burgeoning supply of off-the-shelf software for applications that they wanted to do in their personal and professional lives.

In conclusion, many things about USSR computer circumstances are different from those in the United States. They do not have the abundance of PCs that we do, nor are they likely to have such plenty in this century. Nevertheless, we think the pressure will be to broaden the base of computer usage in Soviet schools from its present algorithmic and programming narrowness. As the new machines gradually make their way into the schools, they will also gradually be used as computational and informational tools in other academic courses and, eventually, as interactive teaching/learning devices.

The speed with which all this happens will depend on Soviet success in meeting and exceeding present plans to supply computers for schools. Equally important, it will depend on a satisfactory solution to the problem of producing, distributing, and supporting educational software in the USSR. Last, but far from least, it will depend on how well teachers are trained in educational computing and on the ingenuity with which Soviet curriculum designers weave computing into the fabric of ordinary course plans.

Despite all the difficulties confronting it, educational computing in USSR middle schools has been launched. Its champions, particularly Andrei Ershov, keep the computer campaign charged with energy. If not all of its champion's hopes have been realized, its accomplishments have been greater than the skeptics expected. As it continues to unfold, the educational computing campaign seems likely to make a significant impact on Soviet education and society.

Notes

1. R. W. Judy and J. M. Lommel, "The New Soviet Computer Literacy Campaign," *ECTJ: Educational Communication and Technology Journal*, 2, no. 34 (Summer 1986), 108–123; S. Kerr, "Soviet Applications of Microcomputers in Education: Developments in Research and Practice During the Gorbachev Era," *Journal of Educational Computing Research*, 1, no. 3 (1987), pp. 1–17.

2. B. B. Szekely (ed.), *Soviet Education*, 28, no. 10 (August-September 1986).

3. J. L. Hoot, "Computing in the Soviet Union," *The Computing Teacher*, 14, no. 8 (May 1987), pp. 8–10.

4. M. Phister, *Data Processing Technology and Economics*, 2nd ed. (Santa Monica, CA: Digital Press, 1979), pp. 350.

5. L. D. Bores, "Agat: a Soviet Apple II Computer," *Byte* (November 1984); R. A. Stapelton and S. Goodman, "Microcomputing in the Soviet Union and Eastern Europe," *Abacus*, 3, no. 1 (1985), pp. 6–23.

6. Its KR588 microprocessor is a Soviet imitation of the Motorola 6502 processor used in the Apple II. Details of the Agat are provided by A. F. Ioffe, *Mikroprotsessornye sredstva i sistemy*, no. 1 (1984), pp. 56–60.

7. See, e.g., "Zaboty shkol'noi informatike," *Uchitel'skaia gazeta* (April 5, 1986), p. 3.

8. The Yamaha computer uses the Intel 8088 microprocessor or one of its clones. It employs Microsoft's MSX operating system and is at least partly compatible with the IBM PC.

9. *Uchitel'skaia gazeta* (April 17, 1986), p. 2.

10. The Elektronika BK-0010 is a small, single board "home computer" whose outward appearance is similar to the British Sinclair PC. It employs the 16-bit Soviet K1801BM1 microprocessor and provides a "Chiclet" keyboard, 32 Kb of RAM, 32 Kb of ROM, plus serial (RS-232) and parallel ports. It accommodates 256 Kb of cassette storage on an ordinary audio tape recorder. Video output is 24 lines of 32 or 64 characters on color monitor or television. Its instruction set and architecture are compatible with the Elektronika 60, which, in turn, derives from the American PDP-11 via the Soviet SM-4 minicomputer family. First produced in 1985, it was initially priced at 840 rubles. Limited numbers were sold at Elektronika retail stores in Moscow, Minsk, Leningrad, and a few other cities. S. N. Kosenkov et al., *Mikroprotsessornye sredstva i sistemy*, 1 (1985), pp. 22–25.

11. The Polish Metranex computers used by Moscow schoolchildren are said to enjoy a reputation for high quality reliability. See *Uchitel'skaia gazeta* (July 30, 1986), p. 1.

12. Designs for school computer laboratories are specified by Minpros. See *Informatika i obrazovanie*, no. 3 (1986), pp. 5–17.

13. *Uchitel'skaia gazeta* (September 25, 1986), p. 2.

14. See the interview with V. V. Men'shikov, deputy chief of the Moscow city executive committee in *Uchitel'skaia gazeta* (July 7, 1987), p. 2. Men'shikov's term *displeinye klassy* is a broader category than *kabinety* since it includes terminal-equipped classrooms as well as those with microcomputers. His 1987 numbers, therefore, are not strictly comparable with the number of *kabinety* previously given.

15. *Uchitel'skaia gazeta* (January 10, 1987), p. 3.

16. *Ibid.* (August 7, 1986), p. 1.

17. *Ibid.* (June 17, 1986), p. 1.

18. For an expression of Georgian resentment on this point, see V. Akhaliia, in *Uchitel'skaia gazeta* (April 8, 1986), p. 3.

19. *Ibid.* (September 9, 1986), p. 1, and (October 30, 1986), p. 2.

20. *Ibid.* (August 12, 1986), p. 1.

21. *Ibid.*

22. *Ibid.* (September 2, 1986), p. 1.

23. See the speech by S. G. Shcherbakov, in *Uchitel'skaia gazeta* (March 4, 1986), p. 3, and that by his deputy A. Korobeinikov, *ibid.* (August 22, 1987), p. 2.

24. A. P. Ershov, *Mikroprotsessornye sredstva i sistemy*, 1 (1985), p. 2.

25. *Ibid.*

26. I. Driga, *Informatika i obrazovanie*, 2 (1986), pp. 66–69.

27. Information about the Korvet is from E. P. Velikhov et al., in *Mikroprotsessornye sredstva i sistemy*, no. 1 (1986), pp. 34–36; M. Sulim, A. Lazarev, and V. Safonov in *Informatika i obrazovanie*, no. 1 (1986), p. 74; E. P. Velikhov in *Vestnik Akademii Nauk, SSSR*, no. 7 (1987), p. 28; Driga, *Informatika* (1986) and no. 2 (1987).

28. MSX is an operating system designed by Microsoft for a series of Japanese PCs. It is not used in the United States. Rapir is a beginner's programming lan-

guage developed in Novosibirsk. See Judy and Lommel, "New Soviet Computer," p. 118.

29. UK-NTs are the initials for *Uchebnyi komp'iuter, nauchnii tsentr*, or "Educational Computer, Scientific Center." Information on this computer is from A. N. Polosin et al., in *Mikroprotsessornye sredstva i sistemy*, no. 6 (1986), pp. 14–16; and Driga, *Informatika*.

30. Driga, *Informatika*, states that the UK-NTs has 128 Kb of "user accessible" memory.

31. For more details of this plan, see A. Iu. Uvarov, in *Informatika i obrazovanie*, no. 1 (1986), pp. 13–17.

32. KUVT stands for *komplekt uchebnoi vychislitel'noi tekhniki* (configuration of educational computer technology). KUVT-86 is a classroom configuration of BK-0010 computers intended to serve as a temporary stopgap until the Korvet and UK-NTs become available. See A. Denisenko, in *Informatika i obrazovanie*, no. 2 (1986), pp. 69–74. The letters UVT are the initials of *uchebnaia vychislitel'naia tekhnika* (educational computer technology).

33. Denisenko, *Informatika*, p. 17.

34. *Infoworld* (October 19, 1987), p. 6.

35. These computer games have gained great popularity among Soviet young people. This phenomenon is viewed by some adults as a good thing because it attracts students to the computer. Others view it with alarm because of the ideology of acquisitiveness and violence said to permeate these foreign games. See A. Shmelev, in *Informatika i obrazovanie* no. 1 (1987), pp. 85–92.

36. See the two-volume preliminary textbook by A. P. Ershov and V. M. Monakhov (eds.), *Osnovy informatiki i vychislitel'noi tekhniki* (Moscow: Prosveshchenie, 1985, 1986).

37. See M. Sokolovskaia, in *Uchitel'skaia gazeta* (January 17, 1987), p. 4.

38. See G. Frolova, "'Schoolgirl' is Coming to School," translated in *Soviet Education*, 38, no. 10–11 (August-September 1986), 39–46; and G. A. Zvenigorodskii et al., in *Mikroprotsessornye sredstva i sistemy*, no. 1 (1984), pp. 50–55.

39. Kerr, "Soviet Applications" (1987), p. 15.

40. See "Programma kursa osnovy informatiki i vychislitel'noi tekhniki," *Mikroprotsessornye sredstva i sistemy*, no. 2 (1986), pp. 86–89.

41. See, e.g., *Algorithms, Computation, and Mathematics: Student Text* (preliminary edition), prepared by the School Mathematics Study Group at Stanford University with the support of the National Science Foundation (1965).

4

THE INFORMATION REVOLUTION AND THE RESTRUCTURING OF HIGHER EDUCATION

*Richard B. Dobson**

In recent years there has been a growing recognition in official quarters that major changes must be made in the Soviet system of higher education. In mid-1986, *Pravda* published draft guidelines for the restructuring of Soviet higher and specialized secondary education—"one of the urgent and most important tasks in the development of society at the present time."[1] Nine months later, in early 1987, the Central Committee of the Communist Party of the Soviet Union (CPSU) and the USSR Council of Ministers approved final guidelines and several resolutions for reorganizing higher education.[2] This chapter examines those aspects of the reform that affect the Soviet ability to exploit modern information technologies and to introduce computers into higher education on a broad scale.

In explaining why reform† is needed, the then USSR Minister of Higher

*Study supported in part by a research grant from the Kennan Institute for Advanced Russian Studies of The Wilson Center, Washington, DC, whose assistance is gratefully acknowledged. The views expressed are those of the author, not of the U.S. government, the United States Information Agency, or any other organization.
†On March 8, 1988, a major reorganization of the educational administration was announced. The USSR Ministry of Higher and Specialized Secondary Education, the USSR Ministry of Education, and the USSR State Committee for Vocational-Technical Education were abolished and replaced by a single educational authority—the USSR State Committee for Public Education. The former USSR Minister of Higher Education, Gennadii A. Iagodin, was appointed head of the new state committee.

and Specialized Secondary Education, Gennadii A. Iagodin, observed that "the higher school system has been transformed from a catalyst of scientific, technological, and economic progress into a 'passive observer' of the nation's economic development." Iagodin went on to stress that the system must boost its contribution to intensive economic development. "For this to happen," he added, "the next step will be to remove, in the very near future, all the obstacles which are holding back our forward movement, to discard all obsolete canons, and to draw practical conclusions from the errors of the past."[3]

Iagodin and other ranking officials are well aware that Soviet higher education must make greater use of computers. "Contemporary computer technology," Iagodin has emphasized, "should become a powerful instrumentality in the intensification and industrialization of the academic process."[4] The system must also, in his view, train specialists who are able to keep abreast of new developments and adapt to rapid technological change.

> Scientific, technological, and sociopolitical information is snowballing, as it were, in a way which makes "education once and for all" a sheer impossibility. In a situation where the volume of society's active informational resources doubles every seven to ten years, a steadily growing portion of those who participate in production have to replenish their knowledge constantly . . . simply in order to maintain satisfactory competence and retain the skill they have acquired.
>
> This consequence of the "information explosion" was first felt by those doing predominantly mental work, by employees in science, education, and management. Today, however, manufacturing methods are being updated at the same brisk pace as information, especially in what are known as the science-intensive branches of industry—in the electronics industry, for example, where they are replaced every three to six years.[5]

The USSR higher educational system will play a major role in efforts to develop, master, and deploy modern information technologies. Whereas secondary schools are expected to instill basic computer literacy, higher educational institutions are charged with training computer programmers, managers, engineers, and other specialists who are able to use computers in their professional work. In addition, universities and institutes play a leading role in diffusing knowledge about computers through their outreach programs, and they are increasingly applying R&D to the new technologies.

The Scientific-Technological Revolution and the Emerging "Information Society"

Sociologists, economists, and futurologists have used various terms to describe the interrelated scientific, technological, economic, and social changes that are transforming advanced industrial societies. Some have characterized the emerging order as a "postindustrial society," whereas others have dubbed it a "knowledge" or "information" society. Regardless of the term used, however, three notable trends are generally identified:

1. A marked expansion of *scientific research,* accompanied both by rapid growth in the store of knowledge and by the ever more frequent application of scientific discoveries in the economy.
2. Intensive rates of *technological innovation,* leading to the creation of new products and services and to further rises in productivity.
3. Major developments in *information technology* and the expanded use of computers and other means for the storage, analysis, and transmission of information.

In advanced Western countries, these trends have been accompanied by various economic and social changes, including a continuing rise in educational levels, an expansion of the service sector, and a growth in the absolute and relative number of highly skilled white-collar workers.[6]

Since the 1960s, leading Soviet scholars have conceptualized these developments as constituting the "scientific-technological revolution" (*nauchno-tekhnicheskaia revoliutsiia,* or NTR). From their perspective, the most noteworthy characteristic of the NTR is the fact that science has become a "direct productive force," which creates revolutionary change in the economy's technological base.[7]

Computerization and the spread of other information technologies are commonly viewed by USSR commentators as an important (some would even say *the* most important) element in the NTR. Several years ago, for instance, the late Viktor M. Glushkov, one of the leading Soviet proponents of computerization, referred to "the appearance of an essentially new man-machine technology for processing information" as the "chief content" of the NTR.[8] Somewhat later, at the June 1985 CPSU Central Committee conference, General Secretary Mikhail S. Gorbachev stressed that microelectronics, computer technology, and the entire information industry serve as "a catalyst for modern scientific-technological progress." These new technologies, he declared, exert a "decisive influence on the effectiveness of the means of labor and of technological systems in all branches" of the economy.[9]

Many of the trends observed in advanced Western countries are evident in the USSR as well. In recent decades the resources devoted to R&D have increased substantially, and the skilled white-collar work force has expanded at a rapid rate. In the Soviet economy, the number of "specialists" (i.e., highly trained white-collar workers) with a higher education quadrupled from 3.5 million in 1960 to 14.5 million in 1985, and the proportion of the employed population with a higher education increased from 3.3 percent in 1959 to 12.2 percent in 1986. The number of persons employed in scientific research (*nauchnye rabotniki*) grew more than fourfold between 1960 and 1985, rising from 354,000 to 1.5 million. During the same quarter of a century, the number of engineers employed in the economy grew from 1.1 million to 6.1 million, increasing more than fivefold.[10]

Yet, despite some similar trends, the differences between the USSR and Western countries remain substantial. In discussing the "Soviet-style information society" in chapter 2, Seymour E. Goodman persuasively argues that the "information revolution" is propelled by different forces and is following a different course in the USSR than it is in the United States and other Western societies. In the West, as a result of decentralized decision making and competitive market forces, information technologies have been developed and disseminated rapidly. On the other hand, Soviet political authorities are attempting to use the new information technologies to accomplish priority tasks, that is to improve economic performance, maintain the economic planning and control mechanism, support their military and internal security objectives, and project the image of a progressive society to the world. Owing largely to state and party controls and the nature of the centrally planned economy, information technologies have spread more slowly and have not penetrated as deeply into the economy and society.

The system of higher education will clearly occupy a central position in the emerging Soviet "information society." Although most commonly identified with teaching and learning, that is, the *transmission of knowledge* from teacher to student, higher educational institutions are also intimately involved with a host of other information activities. These include the *production of information* through scientific and scholarly research and its systematization and certification as "knowledge"; the *processing of information* (e.g., the translation and abstracting of texts or the repackaging of information in textbooks and study programs); the *exchange of information* (e.g., by means of scholarly conferences, the publication of academic journals, electronic data transfers, and the like); and the *storage of information* (e.g. in libraries and data banks). To accomplish these tasks more efficiently, universities and institutes in the USSR are increasingly utilizing an array of new technologies, such as computer-assisted instruction and design systems, word processors, computerized data bases for the storage and retrieval of information sources, and more.

Characteristics of Soviet Higher Education

Before examining the restructuring of Soviet higher education, it is useful to review the main features of the system and to note the ways in which it differs from the American equivalent. In terms of the number of students enrolled, the Soviet system of higher education ranks second only to the American. In 1985 there were slightly more than five million students in Soviet universities and institutes. Of these, about 57 percent studied full-time, the remainder studying in evening and correspondence courses while working full-time. In the United States in 1985, there were 7.7 million students at four-year higher educational institutions and 4.5 million in two-year colleges.[11]

Centralized Government Administration

In contrast to the highly decentralized American system, policy governing Soviet higher education has been spelled out authoritatively on a national level by the USSR Ministry of Higher and Specialized Secondary Education (Minvuz) now replaced by the USSR State Committee for Public Education, and on major issues by the CPSU Central Committee. With the other ministries responsible for particular branches of the economy (e.g., agriculture, public health, culture). Minvuz and republic ministries of higher education have devised and implemented policies regarding admissions, the content of instruction, placement of schools, and so on. Whereas Minvuz has set overall policy, responsibility for administration and financing has fallen to the branch ministries in some cases. In 1987 the 896 Soviet higher educational institutions were under the jurisdiction of 74 union and republic ministries and departments (30 of which had only one or two institutes).[12]

Manpower Planning

The numbers of admissions to USSR higher educational institutions have been planned by the central ministries on the basis of projected manpower requirements. Since these in turn have been derived from enterprise estimates, employers have had considerable indirect influence in determining the number of openings in particular fields. Applicants must choose their specialty (*spetsial'nost'*) when they apply for admission, and upon graduation they are obliged to work for three years at the position to which they have been assigned.

In recent years the Soviet manpower training system has been subjected to sharp criticism by employers, planners, and educators. There have been frequent complaints that many graduates do not report for their obligatory work assignments, especially if they have been assigned to undesirable posts in provincial towns or villages, that the Soviet educational system overproduces engineers, and that the numbers of graduates in various fields do not correspond to enterprise needs. Imbalances between supply and demand are especially likely to occur in rapidly changing fields, such as computer technology, robotics, and computer programming.

Academic Orientations and Types of Institutions

In the United States most students major in the humanities and the social sciences and attend colleges or universities with broad and fairly loosely structured curricula. On the other hand, the majority of students in the USSR study applied specialties at technical institutes. Only 11 percent of all Soviet students are enrolled in universities.

Research

In the USSR the higher educational system does not comprise the primary locus of fundamental research as in the United States. Rather, most basic research is done in institutes under the USSR Academy of Sciences. Minister of Higher Education G. A. Iagodin pointed out that no more than 10 percent of all scientific research is conducted in higher educational institutions, even though they employ about a third of all scientific research personnel and half of all persons with doctorates. Furthermore, the research is unevenly distributed among institutions. Moscow State University reportedly performs more research than all 200 teacher-training institutes put together.[13]

Not only are skilled research personnel not being used effectively, but the training of researchers is also thought to be suffering. Nikita N. Moiseev, a professor at the Moscow Physical Technical Institute (MFTI) and a member of the Information Science, Computer Technology, and Automation Department of the USSR Academy of Sciences, has observed that "the most talented young scientists are rushing from the higher educational institution to the scientific research institute, and fewer and fewer prominent researchers and designers are engaging in teaching."[14] Repeated calls have been made to expand the R&D volume in higher educational institutions, to increase its payoffs, and to coordinate the work more effectively with production enterprises and other research establishments.

Restructuring of Soviet Higher Education

The current restructuring of higher education is, of course, designed to achieve a number of objectives. The most important goals are to improve higher education's contribution to economic performance and to stimulate scientific-technological progress. This section examines efforts to make the system more responsive to enterprise manpower needs, to use more active and individualized modes of instruction, and to increase the effectiveness of R&D. The next section explores efforts to make computers an integral part of the educational process.

"Targeted Training" and Revised Study Programs

The CPSU leadership has determined that economic growth must be achieved largely through "intensification," that is, by using available productive resources more effectively. In this connection, the higher educational system is criticized for having emphasized quantity at the expense of quality, for having provided training in too many narrow specialities, and for not supplying the optimal numbers of graduates needed by the various branches of the economy. To rectify this situation, the basic guidelines stress that the quality of training must be improved and that specialists should be given broader training that would allow them to adapt to changing economic demands.

Restructuring will also entail changes in the manpower planning process, the specialties in which training is offered, and the study programs themselves. Branch ministries will more often enter into agreements with universities and institutes for the training of a certain quantity of specialists and in turn will partially reimburse the institutions for the training. Ivan F. Obraztsov, the RSFSR Minister of Higher and Specialized Secondary Education, has noted that this approach, which has been dubbed "targeted training" (*tselevaia podgotovka*), has been the focus since 1984 of an experiment conducted at 34 higher educational institutions under his ministry.[15]

Proponents of the reform have argued that, through direct contact with branch enterprises, the higher schools will ensure the closest "fit" between the specialist and the job. They have also suggested that if such an agreement is signed five years in advance, an enterprise will be in a position to participate actively in the recruitment of its "own" students. The enterprises, that is, would play a more direct role in vocational-orientation work with secondary school students and in the selection and sponsoring of students who would later be employed by them.

The resolution approved in March 1987 stipulates that for the initial period, 1988–90, the ministries are to pay 3,000 rubles (about $4,870*) per specialist per year for targeted training.[16] These funds are to be used to finance capital investments and the acquisition of equipment, instruments, and computers. Anatolii V. Kaliaev, the rector of the Taganrog Radio Engineering Institute, has pointed out that institutions usually have been "shortchanged" by the ministries and enterprises that they serve under the existing system. As a result the great majority of institutions, including his own, a leading developer of microprocessors, have had to work with unsatisfactory equipment.[17]

The implementing resolution also mandates a thorough review of specialties and training programs. The outcome should be a streamlined list of specialties and new academic programs that are more closely aligned with students' future professional activity. (The revised list of specialties was slated for preparation in time for the 1987–88 academic year and the new study programs for the 1988–89 academic year.) The content of the new training programs will be determined by the central educational au-

---

*Dollar amounts are based on the official Soviet exchange rate in effect on November 1, 1987, namely 1 R = $1.623.

thority, the appropriate branch ministries, and the individual institutions, taking into account the needs of employing enterprises.[18]

Postgraduate certification is another innovation in the restructuring plan. The guidelines state that graduates will be certified as specialists at a particular skill level after they have completed three years of work in the job to which they were assigned. This provision appears designed to strengthen compliance with the mandatory job assignment, to provide a check on quality (analogous to the quality control procedures introduced for industrial products in 1986), and to establish the first step in a regular retraining and recertification process.[19]

Use of Active, Individualized Instruction

In keeping with CPSU efforts to stimulate the economy, the reform envisions changes designed to activate "the human factor"—that is, to train highly motivated specialists who will not only have a firm grasp of the technical aspects of their work, but also show imagination, initiative, and independence. Toward this end, academic programs are to be overhauled, with much more attention given to individualized and active training techniques, such as seminars, simulations, games, and individual projects. The amount of time devoted to lectures is to be cut back; the student-teacher ratio is to be reduced; and more computers are to be made available to students. In the new academic plans slated for the 1988–89 academic year, the amount of time devoted to lectures is cut to 30 hours per week in the first two years and to 24 hours per week in the upper three years, a load that still appears heavy by American standards. To motivate students to achieve high marks, furthermore, the restructuring plan sanctions greater use of stipend differentials and other incentives and states that students who graduate with distinction will begin work with a higher salary than the others.[20]

V. Sokolov, the rector of Krasnoiarsk State University, has asserted that these innovations will entail basic changes in the roles of student and teacher:

> The present state of affairs is such that, paradoxical though it may seem, a student does not bear any responsibility to himself or society for the kind of specialist he becomes. The system of indicators used to evaluate the work of a higher educational institution and the overall regulation of the institution's activities have made the student a passive consumer and ex-

ecutor of someone else's will. It is sad to note that the system of higher
education has absorbed the pedagogy of formalism, irresponsibility, and
infantilism, a pedagogy without risk and without searching, a "who cares?"
pedagogy.[21]

Judging from articles published in recent years, many other educators
share Sokolov's evaluation of the shortcomings of undergraduate education.

The basic guidelines also demand that as much training as possible
should be conducted under conditions resembling those found in producing enterprises. For this reason, the guidelines call for the creation of
more "education-science-production complexes" (*uchebno-nauchno-
proizvodstvennye kompleksy*) that incorporate branches of higher educational institutions, scientific research laboratories, and experimentation
centers. At these complexes, which were first established on an experimental basis in the RSFSR, students can gain on-the-job experience with
production problems and also engage in scientific research.

In addition, the guidelines stress the importance of raising the quality
of research and teaching personnel and of linking them with industrial
enterprises. Accordingly, they propose: (1) to send more teachers and
researchers on assignment to industrial enterprises, where they will be
able to gain on-the-job experience; (2) to recruit more qualified specialists
from industry for teaching and research; (3) to improve graduate studies
and establish doctoral programs (*dokturantura*) at higher educational institutions; (4) to ensure that competitive hiring practices are used for fill-
ing teaching positions; and (5) to expand the programs at higher educational institutions for specialists' periodic skill upgrading (*kursy povysheniia
kvalifikatsii*). Along with the recertification process noted above, these
courses, which specialists would be expected to attend every few years,
will contribute to a system of continuing education.[22]

It should be noted that the qualification-raising courses have played an
important role in spreading knowledge about the new information technologies and training persons already in the work force, such as engineers, secondary schoolteachers, and professors, in the use of computers.
The reform will attempt to enhance their role.[23]

Tapping Higher Education's R&D Potential

As noted earlier, there has been a great deal of criticism of research conducted at Soviet higher educational institutions. At the June 1985 con-

ference of the CPSU Central Committee on accelerating scientific-technological progress, Gorbachev himself addressed this matter:

> Scientific research within the system of higher education possesses great reserves. For two decades, if not more, we have been speaking about the necessity of effectively using this huge scientific potential and about the need to do away with bureaucratic divisions between research institutions, higher educational institutions, and production, but the state of affairs has been changing very slowly.
>
> According to available estimates, higher educational institutions can increase the volume of their scientific research work 2–2.5 times. In order to increase the economic return substantially, it is necessary to change the planning system, introduce new criteria, improve the system of levers and stimuli, and provide the higher educational institutions with enterprises that they can use for experimental work. We will receive a two-fold benefit: on the one hand, we will augment our scientific-technological potential and increase the effectiveness of its use, and on the other hand, we will create conditions for the higher quality training of specialists, who will be drawn into creative work on the improvement of production while they are still students.[24]

Echoing Gorbachev, the basic guidelines state that higher educational institutions should double or triple the amount of fundamental research and approximately triple or quadruple design, technological, and experimental work. They also call for larger investments in research, better coordination among higher educational institutions and scientific institutes, an upgrading of researcher skills, a more flexible system of salaries and incentives, and more intensive student participation in research. Minvuz calculated that research expenditures can be increased to 740 million rubles a year (about $1.2 billion), compared to 380 million rubles (about $450 million) in 1986, through substantial increases in allocations from the state budget and in R&D contracts with ministries and enterprises.[25]

Aside from projecting increased funding for R&D, the restructuring program envisions greater reliance on the education-science-production complexes (mentioned above) and the "self-financing scientific association" (*khozraschetnoe nauchnoe ob''edinenie*). The latter was established under the aegis of the RSFSR Ministry of Higher Education, following an authoritative 1979 decree "On Increasing the Effectiveness of Scientific Research in Higher Educational Institutions." The self-financing scientific association has coordinated research amounting to 678 million rubles (about $1.1 billion) annually that is conducted at 176 higher educational institutions, 38 research institutes, 25 design bureaus, and 35 pilot factories in the RSFSR. According to Obraztsov, it has demonstrated its ability to concentrate powerful scientific potential on the solution of the most important problems and to speed up the economic application of new findings.[26]

In the estimation of leading Soviet authorities, greater reliance on these organizations will improve the effectiveness of research and promote student involvement in the R&D process. By way of illustration, Obraztsov singles out the Taganrog Radio Engineering Institute for special praise. This institute, the first to establish an education-science-production complex, has become a leader in the design and development of microprocessors and multiprocessor systems. Obraztsov maintains that the institute is an excellent example of what the education-science-production complexes can accomplish and of the way in which research activities can be coordinated under the aegis of the self-financing scientific association.[27] Working with ten higher educational institutions and a number of enterprises belonging to the Ministry of the Electronics Industry, the Taganrog Radio Engineering Institute has been acting as the main executor of a complex R&D program targeted on "Multiprocessor Computer Systems with Programmable Architecture."[28]

Increasingly, higher educational institutions are engaging in joint work with institutes at the Academy of Sciences and various branch ministries. Some of these projects relate to the development of new information technologies, such as computer-assisted design and scientific research systems.

Computerization of Soviet Higher Education

Leading officials stress that one of the principal aims of restructuring higher education is "the computerization of the academic process." According to RSFSR Minister of Higher Education Obraztsov, the computerization program will entail uninterrupted utilization of computer technology and information science in the educational process; use of computer-assisted instruction; establishment of combined algorithm and program banks; and widespread application of automated systems, mathematical modeling, and systems analysis.[29]

In recent years a series of steps have been taken to introduce more computers into the Soviet economy. The decision was made in 1983 to organize a department of computer science and technology at the USSR Academy of Sciences, and a number of new institutes were set up, including the Institute of the Problems of Informatics headed by academician B. N. Naumov.[30] At the end of 1985, the "Personal Computer" Intersectoral Scientific-Technological Complex was established, with the Institute of the Problems of Informatics as its central institution. The complex directs efforts to develop personal computers and attempts to coordinate Soviet efforts with those of other East European countries in the Council for Mutual Economic Assistance (CMEA).[31] Soon thereafter, the All-Union State Committee on Computer Technology and Informatics was created (under the direction of N. V. Gorshkov) with broad authority to supervise the creation, development, manufacturing, and servicing of computer technology (both hardware and software).[32] In October 1986, G. I. Marchuk, a mathematician and computer specialist who had been heading the State Committee on Science and Technology, was elected president of the USSR Academy of Sciences. In this new capacity, Marchuk has been playing a guiding role in restructuring the academy and in its efforts to develop new information technologies.[33]

The need to introduce more computers into the educational system has been recognized for some time. During 1984–85 the Soviet government launched a massive campaign for "computer literacy" in the secondary schools. Meanwhile, amid less fanfare, Minvuz took steps to expand the use of computers in higher education. In 1982 Minvuz commended a number of institutions for their outstanding work in developing undergraduate computer education programs, creating instructional software packages, retraining their teaching staffs, and introducing computers in various fields of study. At the same time, however, it noted "substantial shortcomings" in computer training at most institutions and called for vigorous efforts to improve the training.[34]

Obstacles to computerization have extended across the board. Too few teachers had been trained in the use of computers. Hardware has been in short supply and often unreliable or obsolescent. A 1982 report issued by the Scientific Research Institute of Problems of the Higher Schools concluded that nearly 70 percent of the computer equipment used in higher education was outdated. To make matters worse, few suitable computer programs had been developed for instructional use, and computer repair service was slow and undependable.[35]

In December 1983, with an eye to improving the software problem, Minvuz ordered the establishment of a unified Bank of Algorithms and Programs for the higher educational system. The Computer Center of Moscow State University was entrusted with receiving, cataloging, verifying, and disseminating the software that had been developed at universities and institutes around the country.[36] Judging from continuing complaints, however, there are still serious problems with the development and distribution of computer programs.

Basic Undergraduate Computer Training

In December 1983 Minvuz issued a letter of instruction that defined three levels of basic undergraduate computer training:

First level. Designed to familiarize students with the capabilities of computers and microprocessors in their professional work, the first level enables them to master the basic skills of doing calculations on computers and teaches them how to write a simple computer program. Students should acquire general information about mathematical modeling and computer technology, study one or two algorithmic languages, and use the knowledge for problem solving. This level of study is expected to entail approximately 60 to 100 hours of instruction, with more than half of the time spent in seminars and computer laboratories.

Second level. Students learn more about the capabilities of the computer as a research tool and as a means for processing data and solving problems. They acquire further knowledge of methods for developing algorithms and for analyzing and modeling processes and phenomena in their professional work. They also learn additional programming languages, study the architecture and software of microprocessor systems, and solve a broader and more complex series of problems. This level is expected to entail 120 to 250 hours of instruction.

Third level. Students gain mastery of more advanced methods of system programming, optimization methods, and ways of organizing data on computers. They should be able to develop a range of applied programs and debug programs for microprocessor equipment.[37]

Such is the general plan. Specific requirements for basic computer training depend on the student's field of concentration. Those studying to become computer systems programmers are expected to complete the third level; future rank-and-file engineers are in most instances expected to master the second level; and students in the humanities and other less technical fields complete only the first level. Basic training is complemented by specialized training in the use of computers and microprocessors and of computer-assisted design, control, and scientific research systems.[38]

The December 1983 instructions set forth an ambitious program for nationwide computer education. From available evidence, it appears that subsequent implementation has varied widely from institution to institution. At the Moscow Electronic Engineering Institute (MIET), long recognized as one of the strongest in this area, a comprehensive computer education program was functioning at the beginning of 1984, along with an extensive program for teacher computer training.[39] But many other schools have continued to be severely handicapped by a shortage of computer facilities and a lack of suitable instructors. In 1986 it was estimated that computer facilities in higher educational institutions of the Moldavian Republic satisfied only 30 percent of the need for computer time and only 10 percent of the need for display time.[40]

Although it is not known to what degree these figures are applicable to other parts of the country, there is general agreement that computer facilities do not measure up to modern standards. The situation existing at the Tiumen Industrial Institute in 1987 is not unusual, according to then USSR Minister of Higher Education Iagodin:

> At this higher educational institution the material and technical base is such that from 50 to 100 percent of laboratory work in the engineering disciplines has to be replaced by theoretical exercises . . . Alas, this is a typical example. The educational equipment used in many higher educational institutions is five to ten years behind the equipment in advanced enterprises.[41]

Like the rector of the Taganrog Radio Engineering Institute cited earlier, Iagodin is hopeful that when enterprises are required to pay for specialist training, institutes will obtain the funds they need to upgrade their equipment.

Use of Personal Computers in Higher Education

Soviet educators have been debating about what type of computers are most suitable. Is it preferable to have classrooms with display terminals attached to large computers (minicomputers or mainframes) or local networks of personal computers (PCs)? Heretofore, most institutions have favored the acquisition of general-purpose computers, such as the computers of the ES and SM series, though many schools have acquired other types, often in a seemingly haphazard manner.[42]

Increasingly, however, educators and scientists are coming to recognize the advantages of using PCs. Writing in the leading Soviet journal of higher education in 1983, two professors from the Moscow Physical Technical Institute (MFTI) pointed out that PCs are much more versatile for training and professional work than the larger ES models.[43] Later, two professors at the All-Union Correspondence Machine-Building Institute in Moscow argued that microcomputers and PCs should comprise "an average of 80 to 90 percent of all the computer equipment in the higher educational institution."[44] They consider PCs adequate for most student needs and less expensive and more reliable than systems in which monitors are hooked up to a large computer, such as one in the ES series. In their estimation, the PC needed for basic training should be reliable, simple to use, compact, and inexpensive. It should be able to perform the range of tasks commonly encountered by specialists in different lines of work, come with suitable software, be capable of producing graphics, and be mass-produced so that it can be used throughout the country. Yet, *all* of these present problems for the higher educational institutions, because no Soviet model meets these basic demands in an altogether satisfactory manner.[45]

A number of higher educational institutions already have acquired a considerable amount of experience in using PCs for instructional purposes. Classrooms equipped with PCs are found at Moscow State University, the Moscow Physical Technical Institute (MFTI), the Moscow Chemical Technology Institute (MKhTI), the Moscow Aviation Institute, the Leningrad Electrical Engineering Institute (LETI), and Voronezh State University, among others. At the Moscow Electronic Engineering Institute (MIET), there is a training program for small computers of the *Elektronika*-60 class; and at the All-Union Correspondence Machine-Building Institute, about 3,000 students each year receive practical laboratory training with microcomputers. Such programs have also been developed at the Leningrad Polytechnical Institute, the Taganrog Radio Engineering Institute, and other schools.[46]

Although institutions of higher learning will surely continue to encounter difficulties in acquiring proper equipment, the supply situation shows some signs of improving. In recent years the self-financing scientific association has begun to coordinate efforts to utilize computer equipment in institutions throughout the RSFSR, with 20 institutes designated to develop and test programs, methods, and equipment. In addition, the current five-year plan calls for a substantial increase in the number of computers produced. Production of PCs is supposed to reach 1.1 million units during the twelfth five-year plan (1986–90). It is ever more doubtful, however, that this objective will be reached by the target date. According to B. Naumov, "almost half" of the PCs have been earmarked for secondary and higher educational institutions.[47]

Furthermore, the basic guidelines call for approximately 130,000 workstations, equipped with PCs and terminals, to be put into service at higher educational institutions by 1990. They also call for the organization of more computer networks and data bases that can be used by several institutions, for improved information services, and for better coordination of the production and dissemination of computer programs. The additional 130,000 workstations, if installed, will still fall far short of Minvuz's ambitious plans for the computerization of the learning process, but it will be a step in the right direction. In 1986 Minvuz estimated that when the 130,000 workstations are installed, the average student would be able to use computers interactively for more than 200 hours in the course of his or her studies. Since undergraduate studies generally last five years, the 200 hours translates to a meager 40 hours per year. It was also estimated that students at engineering and technical institutes would be able to use computers interactively for about 500 hours during their course of study (i.e., about 100 hours a year).[48] Subsequently, however, these figures were thought to be inflated. The implementing decree issued in March 1987 stipulated that there should be "at least 250 to 300 hours of hands-on experience for students in higher educational institutions that train engineers, technical specialists, and economists and 100 hours of hands-on experience for students in other higher education institutions."[49] These figures are equivalent to between 50 and 60 hours a year for engineers and 20 hours a year for the others.[50] Problems of software and maintenance will no doubt continue to limit use of the hardware.

The Soviet drive to place computers in secondary schools, institutes, and universities is guided by plans formulated at the national level by the responsible ministries. In this respect, of course, the path followed by the USSR differs markedly from that taken by the United States, where the federal government has played a limited role in introducing computers into the educational system. The spread of computers in American higher education has been termed "an accidental revolution," a transformation that was in many ways unanticipated and undirected and that continues at a brisk pace. Today one of its most striking features is the acquisition of PCs by thousands of undergraduate and postgraduate students. There is now the prospect that, in the 1990s, PCs will become as common a possession of American students as typewriters had been forty years earlier.[51]

Conclusion

The current effort to restructure Soviet higher education is propelled by several forces. Chief among them is the leadership's view that intensified efforts to revitalize the economy are necessary, if the USSR is not only to maintain its status as a superpower but also to predominate in the competition between socialism and capitalism. As one Soviet scholar stated pointedly in *Pravda:* "Under present conditions, the winner in the historical competition [between socialism and capitalism] will be whichever socioeconomic system has the higher quality information at its disposal, produces it more rapidly and in larger quantities, and uses it more effectively to achieve its goals."[52]

If implemented as projected, the restructuring will contribute in several ways to the Soviet economy's ability to exploit modern information technologies. One, the plans to revise the list of specialties and study programs, to give students broader training, and to expand "targeted training" based on contracts with enterprises, may well make the manpower planning system more responsive to changing economic needs. Probably the biggest payoffs will occur in areas such as computer science, electronics, and robotics, where the demand for specialists has grown especially rapidly and where the content of the specialties themselves has undergone rapid change.

Two, with respect to the educational process, it is possible that some changes in routines and in academic programs will make Soviet higher educational institutions more open, interesting, creative, and achievement-oriented places than they have been. Plans to reduce the mandatory lecture load, to provide more individualized training, and to increase financial incentives for outstanding performance may promote greater creativity and responsibility among both faculty and students. However, these measures—along with the proposed periodic recertification of teachers, the willingness to widen pay scales, and such—will introduce new elements of competitiveness and uncertainty. They are likely to be resisted by members of the staff who are wedded to the old ways.

Three, the reform will surely add impetus to the drive to computerize higher education. The substantial increase that is called for in funding should enable institutes and universities to purchase more hardware and software. If an additional 130,000 computer workstations are installed, many more students will be able to learn to apply them in their professional work. The quality and quantity of the computers are unlikely to satisfy Minvuz's more ambitious plans for computerization, and long-standing problems of equipment, servicing, and software will no doubt persist. Nonetheless, the changes will make a difference for tens of thousands of Soviet students.[53]

Four, the efforts to increase the amount of research in the higher educational system promise to make better use of the system's research potential. The efforts to create organizations that cut across institutional boundaries, such as the "education-science-production complexes," to have more students engage in research as part of their training, and to recruit cadres from industry and scientific institutes may also help to make the universities and institutes centers of innovation.

Despite these signs of change, however, there is no reason to expect that the restructuring of higher education will move the USSR beyond the confines of the "Soviet-style information society" described by Seymour Goodman. Furthermore, the implementation of the reform plan will no doubt encounter resistance. Iagodin, the highest educational official, has been mindful of the challenges ahead. In the fall of 1987 he observed that enthusiasts and innovators are much less numerous than those who approach the reform guardedly and that in only a few institutions had the implementation gone beyond the very first steps. He saw that "the deeply rooted habit of acting only according to instructions has become the main restraining factor." Passivity and distrust, he said, are contrary to the goal, "a type of higher educational institution where competency and a spirit of search reign and where discussion, not peace of mind, is encouraged."[54]

The system of higher education, like other key institutions in Soviet society, is highly bureaucratized and resistant to change. It has offered professors and students limited incentives for outstanding performance and innovation, and it has long been separated by institutional barriers from science and production. Thus it remains to be seen to what degree the current restructuring will foster initiative, independence, and achievement. To reform the system in a fundamental sense and to make it a true catalyst of change will demand vision and persistence, and much will depend on the long-term outcome of Gorbachev's overall reform package.

Notes

1. "Proekt TsK KPSS: Osnovnye napravleniia perestroiki vysshego i sred-nego spetsial'nogo obrazovaniia v strane," *Pravda* (June 1, 1986), p. 1.

2. "Osnovnye napravleniia perestroiki vysshego i sred

nego spetsial'nogo ob-razovaniia v strane," *Pravda* (March 21, 1987), pp. 1–3. This document is re-printed in K. S. Pavlishchev (ed.), *Narodnoe obrazovanie v SSSR: Sbornik nor-mativnykh aktov* (Moscow: Iuridicheskaia literatura, 1987), pp. 223–45. In translation, see "The Fundamental Guidelines for the Restructuring of Higher and Secondary Education in the Country," *Soviet Education*, 29, no. 9–10 (July–August 1987), 118–64. Five resolutions on the restructuring were published in *Pravda* between March 25 and 29. They concern: (1) improving the training and use of specialists (March 25), (2) improving the training and use of teaching and research personnel (March 26), (3) enhancing the role of scientific research (March 27), (4) raising the salaries of the teaching and research staff (March 28), and (5) improving the material, housing, and leisure conditions of undergraduates and postgraduates (March 29). Four of these resolutions are reprinted in Pavlishchev, *Narodnoe obrazovanie*.

3. G. A. Iagodin, "Following the Course Set by the Twenty-seventh CPSU Congress," *Vestnik vysshei shkoly*, 1986, no. 4, trans. in *Soviet Education*, vol. 29, no. 9–10 (July–August 1987), pp. 28–29.

4. G. A. Iagodin, "The Restructuring of the Higher Education System and Continuing Education," *Politicheskoie samoobrazovanie*, 1986, no. 7; trans. in *Soviet Education*, vol. 29, no. 9–10 (July–August 1987), pp. 109–110.

5. *Ibid.*, p. 98.

6. See, e.g., Daniel Bell, *The Post-Industrial Society* (New York: Basic Books, 1974); Alvin Toffler, *The Third Wave* (New York: Morrow, 1981); Yoneji Ma-suda, *The Information Society as Post-Industrial Society* (Washington, DC: World Future Society, 1981); Tom Stonier, *The Wealth of Information: A Profile of the Post-Industrial Economy* (London: Thames Methuen, 1983); and Tom Forester (ed.), *The Information Technology Revolution* (Cambridge: MIT Press, 1985).

7. There is an extensive literature on the scientific-technological revolution (NTR) and its anticipated impact on Soviet society. See *Nauchno-tekhnicheskaia revoliutsiia i obshchestvo* (Moscow: Mysl', 1973); *Nauchno-tekhnicheskaia re-voliutsiia i sotsializm* (Moscow: Politizdat, 1973); N. V. Markov, *Nauchno-tekhnicheskaia revoliutsiia: analiz, perspektivy, posledstviia*, 2nd ed. (Moscow: Politizdat, 1973); S. V. Shukhardin and V. I. Gukov (eds.), *Nauchno-tekhni-cheskaia revoliutsiia* (Moscow: Nauka, 1976). On the NTR's impact on educa-tion, see V. N. Turchenko, *Nauchno-tekhnicheskaia revoliutsiia i revoliutsiia v obrazovanii* (Moscow: Politizdat, 1973); R. V. Khokhlov (ed.), *Nauchno-tekhn-icheskaia revoliutsiia i razvitie vysshego obrazovaniia* (Moscow: Moscow State University Press, 1974); V. G. Afanasyev, *The Scientific and Technological Rev-olution—Its Impact on Management and Education*, trans. Robert Daglish (Mos-cow: Progress Publishers, 1975); and S. N. Eremin and E. V. Semenov, *Nauka i obrazovanie v strukture NTR* (Novosibirsk: Nauka, 1986). See also Frederic J. Fleron, Jr. (ed.), *Technology and Communist Culture: The Socio-Cultural Impact of Technology under Socialism* (New York: Praeger, 1977); Erik P. Hoffman and

Robbin F. Laird, *Technocratic Socialism: The Soviet Union in the Advanced Industrial Era* (Durham, NC: Duke University Press, 1985); and U.S. Central Intelligence Agency, Directorate of Intelligence, *The USSR Confronts the Information Revolution: A Conference Report* (May 1987), SOV 87-10029. According to D. M. Gvishiani, former deputy head of the State Committee on Science and Technology, "The disclosure of the essence and social role of the scientific and technological revolution is one of the most significant theoretical and political conclusions reached by Marxism in the second half of the 20th century" (cited in Hoffman and Laird, *Technocratic Socialism*, p. 2.). Soviet scholars have argued that the nature and potential of the NTR are determined by the type of society in which they occur. In Western "capitalist" societies, the achievements of science and technology are said to be used for the pursuit of profit and the narrow interests of the ruling class. Only under socialism, they have maintained, will the full benefits of the NTR rebound to the mass of the citizens and promote their all-around development.

8. Cited in Hoffman and Laird, *Technocratic Socialism*, p. 115.

9. M. S. Gorbachev, *Korennoi vopros ekonomicheskoi politiki partii: Doklad na soveshchanii v TsK KPSS po voprosam uskoreniia nauchno-tekhnicheskogo progressa, 11 iiunia 1985 goda* (Moscow: Politizdat, 1985), p. 14.

10. USSR, Tsentral'noe Statisticheskoe Upravlenie, *Narodnoe khoziaistvo SSSR v 1985 g.* (Moscow: Finansy i statistika, 1986), pp. 27, 64, 400–401; and U.S. Department of Education, Center for Education Statistics, *The Condition of Education* (Washington, DC: U.S. G.P.O., 1986), p. 114.

11. *Ibid.*, p. 505. Although both the Soviet and American systems of higher education are very large, the two differ in the relative size of the college-age cohort that they enroll and graduate. Relative to the size of population, the total number of college students was three times higher in the United States than in the USSR in the late 1970s (60 percent to 20 percent). Although many American students are enrolled in two-year programs that do not always lead to the bachelor's degree, the contrast is nonetheless striking—especially in light of the fact that two out of five Soviet students are enrolled in evening and correspondence programs. When it comes to college graduations, the difference between the USSR and the U.S. is still appreciable. The number of undergraduate degrees conferred was equal to 18 percent of all American 22-year-olds in 1960 and 25 percent in 1978. This compares with some 8 percent and 16 percent, respectively, of all Soviet 23-year-olds. This disparity between the two systems has persisted over the past decade. The figures cited are from Catherine P. Ailes and Francis W. Rushing, *The Science Race: Training and Utilization of Scientists and Engineers, US and USSR* (New York: Crane, Russak & Co, 1982), pp. 66–67.

12. "Osnovnye napravleniia," in Pavlishchev, *Narodnoe obrazovanie*, p. 224.

13. Iagodin, "Following the Course," p. 42.

14. N. N. Moiseyev [Moiseev], "'Education and Science—Unity or Opposition,'" *Khimia i zhizn'*, no. 11 (November 1985); trans. by the Joint Publication Research Service (JPRS), UST-86-013 (May 15, 1986), p. 23.

15. I. Obraztsov, "Ispol'zovanie nauchnogo potentsiala vuzov," *Voprosy ekonomiki*, no. 7 (July 1986), p. 13. In 1986 then USSR Minister of Higher Education Iagodin stated that the proportion of students included in targeted train-

ing was 15–20 percent, but that it will increase to at least 60 percent by 1990. Iagodin, "Following the Course," p. 31.

16. See the resolution of the CPSU Central Committee and USSR Council of Ministers of March 13, 1987, "O merakh po korennomu uluchsheniiu kachestva podgotovki i ispol'zovaniia spetsialistov s vysshim obrazovaniem v narodnom khoziaistve," in Pavlishchev, *Narodnoe obrazovanie*, pp. 246–57. The specific reference is to p. 249.

17. A. V. Kaliaev, "Pravo na risk," in *Ekonomicheskaia gazeta*, no. 32 (August 1986), p. 16.

18. The specialties are to be regrouped by type of work, rather than the area in which the work is applied. Thus, similar types of work—e.g., design engineer in the machine-building industry and design engineer in the electronic industry— might be combined in one specialty. The object of the labor or sphere of activity, which formerly defined the specialty, will become a "specialization" (*spetsializatsiia*) within the specialty. According to Minvuz, three actors will make the following contributions to the formulation of the study programs. The general academic training for a specialty will be elaborated and confirmed by Minvuz. The 30–35 percent of the requirements that pertain to the branch of the economy in which the specialists will work will be formulated by the educational methodology association (*uchebno-metodicheskoe ob"edinenie*). This association is to be based on the leading higher educational institution in the particular branch, with representatives from related higher educational institutions. The remaining 15–20 percent will be determined by the specific higher educational institution on the basis of the demand for cadres. See "Na putiakh perestroiki vysshego obrazovaniia" (Editorial), in *Vestnik vysshei shkoly*, no. 7 (July 1986), pp. 4–5.

19. The resolution on training makes it clear that financial obligations will be used to enforce discipline regarding postgraduation job assignments: graduates who do not report to their assigned workplace, who refuse to start work, or who quit or are fired before they complete their three-year work assignment will have to reimburse the enterprise for the stipends that were paid when they studied. No such obligation existed before. "O merakh po korennomu uluchsheniiu," p. 255.

20. *Ibid.*, pp. 246–48, 255; "Osnovnye napravleniia," pp. 229–31.

21. V. Sokolov, "Sovershenstvovat' rukovodstvo, povyshat' otvetstvennost'," *Kommunist*, no. 12 (August 1986), pp. 87–88.

22. See the resolution of the CPSU Central Committee and USSR Council of Ministers of March 13, 1987, "O merakh po uluchsheniiu podgotovki i ispol'zovaniia nauchno-pedagogicheskikh i nauchnykh kadrov," in Pavlishchev, *Narodnoe obrazovania*, pp. 271–75.

23. On the role of the faculties for qualification raising (*fakultety povyshenii kvalifikatsii*), see Stephen T. Kerr, "Innovation on Command: Development and Educational Technology in the Soviet Union," *Educational Communication and Technology Journal (ECTJ)*, 30, no. 2 (summer 1982), 98–116; "Ob izuchenii v sisteme povysheniia kvalifikatsii voprosov, sviazannykh s primeneniem mikroprotsessornykh sredstv i mikroEVM," Letter of Instruction dated November 22, 1982 in *Biulleten' Ministerstva vysshego i srednego spetsial'nogo obrazovaniia SSSR* (hereafter cited as *Biulleten'*), no. 1 (January, 1983), pp. 23–27;

and D. I. Vasil'ev, "Chtoby prepodavateli vladeli EVM," *Vestnik vysshei shkoly,* no. 6 (June, 1983), pp. 47–52.

24. Gorbachev, *Korennoi vopros,* p. 20.

25. According to calculations by Minvuz, only about 15 percent of all expenditures for research at higher educational institutions in 1985 went for fundamental and investigative research. An additional 15 percent was spent on experimental design work (*opytno-konstruktorskie raboty*), and 70 percent went for applied development (*prikladnye razrabotki*). The reform envisions a shift in resources, so that by 1990, the end of the current five-year plan, the proportions will be 20 percent for fundamental research, 30 percent for experimental design work, and 50 percent for applied development. "On the Path of Restructuring," *Vestnik,* p. 7. See also the resolution of the CPSU Central Committee and the USSR Council of Ministers of March 13, 1987, "O povyshenii roli vuzovskoi nauki v uskorenii nauchno-technicheskogo progressa, uluchshenii kachestva podgotovki spetsialistov," in Pavlishchev, *Narodnoe obrazovanie,* pp. 264–70.

26. Obraztsov, "Ispol'zovanie," p. 7.

27. Regarding the success of the Taganrog Radio Engineering Institute, Obraztsov writes: "Since 1980, the amount of research and development has increased threefold, the volume of most important types of R&D has increased tenfold, the economic impact obtained from the introduction [of new technologies and discoveries] has increased fifteenfold, and the number of certificates of authorship for inventions has increased thirtyfold and comes to 150–200 certificates a year. Leading enterprises, scientific research institutes, and design bureaus willingly hire this institute's graduates, who combine a thorough basic training with good practical skills." Obraztsov, "Ispol'zovanie," p. 7.

28. *Ibid.;* Obraztsov, "On the Paths of Restructuring," *Kommunist,* no. 12 (December, 1986), trans. in *Soviet Education,* p. 71; and Kaliaev, "Pravo na risk," p. 16.

29. In addition, Obraztsov maintains that greater attention should be given to new branches of mathematics used for complex quantitative analyses—"information science theory, operational research, decision theory, game theory, linear and nonlinear program design, management theory—in short, everything that goes to make up the mathematical apparatus of general systems theory in its present form." In his view, a firm grasp of such theories is indispensable for an understanding of complex socioeconomic and physical processes. I. Obraztsov, "The Steps of the Higher School System," *Agitator,* no. 16 (1986); trans. in *Soviet Education,* pp. 80–81.

30. B. N. Naumov, "'Drevo tselei' v komp'iuternykh kushchakh," interview conducted by O. Chulkov, *Zhurnalist,* no. 11 (November 1986), p. 73. On the use of computers in the USSR, see S. E. Goodman and Alan Ross Stapleton, "Microcomputing in the Soviet Union and Eastern Europe," *Abacus,* 3, no. 1 (1985), 6–22; and S. E. Goodman and W. K. McHenry, "Computing in the USSR: Recent Progress and Policies," *Soviet Economy,* 2, no. 4 (1986), 327–54; and Ivan Selin, "Communications and Computers in the USSR: Successes and Failures," *Signal* (December 1986), pp. 91–95.

31. Naumov, "'Drevo tselei,'" p. 73.

32. See "Industriia informatiki," interview with N. V. Gorshkov, chairman of the State Committee on Computer Technology and Informatics, *Pravda* (August 17, 1986), p. 2.

33. See G. I. Marchuk, "Perestroika nauchnoi deiatel'nosti akademicheskikh uchrezhdenii v svete reshenii XXVII s"ezda KPSS," *Vestnik Akademii nauk SSSR*, no. 1 (January 1987), pp. 3–13; G. Marchuk, "Nauka na perelome," *Pravda* (February 16, 1987), p. 3; and interview with G. I. Marchuk by V. Konovalov, "Uchenyi i vremia," *Izvestiia* (March 22, 1987).

34. The higher educational institutions specifically cited for having achieved significant success in computer education were the Moscow Steel and Alloys Institute, the Moscow Engineering Physics Institute, the Moscow Electronic Engineering Institute, the Moscow Energy Institute, the Moscow Institute of Management, the Moscow Higher Technical School named after N. E. Bauman, Moscow State University, Dnepropetrovsk State University, the Kiev Polytechnical Institute, and the Moscow, Kazan, and Kharkov aviation institutes. "O merakh po dal'neishemu sovershenstvovaniiu podgotovki studentov, aspirantov i prepodavatelei vysshikh, uchashchikhsia i prepodavatelei srednikh spetsial'nykh uchebnykh zavedenii v oblasti ispol'zovaniia vychislitel'noi tekhniki," *Biulleten'*, no. 9 (September 1982), pp. 12–15.

35. *Opyt ispol'zovaniia sredstva vychislitel'noi tekhniki v vuzakh: Obzornaia informatsiia* (Moscow: Scientific-Research Institute of Problems of the Higher School, 1982), cited in S. V. Cheremnykh and Iu. E. Poliak, "Komp'iuterizatsiia obrazovaniia—problemy massovogo obucheniia," *Ekonomika i organizatsiia promyshlennogo proizvodstva (EKO)*, no. 2 (February 1982), p. 160. There are frequent complaints in the press about these problems. For example, one professor complains about the shortage of software and about how students must go "on excursions" to computer centers. A. Riabov, "V gosti k EVM," *Pravda* (January 1, 1986). Another, working at a military institute, deplores the "extremely weak" software available and rues the weeks and months that enterprising teachers have to devote to developing programs and "reinventing the wheel." V. Shepilov, "Entuziasty est', no. . . . ," *Krasnaia zvezda* (April 5, 1987).

36. "O merakh po dal'neishemu sovershenstvovaniiu funtsionirovaniia otraslevogo fonda algoritmov i programm Minvuza SSSR," *Biulleten'*, no. 3 (March, 1984), pp. 24–29.

37. "Ob osnovnykh napravleniiakh sovershenstvovaniia podgotovki spetsialistov v oblasti ispol'zovaniia vychislitel'noi tekhniki," Letter of Instruction dated December 20, 1983 in *Biulleten'*, no. 3 (March 1984), pp. 24–29.

38. *Ibid.*, p. 27.

39. L. N. Presnukhin, A. A. Sazonov, and V. F. Shan'gin, "Skills in the Use of Microcomputers—for Each Specialist," *Vestnik vysshei shkoly*, no. 4 (April 1985); trans. by JPRS, UHR-85-014, (August 6, 1985), pp. 118–22.

40. I. Sandu, Deputy Minister of Higher and Specialized Secondary Education of the Moldavian SSR, "Kadram—sovremennuiu podgotovku," *Kommunist Moldavii*, no. 6 (June 1986), pp. 49–54.

41. G. A. Iagodin, "VUZ derzhit ekzamen," *Sovetskaia Rossiia* (March 15, 1987), p. 1.

42. The ES (*Edinnaia sistema,* or Unified System) and SM (*Sistema malykh,* or Small System) are produced by CMEA countries and are the most commonly used types of computers throughout Eastern Europe and the USSR. The ES mainframe effort was begun in 1965 and is based on the IBM 360/70 family. The SM program was begun in 1974 and was initially split between the duplication of Hewlett-Packard and DEC architectures. (For further details, see Stapleton and Goodman, "Microcomputing in the USSR," and Goodman and McHenry, "Computing in the USSR.") With respect to the eclectic and seemingly haphazard acquisition of computers, the situation at the Tallin Polytechnical Institute is illustrative. American scholars who visited in the summer of 1987 reported that the institute had some 300 computer workstations. They saw in place not only various ES and SM models, but also Australian MicroBees, Japanese Yamahas, East German Robotion PCs, and a Sharp microcomputer, among others. Personal communication from Seymour Goodman, Peter Wolcott, and Andrzej T. Jarmoszko, Department of Management Information Systems, College of Business and Public Administration, University of Arizona (August 1987).

43. I. T. Gusev and A. G. Filippov, "Vsem vypusknikam—navyki pol'zovaniia mikro-EVM," *Vestnik vysshei shkoly,* no. 3 (March 1983), pp. 13–16. A year later an article by E. P. Velikhov, vice-president of the USSR Academy of Sciences, did much to create an awareness of the advantages of PCs in scientific circles. See E. P. Velikhov in *Vestnik Akademii Nauk SSSR,* no. 8 (August 1984), pp. 3–9.

44. Cheremnykh and Poliak, "Komp'iuterizatsiia," p. 161.

45. Citing a foreign study that compared six personal computers with a powerful minicomputer connected to six display terminals, Cheremnykh and Poliak report that the six PCs cost half as much as the minicomputer with six terminals, that repair costs for the PCs were one-tenth as much as those for the minicomputer, and that, unlike the minicomputer, the PCs did not require additional service personnel. "A special merit of personal computers," they add, "is the reliability of the system as a whole. When one machine breaks down, five of them continue to operate while the breakdown of a microcomputer leads to the interruption of work at all six of the workstations." If the equipment is not reliable, they point out, it is likely to lead to students' developing "a lack of confidence" and "other negative psychological consequences." *Ibid.,* pp. 161–63.

46. *Ibid.,* p. 163.

47. *Ibid.,* p. 160; B. Naumov, "Personal'nye EVM na starte," *Izvestiia* (July 10, 1986), p. 3.

48. "Osnovnye napravleniia," p. 242; and "Na putiakh perestroiki," *Vestnik,* p. 9.

49. "O merakh po korennomu ulusheniiu," pp. 251–52.

50. Although the Soviet target figures for hands-on use of computers may appear low, it should be noted that the first high-level U.S. panel established a goal for the United States near the same level. In its 1967 report, *Computers in Higher Education* (the "Pierce report"), the President's Advisory Committee determined that American undergraduates should receive 30 hours of hands-on instruction for a satisfactory computer education. (The average was based on all

students.) Cited in Robert G. Gillespie, with Deborah A. Dicaro, *Computing and Higher Education: An Accidental Revolution,* University of Washington (1981); available on microfiche through ERIC, No. ED 205068, p. 3.

51. According to Gillespie, the amount spent by American colleges and universities on computers increased from $200 million a year in the mid-1960s to $1 billion annually in 1980. During the same period, the proportion of colleges and universities with computers or access to them grew from 10 percent to 90 percent; Gillespie, *Computing.* See also Carnegie Commission on Higher Education, *The Fourth Revolution: Instructional Technology in Higher Education* (New York: McGraw-Hill, 1972); John W. Hamblen and Thomas B. Baird, *Computers in Higher Education, 1976–77: Fourth Inventory* (Princeton, NJ: ECUCOM, 1979); John Riccobono, *Instructional Technology in Higher Education* (Washington, DC: Corporation for Public Broadcasting, 1986); and *Microcomputer Use in Higher Education,* Executive summary of a survey conducted by EDUCOM and Peat Marwick in cooperation with *The Chronicle of Higher Education,* May 1987.

52. A. Rakitov, "Informatizatsiia obshchestva i strategiia uskoreniia," *Pravda* (January 23, 1987), pp. 2–3.

53. In public discussions of the use of computers in higher education, political concerns have not figured prominently. No doubt increased availability of PCs will heighten concern about students using the computers for purposes other than those approved of by the authorities.

54. G. Iagodin, "Initsiativa bez instruktsii," *Pravda* (October 9, 1987).

5

THE SOVIET UNION AND THE PERSONAL COMPUTER REVOLUTION

Ross A. Stapleton and Seymour E. Goodman

The idea of a personal computer "revolution," specifically in the United States and other industrialized countries, is defensible on the strength of achievements in two areas. In terms of production, personal computing resources have become so profuse as to afford a considerable amount of "slack," or idle time, such that users are not constrained to routines or schedules, but are free to make use of the technology as they may find convenient. Unlike early mainframe systems, to which human resources were sacrificed for the sake of keeping the expensive hardware fully tasked, personal computers remain for the most part idle. When required they can be made fully available to the needs of a researcher, engineer, executive, housekeeper, and student, and make the individual more productive. The first component of the "revolution" is the realization of a sufficient mass of the resource to change its character from that of a scarce commodity demanding human time, to a widespread resource that can be employed at will.

The second component involves the social perception of personal computing. Simultaneous with the evolution from a scarce to an abundant commodity, there has been a steadily growing acceptance of personal computing as a universally applicable tool. Whereas computers have enjoyed extensive application in manufacturing and large business environments, personal computers are proving themselves at all levels in business, engineering, and throughout the economy as personal workstations.

The two components together define a revolutionary transformation of computing, from an exotic technology to a widely consumed resource.

Personal computing in the United States has been far less directed from above than driven by various interests from below. The high degree of slack provided by the surplus of personal computing has served to make it a discretionary resource. Severe economic deficiencies hampering production efforts and a generally poor infrastructure preclude any such condition in the USSR. The Soviets are attempting to introduce personal computing into the economy by fiat, in an environment that may not be ready for it. At the same time there is a degree of experimentation with personal computing by individuals, an introduction from below. A small but steady flow of resources from West to East is providing at least some nourishment to a grass-roots familiarity with PC technology in the USSR and throughout the Council for Mutual Economic Assistance (CMEA) community.[1]

There is no evidence to discount the assertion that the Soviets are "responding" to Western personal computing achievements. Several official decrees, in particular the Politburo decision on promoting secondary school computer literacy, have set ambitious goals for the introduction of personal computers into the economy.[2] Attention is also being paid to Western systems, software, and experience. Empirical study shows the Soviets willing directly to transfer Western technology, adopting many of the same architectures, in the interest of accelerating the development of personal computing resources.[3] It is difficult, however, to see how fundamental obstacles can be overcome to permit a comparable revolutionary advance in the Soviet economic and social environment.

Scope and Nature of U.S. Personal Computing

The PC production industry in the West has without question passed through its initial phases of growth, and personal computer hardware and supplementary software are well-established technologies. The industry leaders such as IBM and Apple have succeeded in promoting a viable set of standard systems produced in sufficient quantity to support subsequent software production.[4] The later success of "scavenging" second-source producers in duplicating the leaders' systems has given the industry a sufficient coherence and mass to project personal computing systems into wide application.[5] We are now seeing evolutionary changes in a considerably matured industry. A current concern of the leading U.S. producers is to maintain control in an environment fast becoming a commodity market, that is, to wrest back portions of the market lost to clone and compatible producers.[6] Regardless of whether the industry leaders manage to retain their share, the last several years have seen a strong growth in a market of proven architectures and software to complement them. The supply of personal computing in the United States and elsewhere in the West has grown enormously as a result.

Looking at the scale of the industries as a whole, the value of the U.S. personal computer hardware and software markets was in excess of $16 billion in 1984, and is expected to reach more than $53 billion by 1989.[7] The number of PCs being absorbed by the U.S. business sector has risen steadily from some 300,000 in 1981 to an estimated 3.7 million new PCs in 1986.[8]

At the same time, a sizable percentage of the personal computer market is devoted to home and school use. A 1985 Future Computing Inc. survey of IBM PC and Macintosh purchases placed 2 percent of the 1.8 million IBM PCs and PC/XTs versus 17 percent of the 292,000 Macintoshes in the schools, and 20 versus 49 percent, respectively, in homes.[9] A 1986 survey of U.S. public school districts showed microcomputers in 91.4 percent of all schools, up from 16 percent in 1981–82.[10] At the same time the ratio of microcomputers to students increased from one per 750 students in 1981, to one per 30 in 1986.[11]

In terms of application, the latest PCs have enabled some work previously impossible or uneconomical. For example, office word processing and desktop publishing promise to make professional quality presentation affordable to small firms and even individuals.[12]

A five-phase "pervasiveness" model may be employed to describe the progress of a technology from inception to complete absorption by society:[13]

1. An experimental rarity, often an entrepreneurial or laboratory discovery.
2. An exotic tool or toy used by a small group of experts.
3. Products that are well known and manufactured in modest quantity, but direct use is limited to a small fraction of industrial or other institutional environments.
4. Widespread production and availability, with direct use requiring little or modest training in a broad domain by a sizable minority of the population.
5. The technology has become part of the fabric and infrastructure of

daily life, and its absence is often more noticeable than its presence.

Despite significant barriers that still exist to making PCs useful to (and usable by) all classes of people, personal computing in the United States is, by this model, squarely in the fourth phase.[14]

It would be optimistic to predict a rapid transition of personal computing to a phase five technology. The utility of the telephone and television is clear, but only a small part of the U.S. population has an immediate need for personal computing, or would suffer greatly from its absence. And the enormous reduction in prices seen over the last several years notwithstanding, a personal computer system configured to meet the average user's needs is still several times more expensive than the most expensive of "indispensable" household appliances. But personal computing, coupled with an enhanced communications environment afforded by such advances as Integrated Services Digital Network (ISDN) technology and various commercial network services, may closely integrate with, and certainly augment, both telephones and television as a component in the global information system in the decades to come.

Personal Computing in the Soviet Setting

The study of USSR developments in personal computing should be considered not only with regard to the technical level attained, but in comparison to the market success attained in the West. That is, whereas the Soviets may have achieved an equivalent technical proficiency for a given system, the more important question is whether or not that system can be expected to be replicated in sufficient quantity, disseminated with sufficient support, and accepted in its application. By "sufficient" we mean at least in quantities to encourage wider use and continued growth. A key component in the transition of a technology from phase three to phase four in the pervasiveness model is the widespread dissemination of the technology outside of an initial, narrow user community.

Some of the factors that have led to the growth of personal computing as an industry in the West may have some bearing on future Soviet developments. For example, the rising level of participation by foreign producers of the industrialized and newly industrializing countries of the Pacific rim in the supply of the U.S. personal computing resource pool suggests a number of options heretofore unavailable to the Soviets.

Technically, the strategies of the American industry leaders may exert considerable influence on Soviet choices. As with previous programs in mainframe and minicomputer systems, the Soviets are basing many of their personal computing decisions on U.S. research and development, through replication of American systems. Various deficiencies in the Soviet economy, and incentives to be risk averse in order to safely meet planned quotas, make the transfer of proven technology a reasonable course of action.

The basis for an evaluation of the current USSR personal computing capability, and leading from that to an estimate of its potential through the end of the century, is a profile of personal computing resources in their generation and consumption by the Soviet economy. To this end, we examine the phenomenon in a four-stage process. The stages—design, production, installation, and perception—proceed up from technical incarnation to application. This examination also needs to be aware of world developments applicable to the USSR economy. At each stage, therefore, internal developments are considered in parallel with external options. More than in many other areas, the Iron Curtain is proving permeable to Western personal computing achievements and experience.

Developmental Stages

Design

Indigenous technological capability. Clearly, Soviet developments will remain in the context of their own domestic technological capabilities. Soviet R&D will not be designing systems that Soviet industry is incapable of producing. Although imports may help meet Soviet personal computing needs, a domestic production capability is critical given the USSR's position as a military superpower and desirable for a number of other reasons. From a pedagogical perspective, the lack of Cyrillic-based programming languages and applications packages may have a negative impact on the acceptance of computing; the need to "russify" Soviet computing has been discussed in the literature.[15] And even if the needs for computing resources could be completely satisfied through imports, the PC production technologies are necessary to many other sectors of the economy. Neglect in promoting a domestic industry capable of PC production can be expected to impact on many of the other features that distinguish a self-sufficient industrialized economy. Telecommunications and production automation, both of which are relying more and more heavily on the microelectronics industry, grow from the same research and development roots. Indigenous system design will proceed apace with the supply of the necessary component technologies by that domestic industry. At the same time, the external developments of the West can be expected to have both "trailblazing" and "bootstrapping" effects on Soviet planning.

External models. The West has provided "proof-of-concept" research and development in the successful systems now on the market. For example, Apple took considerable risks in its design of the Macintosh, with its then radical architecture. The market failure of the Lisa, the Macintosh's immediate predecessor, was part of the price to produce one of the most successful personal computers now available. The now-proven Macintosh, with its successors, is a potential architecture for Soviet developments in the next decade. Western industry leaders have presented the USSR with a set of technically sound options, in effect blazing a low-risk trail.

At the same time, the compatibility with existing Western systems permits bootstrapping in an environment where all the supporting industries may not have been sufficiently formed to support a wholly indigenous effort. The Western software sector experienced its strongest growth only some time after the hardware industry, as might be expected. The success of such producers as Microsoft and Lotus Development Corporation, once the hardware became available in quantity, has been considerable. Lotus's 1-2-3 spreadsheet software has been identified as one of the major contributing factors to the IBM PC's popularity, that is, the initial hardware base supported software that then demanded that level of power and functionality.

The Soviet software industry is primitive by comparison. For it to grow and match planned hardware growth from what is essentially a standing start would have to involve substantial modifications to Soviet economic practice. Whereas there has been a good deal of experimentation in organizational and economic reform under Gorbachev, the USSR simply cannot match the enormous growth that such entrepreneurial corporations as the now major software producers enjoy in the United States. At the same time, whereas the lack of hardware has been commented on and used as a focus for economic reforms to enhance production, it is not clear that Soviet planners properly perceive the need for comparable growth in the software and supporting industries. By selecting compatible systems architectures, however, the Soviet PC producers can put their systems into use despite an inadequacy in domestic software production, making use of widely available Western software.

Three systems serve as illustrations: the IBM PC, and its clones and compatibles, the Apple Macintosh, and the Elektronika BK-0010. The IBM PC has been chosen explicitly as a standard model for both Soviet and CMEA production.[16] Because of a high degree of correspondence between current Soviet microelectronics capability and the requirements of what is a proven Western design, the IBM PC almost ideally fits current capabilities.[17] The microelectronic basis for the IBM PC, that is, the microprocessor and its support chips, was probably identified by the Ministry of the Electronics Industry (Minelektronprom) as its next logical step, after introduction of the first major microprocessor families at the end of the 1970s.[18] The IBM PC was designed as basically an open system with off-the-shelf technology. That is appealing, given the Soviets' component supply sector, which has offered little in the way of production of "equipment-oriented" circuits custom designed for specific applications. The wide availability of IBM PC-compatible software only increases its suitability.

The Macintosh, on the other hand, although proven in the Western market, is unbuildable given mid-1987 Soviet technological capabilities. It has received almost no attention in the CMEA literature. As the Soviet microelectronics industry has closely followed the U.S. Intel line (8080 and 8086) and does not produce equivalents of Motorola microprocessors, this is not surprising.[19] It is possible that both the Motorola 68000 (the basis for the Macintosh) and the Macintosh itself may be pursued in the next decade, depending on the level of growth achieved in microelectronics production, which thus far is restricted in both volume and scope.

The BK-0010 represents a response based on a purely indigenous current capability. Whereas the BK-0010 is actually a derivation of minicomputer technology taken directly from Western developments (the DEC PDP-11 family), it is not patterned on a Western microcomputer design and has minimal compatability with Western personal computing resources. For example, the BK-0010's ROM-based programming language is DEC's "Focal," not Basic.[20] As such it is unable to achieve much in the way of bootstrapping, as discussed above. Consequently, it has been reported as being inadequately supplied with software and peripherals, poorly documented, and is meeting with little acceptance.[21]

An additional benefit accrued by adoption of an externally proven design is in the use of imports of complete systems to augment domestic production.

Responsibility. Whereas the production volume of all Soviet PC models is very low, the number of ministries, institutes and other organizations experimenting with PC design is rather large, and can be attributed both to the ease of designing microprocessor-based hardware and to the fact that no final distribution of responsibility for PC production has yet been seen in economic plans. Given that a PC might be little more than a microprocessor, with some supporting components relatively easily acquired in small quantities, it is not surprising that such models as the Timur, Irisha, and Mikrosha have been seen as prototypes, constructed by institute design groups and individuals at scientific and academic organizations.[22] Additionally, the USSR has provided considerable support for amateur radio as a hobby, which could support "homebrew" efforts. The Soviet journal *Radio* detailed a microcomputer, the Radio-86RK, which could be built from schematics supplied in the magazine.[23]

The two ministries responsible for mainframe and minicomputer production, the Ministry of the Radio Industry as well as the Ministry of Instrument Making, Means of Automation and Control Systems, produce personal computers in one form or another as does Minelektronprom itself. Whereas minicomputers and mainframes have always been produced by Minelektronprom's consumers, the ease of microcomputer production coupled with the lack of specific tasking to any ministry or group of ministries has encouraged all related parties to make some efforts. Similarly, both East Germany's Microelectronics Combine and Hungary's Microelectronics Enterprise have designed their own computers for the first time, in bids to enter the PC market.[24]

Production

One of the most significant barriers to the promotion of personal computing in the Soviet Union is the poor production capacity demonstrated by its domestic industry. The USSR suffers from low production rates, incoherence in production responsibility, and a generally poor level of quality control. To some extent difficulties in production have provided for more slack in the previous stage; there is no great pressure to apply computer-aided design (CAD) resources to computer system design, for example, as even the simplest models have yet to go into large-scale production. On the other hand, production difficulties will seriously impact upon later stages.

At the same time, the world market's character has changed substantially toward a more "generic" or commodity perception of personal computer systems, and a freer market for lesser players and less-industrialized nations.[25]

The commodity nature of PC technology has made it easier freely to substitute components by different producers and to form secondary sources. The generic IBM PC is now the market standard in the United States, and less and less distinction is being made between an original and a "clone." The enormous increase in personal computer imports by the United States, both of complete and semifinished systems and components, is a measure of the degree to which the various technologies have been farmed out to alternate producers.[26]

As of early 1987 no Soviet personal computer model had achieved a cumulative production of more than a few thousand units, with the possible exception of the BK-0010. Whereas various production figures and evidence of some sales may place the BK-0010 in the range of up to 10,000 units or so, the vast majority of machines mentioned in the Soviet press are at the prototype stage only.[27] The Agat, an Apple II clone widely discussed as the first Soviet personal computer, has been discontinued due to a problem of obtaining components like disk drives.[28] Total production of Agats probably did not exceed from 2,000 to 3,000 units. The BK-0010 represents a retrenching at a technical level more compatible with Soviet industry and is reminiscent of the earliest American PCs, using a television set as a monitor and cassette recorder for program storage.[29] Such personal computer models seen as prototypes at exhibitions and trade fairs show little evidence of mass manufacture. Nothing has been available in the literature to imply that any Soviet facility has begun serious production of PCs.

One step to try to rectify this problem was taken with the creation of an MNTK (Inter-Industry Scientific and Technical Complex) for Personal Computers (the MNTK PK) in December of 1985.[30] A number of different MNTKs for critical technologies, for example, fiber optics, robotics, membrane technology, have been formed. The MNTKs are intended to better integrate research organizations with production facilities, to cut across ministerial boundaries, with some reliance on Soviet Academy of Sciences institutes for leadership.[31] There appears to be little interest in supporting the MNTK PK from the production ministries, however.[32] The Academy institutes are only minimally funded for the task of organizing these complexes and, without strong support by the industrial partners, may not have the resources to succeed.

At the same time, there is a growing possibility of beefing up the Soviet domestic production capability through acquiring complex components (such as Winchester drives, which have proved difficult to manufacture for all the CMEA countries that have attempted them) and purchase of production automation tools.[33] The acquisition of integrated circuit manufacturing technology and equipment has been ranked as high priority by most analyses of USSR covert technology transfer policy and practice.[34] The Soviets have also evidenced some desire to purchase entire factories for PC production.[35]

Although we know of no incidents of sizable USSR purchases of PC production equipment from the West or setting up a joint venture for PC production within the Soviet Union under the terms of the new economic reforms, both have happened in other countries of the CMEA community. The Pravets Combine for Microprocessor Production in Bulgaria is using Japanese assembly and test equipment to produce IBM PC and Apple clones on the basis of largely imported components.[36] The Polonia enterprises are joint venture companies formed by emigres supplying capital to enable Polish import and assembly of components unavailable throughout the CMEA.[37] Just why the Soviets have not done so themselves is not entirely clear.

Installation

The increased availability of systems and components on the world market would suggest benefits to the USSR in the way of augmenting or preceding domestic production with imports. A number of economic barriers to this are not likely to be greatly diminished in the near future. These include (1) a monolithic organization of import/export practice, (2) a poor facility for the use of hard currency and investment capital, and (3) various trade and technology embargoes.

The first two problems make the purchase of PCs from abroad possible only to such massive organizations as Elorg (the Soviet foreign trade organization that covers computer technology), far removed from the area of application. There have been a number of changes begun under Gorbachev to widen the range of options, permitting smaller organizations to deal directly with Western corporations, but it is not clear if this will be much of a solution given the poor environment for capital invest-ment.[38] It may be of little use for a Soviet institute to contract directly with a Western PC supplier. Without the ability on the Soviet side to borrow against the anticipated profit, and with trade restricted to such mechanisms as barter, Western firms may not find the prospects attractive.

Export controls have done little to deny Soviet access to most personal computer products. Even before softening of the Coordinating Committee on Multilateral Export Controls (CoCom) restrictions on low performance PCs in 1984, Western PC systems were making their way east in modest numbers.[39] The Soviets have demonstrated an ability to acquire nearly anything, up to VAX systems and above, on a single unit basis. There is no reason to believe that they do not have adequate "competitive" information on the relevant personal computing technologies, with the exception of advanced microelectronics.[40] The Soviet lag in basic production capability also relieves some pressure to acquire "state-of-the-art" information. If, for example, the USSR chooses to clone the Apple Macintosh, it will have to widen its microelectronics base and master the Motorola 68000 (on the Western market since the end of the 1970s) before it needs to reproduce the rest of a system. That system itself is available for dissection and reverse-engineering now and eminently suited to being smuggled across the border in a diplomatic pouch, if not merely trucked in across historically permeable borders in Austria or Finland. The ease with which the newly industrializing nations are cloning American PCs is additional evidence of the lack of secrecy regarding basic PC technology. Apple is pressuring the Brazilian government to curtail the cloning of the Macintosh by Unitron. Unitron's copy of the Macintosh is a case of straightforward pirating of all of Apple's proprietary components.[41]

Where the trade restrictions have had a much stronger effect is in making the large-scale purchase of systems and components a great deal more difficult. Whereas systems have been trickling across East-West borders in ones and twos (in the more Westernized CMEA countries such as Hungary and Poland, modern Western PC systems such as the PC/AT and its clones now number somewhere in excess of several thousand), coordinated purchases of powerful systems have been few.[42]

Recently, negotiations occurred between the USSR and two South American countries for the sale of personal computer systems. A purchase in the range of up to 100,000 microcomputers from Brazil ultimately fell through, and a comparable deal, totaling between $450 and $500 million, was signed with Novotec, a Peruvian company.[43] The latter agreement involved the purchase of 100,000 IBM PC-compatibles over a period of several years, in exchange for a package from the Soviets including cash, barter, and cancellation of debts.[44] This requires that the Peruvian government act as an intermediary, with the local firm ultimately receiving payment in cash. This sale illustrates the considerable difficulty in arranging for trade in computer systems; most Western corporations would be unwilling to undertake the lengthy negotiations or be able to accommodate the Soviet problems with substantial hard currency expenditures.

Novotec's own success can be attributed to the same factors described above for possible increases in USSR production with the growth of the world component market. Whereas Novotec manufactures its own circuit boards and required systems software, virtually all of the components, for example, chips and disk drives, are obtained on the world market. More and more countries are acquiring the ability to ship finished systems. As discussed in the previous section, even Bulgaria could be counted as a potential supplier of IBM PC-class machines to the Soviet Union.[45] Even if the USSR does not follow the same course and augment its production facilities via component import or acquisition of foreign manufacturing technology through direct purchase or the establishment of joint ventures, it will still be able to count on a much broader supply base for the import of finished systems.

With the availability now of IBM PC-class personal computers on the world market, the purchase of foreign systems is more appealing. The up to 10,000 non-IBM PC compatible MSX computers purchased by the USSR in 1985 from Japan's Nippon Gakki, for example, proved to be suitable for little more than unsophisticated games.[46] With adoption of the IBM PC architecture by the Soviets and the rest of CMEA, imported IBM PC clones could be integrated with domestic machines to provide PC resources better suited to the USSR's needs. The use of imported PCs, however, suggests certain caution. The Peruvian PCs have been described as unreliable, placing additional demands on Soviet sources for service and maintenance.

Such service and related infrastructural needs are also of considerable concern to the installation of personal computing resources, perhaps as important as acquiring the systems themselves. The United States has had a very strong infrastructure long before PCs required it, including a reliable telephone system and power network, and a flexible retail market that has taken over many of the needs of service and supply. Prior to freezes and cutbacks on their dealerships, as a result of the considerable price cuts that have occurred in the last few years, Apple and IBM each had in excess of 2,000 authorized dealers for their PCs.[47] IBM's use of dealers to establish a wide sales and service base, instead of relying solely on direct sales, has been credited for the quick accumulation of several million IBM PCs in a wide range of applications.[48]

The USSR infrastructure, by contrast, is poor to nonexistent. The Soviet telephone system will require substantial investment merely to serve as a tool for person-to-person voice communications.[49] Despite some increase in attention to the telephone system as a consumer need, it is likely to be some time and probably not before the end of this century before the system will be substantially improved. And that is only if current efforts can be kept up.[50] Comparatively, the USSR telephone system handles far fewer calls than the U.S. system, with substantially fewer units (28 million telephones as opposed to 170 million for the United States), only 2 percent of the U.S. volume in long-distance calls, and more than two orders of magnitude fewer international calls.[51] And the quality of Soviet connections is notoriously bad. Even in Moscow, where the system might be expected to be the most modern and best serviced in the USSR, the transmission quality is poor, to the point of being unable to support data communications, and wrong numbers are extremely frequent. The Soviet Ministry of Communications, Minsviazi, has been singled out for severe criticism concerning the poor state of the system and the scarcity of telephones.[52]

Another likely bottleneck in the process of making PC resources usable is in the area of service, including preventative maintenance and repair. Service even of large computer systems has been notoriously poor, and horror stories exist where several systems have been routinely cannibalized to keep one working.[53]

The U.S. personal computer boom gave rise to, and in turn expanded from, a strong base of retail sales of hardware, software, and services. It is difficult to see any potential for an analogous growth in the Soviet economy. The collection of USSR ministries that shares the responsibility for the PC infrastructure and production are far less cohesive than the producers in the American market. Gaps, where a given need is not filled by any of the ministries, have caused the supply of resources to be jerky and uncoordinated. The entrepreneurial opportunities in the U.S. economy that produced companies like Apple, and virtually all of the personal computer software firms, are absent from the Soviet economy. Whereas the new USSR reforms permit limited free enterprise, they do not address undertakings above the level of cottage industry. It should be noted that elsewhere in the socialist bloc, particularly in Hungary, entrepreneurial enterprises have been permitted to foster the growth of personal computing.[54] Whereas the Hungarian economic work associations (GMKs) have been faulted for drawing skilled workers away from conventional enterprises, GMKs, and firms that have grown out of GMKs, have served to fill gaps in the economy.[55] Similar developments have occurred in Poland.[56]

Perception

The final stage of introduction of personal computing to the Soviet economy involves its perception, that is, given that systems have been selected, produced or otherwise acquired, and incorporated into work environments, they then have to be used. Personal computing being a mass phenomenon, one measure of the progress in this stage can be taken from the portrayal of personal computing in the media. In the United States, substantial attention was paid to computing as it began to become pervasive outside of centralized data processing and strictly industrial applications. Recall that *Time* magazine named the computer as "Man" of the Year for 1982.[57] The initial fascination with PCs in their own right may be considered as having passed; topics of interest have progressed to desktop publishing and laser printing, powerful scientific workstations, and considerably expanded graphics capabilities. The PC itself is being submerged as a technology beneath the rapidly emerging applications it now supports. The final step will be taken when PCs become so universally accepted as to be "more noticeable by their absence than by their presence."[58]

Surveying the Soviet literature provides a very different perspective on personal computing. Among the few articles seen in the popular press, the personal computer is portrayed as a very exotic technology. An article from *Sovetskaia Belorussiia* of 1987 discusses how the article was itself prepared on the personal computer being announced, a Soviet copy of the IBM PC, as if this were a novel occurrence.[59] The vast majority of articles about personal computers in the more technical literature have to do with first uses of computing within an application, for example, the use of PCs by pilots to calculate fuel consumption, previously done manually.[60] Almost nothing has been seen of PCs accessing electronic bulletin boards, even using modems or advanced peripherals.

One of the few areas where the Soviet government has been at least talking about a major effort to introduce personal computing for the economy is the use of PCs in the secondary schools as well as in the promotion of computer technology and programming as a "second literacy," a reference to the push for universal literacy undertaken in the 1920s.[61] As part of a program for universal secondary school technical literacy initiated by the Politburo in 1985, a course on Fundamentals of Informatics and Computer Technology is now being taught in the ninth grade.[62] At the same time, plans for massive introduction of PC hardware in the form of microcomputer laboratories have achieved very little.[63] Some schools in the larger cities (Moscow, Leningrad, Novosibirsk) seem to have been well supplied. Moscow Public School No. 117, for example, was the beneficiary of 100 personal computer workstations supplied by the Institute of Cosmic Research.[64] More commonly, stopgap measures, use of university and industry facilities, and "mobile labs" with computers bused to the schools have been seen. It is reasonable to assume, therefore, that a great many schools have no computer resources at all.[65]

The level of general "noise" in the media on personal computers may also be thought of as contributing to the nonformal computer literacy, inasmuch as it can create a demand for personal computing in the workplace, hasten its acceptance, and encourage an extracurricular interest among the youth, the next generation of the work force. Thus far the level of personal computer-related information in the media has been minimal compared to the high levels in the West. The dozen or so magazines now published in the West and devoted to each of the popular PCs are matched by a small collection of articles in newspapers such as *Komsomolskaia pravda* or radio hobby journals.[66] A number of personal computing clubs have been reported in major cities like Moscow and Leningrad, where PCs can more readily be used, but they afford only a small fraction of Soviet youth limited access to computing.[67]

Conclusions

The Soviet Union is experiencing great difficulties in all of the four stages discussed above, from design to incorporation into the economy. In many respects, the USSR is at square one in terms of matching the tremendous Western success at disseminating personal computing technology throughout the economy and society. Unquestionably, however, the Soviets have identified widely disseminated resources as a critical need, demanding increases in both resource production and in technological awareness among the work force. At the same time, there lies a substantial gulf between words and the deeds. Without trying to stretch the analogy too far, the USSR's economic situation, of which the push for personal computing remains a particularly potent indicator, is comparable to that of an addict crippled by his or her condition, capable at the conscious level of seeing past systemic problems, but incapable of overcoming them without great anguish.

In principle, the Soviets have received sufficient direction from Western achievements to enable them to begin the first major investment in PC resources, and the products of American industry are being embraced as models. Particularly indicative of this is the decision to use the IBM PC as a CMEA-wide standard, dictated by the indigenous technical capabilities of CMEA members, the increasing availability on the world market of components and experience, and confidence that deficiencies can be met through imports.

Despite the fact that USSR design decisions have been made in many ways by the momentum of the world market, problems in production represent a bottleneck to any growth. Computer systems, with considerable requirements for quality control and precision assembly, have fared poorly in large-scale production. Such systems being produced are poorly supplied with peripherals. Supporting industries like service and software, whose growth in the West followed directly on that of the hardware supply itself, are rudimentary at best in the Soviet Union. In part this can be ascribed to the scarcity of hardware requiring the complementary industries, but one also has the impression that a great many of the steps necessary to promote personal computing as a resource are not being taken. Certain major policy decisions have been made, like creation of the MNTK PK to enhance interorganizational cooperation, but in too many other areas underlying problems remain unaddressed.

Were the production problems to be solved, or sufficient economic flexibility acquired to make substantial imports from the West a viable alternative, there would still be a need for investment in the infrastructure. The poor operating environment in most USSR facilities, including problems with reliable power and sources for service and maintenance, is a considerable barrier to keeping a personal computer system up and running. The Soviet telephone system is poor at best, and the question of whether or not networked personal computing and PC bulletin boards might aid in the dissemination of dissident material is more or less rendered moot.

At their current rate of growth in all of the underlying and dependent technologies, the Soviets are failing to make personal computing available in the economy. The four stages noted above only take personal computing to the level of first perceptions in society, but it is not possible to look much past that. In terms of the five-phase model of technological introduction, personal computing in the United States is well into the fourth phase. The USSR is at best just entering the third, slowly. A number of Soviet PC designs, like the Agat, were merely experiments with the technology, as if to make the claim that "we can do it, too." Only in the last year or so have there been signs of intent to begin serious production of PCs. If the models now being introduced for serial production prove viable as useful tools, we might expect personal computing in the Soviet Union to attain a solid foothold in the third stage of the model by the end of this century. If, to be optimistic, the USSR can manage to both reform the domestic economy and take advantage of the world market in the component technologies, it is even conceivable that it could be approaching the fourth.

The answers to the following questions then should serve as indicators of the future for personal computing: How will the Soviets take advantage of a new world market in PC-related technologies? What is the strength of their commitment to making substantial changes in the domestic economy? The enhanced opportunities for exploiting the world economy for components and systems, should the USSR improve its flexibility and willingness to trade, could help it to fill in many of the deficient areas, while it organizes the rest of the sectors necessary for what is truly a massive new economic investment. The extent to which Moscow moves to take advantage of such opportunities to foster personal computing may be a gauge for many other economic areas. The few steps that have been taken need to be followed with concerted action. A third question is: To what extent will the West serve as a model for further Soviet developments in personal computing? There are strong indications that the evolution of world standards such as the IBM PC will be embraced by the USSR due to its minimizing of research and development expenditures, and a bootstrapping effect through the availability of a pool of compatible resources already well developed in the West.

It is not clear that the Soviets are wholly prepared to make the commitment required to turn the domestic situation around. In some respects, personal computing could be called a "critical but not necessary" technology for the USSR. Should it continue on the current path of economic development, personal computing will remain a nascent technology. The alternative is to institute considerable reforms and serious investment in a great many contributing sectors of the economy, all requiring substantial improvement before personal computing will be able to flourish.

Expectations of personal computing having an overall effect on the Soviet economy must necessarily be couched in rather pessimistic terms. Clearly, certain conditions must be met before some of the uses of PCs in the West can even be possible in the USSR. For example, without substantial upgrades to the telephone system and without the production of modems as PC peripherals, there can be no personal access to subscriber networks, or the creation of bulletin boards. Whether or not that will come about remains a question. In a way, the severe deficiencies of the Soviet PC-related industries reduce the study of PC impact by several dimensions. This work does not purport to deal with the larger question of an "information society," which the USSR quite obviously is not, but which it may have incentives to try to become (see Note 13 for a treatment of that question). Personal computing by itself probably will not be a strong force in the creation of such an information society in the USSR; its considerable success in the United States has been based on previous strong growth of other sectors, like telecommunications and the support infrastructure of the service industries. And, whereas PC use requires these components to be enhanced and integrated, the technology is more dependent on rather than determining of the progress toward their improvement. Yet personal computing has been recognized by the Soviets as a useful technology, as a component of the future economy, and steps are being taken to foster its growth.

The results of Soviet intentions toward the promotion of personal computing will be evident only at some time in the future. It is not enough to make an evaluation that the Soviets have up to now "succeeded" or "failed" to equal, or compensate for, or absorb, Western achievements as if this were merely a question of relative success. Even from the above cursory examination, it is clear that that sort of evaluation would find the USSR sorely wanting. It is likewise probable that the Soviet technological lag will continue, and perhaps increase, as the West advances. An absolute comparison of the USSR with the West, although certainly valuable in its own right, is not the sum total of what we can obtain from an analysis such as the one above. What is equally as important is to determine how opportunities provided by both the development of new technologies and new concepts might be employed in the Soviet economy. It is important to note what the USSR does or does not extract from the Western model and to explore the degree to which Soviet choices are influenced by Western and world technological developments. Research in progress will also serve to better place the USSR within both the CMEA and world communities in terms of trade and transfer of PC technologies, and go into more detail on pre-PC small computer technology and its significance to the development of modern personal computing resources.[68]

Notes

1. Victor Yasmann, "Black Market in Computer Games in Moscow," *Radio Liberty Research Bulletin*, no. 160/87 (March 27, 1987), pp. 1–3.
2. "Horizons of Computer Technology," *Ekonomicheskaia gazeta*, no. 15 (April 1985), p. 2; "Tasks of New Drive to Put Computers in Classroom," *Izvestiia* (April 3, 1985), p.. 3; "In the Politburo of the CPSU Central Committee," *Pravda* (March 29, 1985), p. 1.
3. Ross Stapleton and Seymour Goodman, "Microcomputing in the Soviet Union and Eastern Europe," *Abacus* (NY), 3, no. 1 (Fall 1985), pp. 6–22; Stapleton, "Soviet and East European Microcomputer Systems," *Signal*, 40, no. 4 (December 1985), pp. 69–76.
4. Paul Bonner, "Whither goeth 8088-based PCs? Obsolescence is just a year away," *PC Week*, 3 (September 23, 1986), p. 27.
5. Paul Karon, "Buyers no longer think it has to be IBM to be reliable; corporations are turning to compatibles as the IBM mystique fades," *PC Week*, 3 (August 5, 1986), pp. 55–58; Michele S. Preston, "Rebuilding micro muscle," *Datamation*, 3, no. 1 (January 1, 1987), pp. 73–76.
6. Stapleton, "Microcomputing's Shifting Focus From High Tech to Mass Market," paper presented at PERSCOMP '87 conference, April 21–24, 1987, Sofia, Bulgaria.
7. William F. Ablondi and Laura Lundquist, "IBM, Apple rule office market," *Mini-Micro Systems* (June 1985), pp. 123–32.
8. Patrick Honan, "Trends," *Personal Computing*, 10 (October 1986), p. 53.
9. Michael W. Miller and Erik Larson, "Desktop Duel: Apple Stakes Future On Battle With IBM For the Office Market," *Wall Street Journal*, CXII, no. 52 (March 15, 1985), pp. 1,18.
10. "VCRs Hailed as Educational Tool," *Tucson Citizen* (November 24, 1986), p. 4A.
11. "Classroom Computers," *New York Times* (October 12, 1986), p. 1F.
12. Bonner, "Whither goeth . . ."
13. Goodman, "The Information Technologies and Soviet Society: Problems and Prospects," *IEEE Transactions on Systems, Man, and Cybernetics*, SMC-17, no. 4 (July–August 1987), pp. 529–52, modified from Joel S. Birnbaum, "Toward the Domestication of Microelectronics," *Computer (IEEE)*, 18, no. 11 (November 1985), pp. 128–40.
14. *Ibid.*

15. U. Mannanov, "Computer Language, What Should it Be?," *Pravda vostoka* (Tashkent) (August 12, 1986), p. 3.

16. Ye. P. Velikhov, "Personal Computers, Current Practice and Prospects," *Vestnik Akademii Nauk SSSR*, no. 8 (August 1984), pp. 3–9; Peter Broczko, "Microcomputer Manufacture 1985, Socialist Countries," *Szamitastechnika* (Budapest), no. 5 (May 1986), pp. 4–5; G. Sharayeva, *Sovetskaia Belorussiia*, no. 86 (April 12, 1987), p. 4; authors' notes.

17. Broczko, "The Socialist Market; Microcomputers Compatible With the IBM PC," *Szamitastechnika-Computerworld*, no. 1 (September 17, 1986), pp. 24–25.

18. S. V. Iakubovskii, N. A. Barkanov, B. P. Kudriashov, L. I. Nissel'son, M. N. Topeskhin, and L. P. Chebotareva, *Analog and Digital Integrated Circuits*, Sovetskoe radio, Moscow, 1979; Radio i Sviaz, Moscow, 1984; V. S. Borisov, A. A. Vasenkov, B. M. Malashevich, V. A. Sakhnov, and L. Ia. Ivanova, *Integrated Circuit Microprocessor Families: Composition and Structure: Handbook*, Radio i sviaz, Moscow, 1982.

19. "Microprocessors Produced in the Socialist Countries," *Mikroszamitogep Magazin* (Budapest), no. 4 (1984), p. 47.

20. "Microcomputer Elektronika BK-0010," *Ecotass*, no. 33 (1985), p. 25; Iu. Kogtev, "Who is Last in Line to Buy a Computer?" *Leninskoe znamia* (December 25, 1985), p. 3; Modris Eglays, "Computer in the School," *Nauka i tekhnika*, no. 7 (July 1986), pp. 14–16.

21. Yasmann, "Black Market"; Kogtev, "Last in Line"; Eglays, "Computer"; S. Beliaeva, "How I Bought a Computer," *Komsomol'skaia pravda* (Moscow) (January 11, 1987), p. 4; V. Tolstov, "Electronic Equipment in Our Homes," *Izvestiia* (March 21, 1987), p. 1.

22. Beliaeva, "How I Bought"; Z. I. Aleksandrova, I. A. Saruivanov, E. I. Alekseeva, and G. M. Marinov, "The Izot 1030S Microcomputer—A Means for Developing 8 and 16-Bit Microprocessor Systems," *Elektropromyshlennost' i priborostroenie* (Sofia), no. 2 (1985), pp. 4–6; V. Baranov, "Computers in the Class," *Ekonomicheskaia gazeta*, no. 27 (July 1985), p. 24; Brian Moran, "Personal computer foes double-team IBM; Compaq's Deskpro leads onslaught," *Advertising Age*, p. 57 (September 15, 1986), p. 52; S. Riabchuk, "The 'Irisha' for Irisha," *Tekhnika i Nauka*, no. 6 (June 1986), pp. 33–35.

23. D. Gorshkov, G. Zelenko, Iu. Ozerov, and S. Popov, "The Radio-86RK Personal Ham Computer," *Radio* (USSR), no. 7 (July 1986), pp. 26–28; A. Osokin, "We Take a Look: Homebrew Computers Have Appeared! How Much Does a Memory Cost Now?," *Nedelia*, no. 9 (February 27, 1986), p. 11.

24. "Home Computer HC 900 Developed," *Neues Deutschland* (East Berlin) (May 17, 1984), p. 4; Klaus Krakat, "Microelectronics Exhibits at 1984 Leipzig Spring Fair," *Computerwoche* (Munich) (April 6, 1984), pp. 44–45; Peter Broczko, "Microcomputer Manufacture of Socialist Countries in 1984: The Year of the 16 Bit Microcomputers," *Szamitastechnika* (Budapest) (April 1985), pp. 8,9; Ivan Salgo and Agoston Dibuz (eds.), *Microcomputers, Integrated Circuits*, Budapest: LSI Alkalmazastechnikai Tanacsado Szolgalat, 1986.

25. "VCRs Hailed."

26. Jesse Berst and James Cavuoto, "Makers of PC AT compatibles provide

low cost-cost products with more features," *PC Week,* 3 (August 5, 1986), pp. 99–105.

27. "Application of Computer Technology in Schools," Moscow Home Service Broadcast, 1985; E. Dikun, "View from the Store; Why is 'Zero-Zero-Ten' So Slow in Getting to Us," *Nedelia,* no. 9 (February 27, 1986), p. 11.

28. Baldurs Apinis, "Educators View Scope, Prospects for Computer Literacy in Latvia," *Padomju Jaunatne* (Riga) (September 27, 1985), p. 2; Fred M. Hechinger, "Soviet Schools Begin a Computer Curriculum," *New York Times* (November 13, 1985); "We Should Elevate Computerization to Superproject Status," *Business Week* (November 11, 1985), p. 102.

29. Broczko, "Microcomputer Manufacture 1985"; Kogtev, "Last in Line"; Apinis, "Educators View."

30. B. Naumov, "Personal Computers at the Starting Line," *Izvestiia* (July 11, 1986).

31. "Moscow First," Moscow Broadcast, 1100 GMT, February 4, 1986; A. Lepikhov, "Interbranch Interaction. Academician G. Marchuk Responds to the Questions of *Sotsialisticheskaia industriia* and *NTR: Problemy i resheniia,*" *NTR: Problemy i resheniia,* no. 17 (September 2–15, 1986), pp. 4–5.

32. Naumov, "Personal Computers."

33. Broczko, "Microcomputer . . . 1984."

34. Christopher Simpson, "What Are the Soviets Doing in Silicon Valley?," *Computerworld* (February 9, 1981), pp. 1–8; "Hi-Tech Trail to Moscow," 60 Minutes, CBS Television, broadcast October 2, 1983; Gus Schoone, "The Role of Technology Transfer in Soviet Computing," draft report, November 1983; Robert C. Toth, "Soviets Seem Making Dual Use of Pirated Computers," *Los Angeles Times* (December 18, 1983), pp. 1,24,25; "Soviet Acquisition of Militarily Significant Western Technology: An Update," unattributed U.S. government publication, September 1985, 34 pp.

35. "ICL Eying Soviet Plant?" *Computerworld,* XIX, no. 6 (February 11, 1985), p. 6; Angeli Mehta, "ICL Talks Trade With Soviet Delegation," *Computer Weekly* (UK) (February 7, 1985), p. 1.

36. Authors' notes, PERSCOMP '87 conference, Sofia, Bulgaria, April 24–27, 1987.

37. Broczko, "Microcomputer Manufacture 1985."

38. Peter Gumbel, "Moscow Enigma. Soviet Plan to Let in Foreign Firms Proves Frustrating in Practice," *Wall Street Journal,* CXVII, no. 13 (July 17, 1987), pp. 1,11.

39. George Anders and Richard L. Hudson, "Computer Firms Rush to Sell the Soviet Union Low-Power Units After West Eases Restrictions," *Wall Street Journal* (July 19, 1985), p. 24; Brian Bremner, "Red PC Boom? Nyet Yet!," *MIS Week,* 6, no. 41 (October 16, 1985), p. 1; Hiroshi Egoshima, "Economic Cooperation with Soviet Union Discussed: Trade Expansion Anticipated," *Nikkei Business* (Tokyo) (November 25, 1985), pp. 148–52.

40. "Soviets Want Computers for Defence, Paper Says," *Arizona Daily Star* (December 19, 1983), p. A5; Allocation of Resources in the Soviet Union and China—1984: Hearings Before the Subcommittee on International Trade, Finance, and Security Economics of the Joint Economic Committee, U.S. Con-

gress, Part 10, November 21, 1984 and January 15, 1985., U.S. GPO, Washington, DC, 1985.

41. *Gazeta Mercantil* (June 15, 1987), p. 7.

42. "Private Import on the Hardware Market," *Szamitastechnika-Computerworld*, no. 2 (October 1986), p. 2.

43. *O Estado de Sao Paulo* (Brazil) (April 19, 1985), p. 22; Gladston Holanda, *Correio Braziliense* (April 13, 1985), p. 14; Jeff B. Copeland and Robert B. Cullen, "Easing the High-Tech Sales Ban," *Newsweek* (January 26, 1987), p. 28; Barbara Durr, "USSR to Buy Peruvian PCs," *Journal of Commerce* (January 8, 1987).

44. *Ibid.*

45. Authors' notes, PERSCOMP '87.

46. Yasmann, "Black Market"; Hechinger, "Soviet Schools"; Bremner, "Red PC Boom?"; Paul Tate and David Hebditch, "Opening Moves," *Datamation* (March 15, 1987), pp. 43–56.

47. Preston, "Rebuilding micro"; Andrew Pollack, "Apple to eliminate 600 of its dealers; price cutting is one factor," *New York Times,* 135 (April 7, 1986), p. 42,D3.

48. Karon, "Buyers."

49. Alain Le Diberder and Francis Wasserman, "Communications Technologies in the USSR," *Futuribles* (Paris), no. 82 (November 1984), pp. 3–19; "Make Means of Communication Reliable and Efficient," *Pravda* (September 26, 1985), p. 1.

50. R. W. Campbell, "Current Party Plans for Developing Telecommunications," presentation at the IREX/USIA Conference on Communications and Control in the USSR, Washington, DC, September 17, 1986.

51. *Ibid.;* A. Troitskii, "In a Paper Merry-Go-Round. Use of Computers in Regional Communications Center is Still Far Away," *Leninskoe znamia* (August 21, 1985), p. 2.

52. Iu. Nesterikhin, "Problems with Computer Technology and its Servicing," *Trud* (January 28, 1984), p. 2; Iu Nesterikhin, "Computers: Possibilities and Problems," *Trud* (January 20, 1984), p. 2; A. Petrov, "The USSR Supreme Soviet Between Sessions: Communications is a Key Service," *Izvestiia* (September 3, 1985), p. 2; "In the Presidium of the USSR Supreme Soviet," *Pravda* (September 1, 1985), p. 2.

53. E. Zamura, "The Computer—For Interior Decoration," *Sovetskaia Moldaviia* (October 5, 1984), p. 4.

54. Andras Ulok, "Employment and Income," *Szamitastechnika-Computerworld*, no. 4 (December 10, 1986), p. 6; Zoltan Tompe, "Dispute: Small Hungarian Computer Engineering—Or The Findings of a Survey," *Magyar Elektronika* (Budapest), no. 1 (1986), pp. 82–85; Tamas Samathy, "Software Balance; Primarily in Work for Hire," *Impulzus,* no. 4 (February 21, 1987), p. 22.

55. Tompe, "Dispute"; Kristof G. Kocsis, "Software Competition, SZAMALK and the SZKI Weigh it Soberly: A Small Undertaking Does Not Pay; Extra Burdens on GMK Not Advantageous for Export," *Magyar hirlap* (Budapest) (May 4, 1985), p. 6; Attila Kovacs, "MXT, the new Microcomputer of Muszertechnika," *Szamitastechnika* (Budapest) (August–September 1985), p. 20;

"Successes and Traumas," *Figyelo* (Budapest), no. 6 (February 6, 1986), p. 6; Janos Kis, "A Hungarian Success—in the 'Apple Manner,'" *Impulzus,* no. 2 (January 24, 1987), p. 7.

56. Marek Rostocki, "A Dream About 'a Hard Zloty,'" *Export-import politika,* no. 3 (February 1986), pp. 13,15; "Last Week: At Home," *Zycie gospodarcze,* no. 17 (April 27, 1986), p. 2.

57. "Machine of the Year," *Time* (January 3, 1983), special issue.

58. Goodman, "Information Technologies"; Birnbaum, "Domestication."

59. Sharayeva, *Sovetskaia.*

60. A. Lobanov, letter to the editor, *Krasnaia zvezda,* no. 161 (July 11, 1986), p. 2.

61. "The Second Literacy," *Uchitel'skaia gazeta* (January 15, 1985), p. 1; R. W. Judy and J. M. Lommel, "The New Soviet Computer Literacy Campaign," *Educational Communications Technology Journal* (Summer 1986).

62. "Horizons"; "Tasks of New Drive"; "The Ministry and the Reform: Entering the Second Year," *Uchitel'skaia gazeta* (August 22, 1985), pp. 1–2; A. Iakovlev, "The Student and Computers," *Sotsialisticheskaia industriia* (February 19, 1986), p. 3; A. P. Ershov, "Algorithmic Language In the School Course Informatics and Computer Technology," *Mikroprotsessornye sredstva i sistemy,* no. 2 (1985), p. 48.

63. Hechinger, "U.S. and Soviet to Share Insights on Computers," *New York Times* (December 10, 1985).

64. A. Tsyganov, *Sovetskaia Moldaviia,* no. 204 (September 3, 1985), p. 4; Anatoli Komrakov, "Hello Kids! I'm Your School Computer," *Soviet Life* (Washington), no. 9 (September 1986), pp. 21–23.

65. A. P. Ershov, "Man and the Computer," *Izvestiia* (February 3, 1984), p. 2; A. Smolyuk, "Universal Computer Education," *Sovetskaia Latvia* (Riga) (June 18, 1985), p. 2; E. Taranova, "Electronic Universal Education: Learning to Interact with Computers," *Sovetskaia Kirgiziia* (August 2, 1985), p. 3; L. Levitskii, "Computer Class in a Bus," *Izvestiia* (September 3, 1986), p. 3; L. Shurukht, "On Computer Games and . . . Bureaucratic Games," *Sovetskaia Estoniia* (June 10, 1986), p. 2.

66. Beliaeva, "How I Bought . . ."; Gorshkov et al., "Radio-86RK"; S. Kushnerev, "The Computer Poses the Questions: Computerization of Education—Fashion or Economic Necessity?" *Komsomol'skaia Pravda* (Moscow) (November 22, 1984), p. 2; "Conversation With a Computer," *Komsomol'skaia pravda* (Moscow) (January 4, 1986), p. 3.

67. Yasmann, "Black Market"; John-Thor Dahlburg, "Soviet Computers," Associated Press (March 13, 1987); S. Kozyrev, and S. Sokolov, "Computer with an Accent," *Komsomol'skaia Pravda* (Lithuania) (March 13, 1987), p. 1.

68. Stapleton, Ph.D. dissertation (in progress).

6

COMPUTER NETWORKS AND THE SOVIET-STYLE INFORMATION SOCIETY

*William K. McHenry**

> In principle, the day is no longer very far away when each production organizer, economist, and scientific-technical worker will receive all the information he needs directly from his terminal or personal computer station.[1]

The above quotation could be taken as in part defining an information society. It describes a situation in which computer-based telecommunications applications have saturated the markets for which they have been intended, reaching the highest stage of pervasiveness in which "the absence [of computers] is more noticeable than their presence."[2] The personal computer and modem, under individual control and connected to an external information source, is the quintessential symbol of the information society in the West and Japan, and is the key to achieving many of the goals associated with it: instantaneous communication, previously unknown communications patterns and styles, dissemination of information, and increased decentralization and democracy.[3]

Although there is a superficial similarity between the conception of an information society as represented in this quotation and the Western con-

---

*The author gratefully acknowledges the assistance provided by the Management Information Systems Department of the University of Arizona in preparing this chapter.

ceptions, the Soviet goals for computerization are quite different. In the formulation of Professor Seymour Goodman, a Soviet-style information society is based on the pervasive use of computers and communications technologies to: (1) attain real gains in productivity and to modernize the industrial base, (2) maintain and improve the economic planning and control mechanism, (3) support both military and internal security needs, and (4) present the image of a progressive society, both to the people of the USSR and to the outside world.

These four goals can be divided into two groups for the purposes of this chapter. The first two are directed toward improving the economic performance of the Soviet Union. The other two could lead to contradictory positions on networking. On the one hand, as the evidence of the *glasnost'* campaign so aptly demonstrates, freer communications due to networking will undoubtedly foster the image of a more progressive society. On the other hand, such a development may threaten political control. This chapter first presents an overview of the current networking infrastructure in the USSR. Then it examines the relationship between networking and the achievement of economic goals. The third section discusses the potential for the free flow of information that networking may foster. The last section considers how the networking picture might change in light of the reforms introduced by the June 1987 communist party plenum.

The Networking Infrastructure

The networking infrastructure consists of two parts. One is the existing telecommunications structure, and the other comprises the set of computers and protocols that support communications among computers.

Telecommunications

The Soviet telecommunications[4] infrastructure is more fragmented than its American counterpart, consisting of several general and special purpose telephone and telegraph networks, some connected to one another only in part. None of the various choices for networking is particularly palatable.

In all major aspects—extensiveness, ability to interconnect, level of technology used, and quality—the USSR telecommunications system is backward. The number of channel-kilometers in the Soviet system is less than half of what one would expect on the basis of the number of telephones. There are 10 to 15 million people on waiting lists to obtain phones, and the number of phones connected to the public network in the early 1980s was about one-sixth of that in the United States. In 1985 only 65 percent of the Societ public telephone network had direct long-distance dialing. A large percentage of the urban population and the vast majority of rural residents do not have private phones, and the number of pay telephones is minuscule in comparison to demand.

In the United States computerized digital switches have made an enormous, fully automated network a reality. In the Soviet Union most exchanges are still electromechanical. Even by 1990 stored-program switches will cover only a small percentage of the numbers in the system.[5] In the mid-1980s the USSR Ministry of the Communications Equipment Industry (Minpromsviazi) continued production of obsolete switching equipment that foreign countries had ceased producing by the 1970s.[6] The Kvarts system, which went into series production in 1985, is 1960s-style analog technology.[7]

Most importantly, the general telephone network in the USSR cannot support data communications at any appreciable speeds. Without sophisticated error-correction devices, only about 300 bits/second can be transmitted. It is sometimes necessary to try out many lines before one can be found that will support data communications, and even then the connection may be difficult to maintain. In any case, the use for data transmission is limited by statute to nine minutes out of every hour, although it is not clear how or whether the Soviets enforce this rule.[8]

In the United States the high quality of the general telephone system has meant that anyone with a phone line, a computer, and a modem can become a sender or receiver of digital information. Businesses can lease lines for heavy traffic and use the general purpose network in peak periods. Since the breakup of the Bell Telephone Company, more and more American users are installing bypass technology which gives them direct access to long-distance lines. Digital lines are a fast-growing market segment.[9]

In the Soviet Union the low quality general purpose telephone system has led to the development of a variety of other systems for transmitting data. An overview of major options is presented in Table 6.1. Of these, leased telephone lines are of the highest quality, but they are also quite expensive if they are long-distance lines. Within a city, the cost is about 1,000 rubles per year.[10] A Moscow-Leningrad line can cost 50,000 rubles

Table 6.1
Telecommunications Infrastructure in the USSR

Type of transmission media	Name	Characteristics
Telegraph	AT-50	50–200 bits/per second, switched.
Switched telephone	TF-OP	Difficult to maintain connections, maximum speed 300 bits/per second without sophisticated error correction equipment; lines are often down; establishing connections takes a long time.
Dedicated telephone	PD-200	Designed for 200 bits/second; allows line switching to bypass lines that are down; requires specialized equipment; being upgraded to 1,200–2,400 bits/second.
Leased telephone		Can handle 2,400 bits/second, sometimes higher; quality 1–2 orders of magnitude better than switched telephone network; quite costly.
Satellite		Extent of use of satellites for data communications small.
Digital lines	EASS	Development planned for the future.

Sources: R. W. Campbell, "Current Party Plans for Developing Telecommunications," presentation at the IREX/USIA Conference on Communications and Control in the USSR, Washington, DC (September 17, 1986); McHenry, "Computer Networks in the Soviet Scientific Community," in *The Status of Soviet Civil Science,* Craig Sinclair (ed.) (Dordrecht: Martinus Nijhoff, 1987), pp. 151–176.

per year, and a Moscow-Novosibirsk line, about 80,000 rubles.[11] Lines cannot be rented in units of less than 24 hours.[12]

In the early 1970s it was recognized that the general purpose telephone system and telegraph lines were insufficient means for transmitting data. Under the umbrella of programs for an All-Union State Network of Computers (GSVTs) and a Unified Automated Communications System (EASS), the first design of the All-Union System of Data Transmission (OGSPD) was completed by 1977. By 1982 about 129 main automatic switching nodes and substations had been installed throughout the country. These nodes are part of the PD-200 network, which is the first stage of the OGSPD and which was being completed in 1986. One major advantage of the PD-200 is that it provides automatic circumvention of lines that are down. However, the terminal hardware for this system has been difficult to obtain, and each PD-200 connection is limited to 18 minutes per hour. The OGSPD is eventually supposed to become the backbone network for most data communications in the USSR, but its predominance is being threatened by the creation of independent ministry networks.[13]

According to Robert Campbell, the telecommunications infrastructure has been retarded by low priority in serving the general population, by low investment, and by the fact that the Ministry of Communications (Minsviazi) has had difficulty in obtaining necessary equipment from its suppliers. In the past few years the priorities of the Soviet leadership have changed, and telecommunications investment slated for the current Five-Year Plan (1986–90) is double that of the previous one.[14] The capacity of exchanges is to increase by 50 percent, quasielectronic exchanges will be installed, and fiber optics and satellites will see greater use for data communications. The Soviets have begun the construction of the Unified Automated Communications System (EASS), which should eventually be something akin to an integrated digital network. Included in the second and third stages of EASS development are: electronic mail, facsimile, digital transmission of newspapers for local printing, information retrieval through the telephone network, video conferencing, computer networks, television, radio, and broadband local area networks. Digital switches of 150, 300, and 1,200 bits per second have already been "mastered by industry," and switches of 4,800 and 19,200 bits per second are being introduced into series production.[15]

Computing

Computer networks exist in varying degrees of sophistication, speed, and distance. Wide area networks involve two or more host computers, which are located far enough away from one another that they cannot be directly connected. They must use ordinary telephone lines, dedicated lines, or microwave, fiber optics, or satellite connections to transmit data. In local area networks, machines are close enough together that they can all be connected to one another by direct lines. Local area networks can support much higher rates of transmission, which in turn permits the use of a different class of transmission protocols. The transmission of data to and from a computer can be accomplished by a variety of means, only some of which actually qualify as computer networks. Computer networks are defined by the protocols that govern how and when various devices can communicate with one another.[16] These protocols are usually divided into well-defined layers, each of which carries out certain functions.

The Soviets have developed networks strongly influenced by the available hardware. Since they created the unified system of computers, which copied the IBM 360 and 370 computer architectures and now make use of considerable IBM systems software, it is natural that they have adopted elements of IBM's Systems Network Architecture (SNA).[17] The hierarchical nature of SNA fits the hierarchical structure of the USSR economy quite well. However, it does not appear that the Soviets have implemented the most sophisticated features of SNA, including peer-to-peer communications and remote network management. Undoubtedly the low reliability of USSR mainframes, their smaller memory sizes, and the small size and slow speed of their systems disk drives renders the use of SNA considerably less effective. Not all large-scale networks use SNA.[18] Many of the Soviet minicomputers are based on the DEC PDP-11 architecture, so installations of DEC's DECNET can also be found, although there is a greater variety of architectures in use. Local area networks (LANs) are also based on microcomputers, many using the Soviet copies of the Intel 8080 chip. There are few, if any, specialized chips that implement parts of networking algorithms in hardware. This tends to limit the speeds at which LANs can run.

In conclusion, both the computing and telecommunications infrastructures have definite limitations, but neither present such tremendous barriers that networking cannot be carried out. As in other parts of the computing industry, users must shoulder a considerable portion of the responsibility for putting all the pieces together to make networks.

Improving Economic Performance

Since the late 1960s, the introduction of computers in Soviet industry has proceeded in two directions. The first is the application of "intelligence" on the shop floor in order to enhance labor productivity. The second is the use of computers to reform and improve the centralized planning mechanism. Computer networks have not played a particularly important role in achieving the former goal, but have been intimately connected with the success of the latter.

Networking in Support of Modernization

There are three main applications of networking at the enterprise level. The first is the use of local area networks for production control, leading ultimately to computer-integrated manufacturing. The second is the use of local area networks for internal transmission, which often is defined as office automation in the West. The third is the use of networks to connect to external organizations, such as production associations.

Computer-Integrated Manufacturing (CIM). A wide variety of technologies fall under the rubric of computer-integrated manufacturing. At the bottom level are computer-controlled machine tools, programmable controllers, and robots. These are organized into cells, which are linked to one another and to facilitywide information systems. CIM also includes computer-aided design routines that can download manufacturing instructions to machines and query production data bases. In the United States different networking technologies have evolved at each of these levels, and most of the networks in use to connect programmable controllers are incompatible. The Manufacturing Automation Protocol (MAP) of General Motors is an attempt to develop a standard that can connect any device in use on the shop floor. The use of local area networking technologies in CIM is a good indicator of the technological sophistication of the systems.

Starting with the 11th Five-Year Plan (1981–85), the USSR began a major drive to upgrade the machine-building industries through the introduction of CIM technologies. More than 13,000 robots were produced in 1985 versus only 2,500 in 1981. Estimates on the number of robots produced during this Five-Year Plan vary from 33,500 to 40,000 to 47,000. Many of these robots are of the pneumatic "pick and place" variety and do not have microprocessor-based control systems. Despite efforts at centralized coordination, about 20 ministries have built as many as 400 different models, many that functionally duplicate one another. Without the necessary support structures from these sundry producers, users are left largely on their own to provide whatever finishing touches are necessary to get the robots to work. This in part accounts for the dramatic difference between the number of robots produced and the much smaller number actually assimilated into production. For example, between 1981 and the first half of 1984, a total of 26,500 robots were produced, but only 14,500 were installed.[19]

In comparison to the number of robots, few flexible systems have been introduced. The Soviets distinguish among machining centers, flexible production modules and systems, and flexible automated production systems. Machining centers combine two or more robots into a unified complex that carries out a set of operations. Flexible production modules and systems may tie together several machining centers, whereas a flexible automated system as a whole may refer to an entire line or factory that consists of connected flexible production systems. By downloading new programs, these machines can rapidly adjust to the production of new goods. By 1985 the Soviets had created 60 to 70 flexible systems of all types, versus 230 to 250 in the West. Four-hundred machining centers and 2,000 flexible modules and systems were scheduled for introduction in 1985.[20]

During the 12th Five-Year Plan (1986–90), some 31,000 flexible automated production modules; around 1,400 flexible production systems, lines, and sections; and more than 1,800 flexible production system complexes are to be produced. Other goals include establishing 1,800 control computer complexes, about 5,500 workstation complexes for computer-aided design, some 89,800 programmable controllers, over 100,000 industrial robots, around 200,000 sensors, and more than 125,000 machine tools with program control (including 31,000 machining centers).[21]

Conspicuously absent from these plans are target dates for introducing local area networks in flexible production systems. One reason for this may be the absence of developed LAN technology. A number of the largest scientific research centers have built LANs of various types, but most are rudimentary by Western standards. Many of the connections would not even be considered LANs, because they consist only of hierarchically subordinated computers. Some do use more sophisticated protocols, but have slower transmission speeds. This is a function both of the lines they are using and of the speeds of the computers used in the networks. There is an absence of special-purpose integrated circuits that are necessary to execute network protocols at high speeds.[22]

Consequently, it is difficult to buy off-the-shelf LAN technology in the USSR. The KONET LAN, which was developed at the Institute of Cybernetics of the Estonian Academy of Sciences in collaboration with the Hungarian firm Videoton,[23] is a good example. At one megabit per second, this was one of the highest speed LANs in the country. Up to 64 nodes could be connected. In 1984 it passed international testing at the Institute of Electronic Control Machines. It used a 34-bit frame, and the original intention of its creators was to make it into a standard industrial LAN for Eastern Europe. However, it has not progressed beyond a prototype on the shelf at the Institute.[24]

Before worrying about LANs, the base technologies have to be improved. P. Belianin wrote the following in 1985:

One can expect that in a number of branches of machine-building at the turn of the century a significant portion of production equipment will be unified into complexes which are controlled by computer. But these are the desirable horizons. For now it is necessary to solve some fundamental problems. First and foremost is raising reliability and increasing the use of resource-exploiting and emerging systems, and all the components which comprise them. It is necessary to raise the mean time between failures (MTBF) of a numerical control machine tool from 30–50 hours to 500–1,000 and more hours, to increase the MTBF of control computers to not less than 4,000–5,000 hours, to increase the reliability of machine tools by a factor of 2–3, and to raise the durability of instruments by a factor of 5–8.[25]

Flexible production systems have been breaking down at least once a shift, too often to support multishift use.[26]

Apart from problems with reliability, many of the robots are not controlled by microprocessors, and, therefore, cannot communicate with other devices. Software for each machine is being created independently, making it difficult for machines to exchange information.[27] This situation is not unique to the USSR. In the United States there are over 2,000 different protocols for numerical control machine tools and several protocols for programmable controllers. One of the biggest growth areas is in third-party systems integration.[28]

The creation of flexible systems in Soviet enterprises faces significant barriers. The economic returns from automation have been disappointing, partly because of the "forced" distribution of a small quantity of robots or flexible modules among enterprises with the instruction to integrate them into existing production lines. Users are often left on their own to do the integrating, and not all the necessary parts may be available. In order to pay off the extremely high cost of such systems, it is necessary to run the factory in three shifts, which is difficult under Soviet circumstances. Meanwhile, some enterprises acquire the robots just for the sake of prestige. Planning agencies have difficulty factoring flexible production systems into their calculations, which are based on fixed norms for specific pieces of equipment. Finally, CIM requires that all necessary parts be present. The Soviets have had difficulty introducing two key technologies for CIM: manufacturing resources planning (MRP) and computer-aided design (CAD).[29]

The market for CIM products in the United States has held steady at about $17 billion for the past several years, but it is expected to grow to

$28 billion by 1991. There are numerous MRP and CAD packages and several manufacturers who have brought out boards and other products that implement shop-floor networking protocols such as MAP. Sales of MAP products are expected to reach $21 million in 1987.[30] In the United States the next few years will see continued steady growth in the use of local area networks to link shop-floor devices to higher levels in the control hierarchy. Despite the large number of Soviet robots, it appears that a similar stage of development will not take place until a number of more fundamental problems have been solved.

Office automation and intraorganizational networking. The literature contains almost no examples of networks that have been created to support office automation. A representative of the State Committee for Science and Technology (GKNT), V. Vasil'iev, wrote in 1984 that "the installation of an efficient system of communications in the factory of the future is becoming yet another problem on tomorrow's agenda, so that all production and business activities will function without paper flows of information."[31] The author did not expect such networks to appear, however, until the "eve" of the new century. Since Vasil'iev also discusses the "All-Union Scientific Program for Work in 1986–1990 and to the Year 2000 in the Area of the Creation of Flexible Automated Production and its Use in the National Economy," which was adopted by GKNT, the State Committee for Planning (Gosplan), and the Academy of Sciences, it is possible that this forecast is based on concrete plans rather than speculation.

One example that has been located is called *Estafeta* ("relay"), and is a product of the State Design Engineering Institute of Automated Management Systems in Ivanovo. Estafeta has a ring architecture, uses regular twisted pair wires at distances of more than one kilometer, and can link up to 125 devices. It is in use at the International Center of Scientific Technical Information. "On its basis it is planned to create an office automation system, use it for flexible manufacturing, and of course, for collective use information."[32]

Networking in Support of Centralized Planning

The USSR economy would appear to be ideally suited for networking applications. It is organized hierarchically and official information flows are well-defined. The Central Statistical Administration (TsSU)[33] collects data from tens of thousands of organizations and aggregates it for use by various policymaking bodies. Enterprises report directly to a variety of other bodies, including their production associations and ministries, the Ministry of Finance, and state committees on prices, standards, supplies, and planning.

The potential gains from networking did not go unnoticed by the early developers of Soviet computers. In 1963 plans were first formulated for a state network of computer centers (GSVTs), and a large-scale analysis was carried out in 1964–66. For several reasons, the GSVTs could not be launched during the 1960s. It was not until the end of the decade that the Soviet computer industry mastered the production of reasonably capable and reliable second-generation computers. These machines, however, were not suitable for implementing the GSVTs. In addition, the network was the victim of a tug of war between various agencies.[34]

OGAS: Centralization as the key to economic revival. At the 24th Communist Party Congress in 1971, the GSVTs idea was incorporated into plans to create OGAS, the All-Union System for the Collection and Processing of Information for Accounting, Planning and Management of the National Economy. OGAS was placed at the top of an entire hierarchy of computer-based management information systems, called "automated management systems" (ASU). The ASU program stretched from state-committee level systems, to ministry, departmental, and regional systems at the next level, to enterprise and association systems at the lowest level. Within enterprises one more type of ASU was defined, for process control (see Table 6.2). The ASU program was a massive attempt to rationalize the Soviet economic system by introducing new management methods at all levels of the economy.[35] The following account by one of the major proponents of OGAS, Viktor Glushkov, is typical of the grandiose benefits claimed for computerization and is representative of the Soviet vision for an information society:

> In the future OGAS will make it possible to instantaneously and precisely obtain any information, even at the most detailed level, about everything that is happening in the economy, and on the basis of this to quickly work out optimal planning and management decisions. Today it is difficult to imagine the colossal economic effect that our economy will receive from OGAS. Here it is enough to list only a few of the expected effects: a high level of synchronization of production (which is precisely coordinated in time) at all levels of the economy; the rational reduction of the quantities

of raw materials and equipment which are stored in hundreds of thousands of warehouses and sometimes are not in use in the material production for long periods of time; and a much more flexible planning which precisely takes into account the available capabilities and resources.[36]

OGAS is presented as yet another panacea for the well-known ailments of the Soviet economy. It represents a deliberate policy of centralization, which emerged as the 1965 reforms of Prime Minister Aleksei Kosygin were circumvented and undermined by bureaucratic resistance and the re-establishment of the ministerial system.[37]

As the statistics cited in Table 6.2 indicate, it is only at the highest levels of the economy that the ASU program has been universally embraced. Once past the ministry level, the vast majority of enterprises do

Table 6.2
Top Level Systems and Major Categories of Automated Systems

Acronym	System	Number
ASPR	Automated System of Planning Calculations of the State Planning Committee	1
ASGS	Automated System of State Statistics for the Central Statistical Administration	1
ASFR	Automated System of Financial Calculations of the USSR Ministry of Finance	1
ASU MTS	Automated Management System for State Committee on Material Technical Supply	1
ASOItsen	Automated Data Processing System for State Committee on Prices	1
ASUNT	Automated Management System of the State Committee for Science and Technology	1
OASU	Branch Automated Management Systems	339
RASU	Republic Automated Management Systems	15
ASUP	Enterprise Automated Management Systems	3,672
ASUTP	Automated Process Control Systems	4,651

Note: The number of systems is given as of the end of 1985.
Source: SSSR Narodnoe khoziaistvo v 1985, Moscow: Finansy i Statistika, 1986.

not have their own computer-based management information systems. The original design for OGAS, which was developed in the early 1970s, envisioned the creation of 25,000 ASUs for enterprises and production associations (ASUP).[38] At the current rate of development of 200–300 ASUPs per year, it will take the Soviet Union another 70 years to complete the lowest level of OGAS!

Recognizing that the ASU program was not providing computing services to the large numbers of organizations that needed them, a second front of computerization was opened based on "collective use" of computing resources. Ministries established branch computer centers (KVTs) and specialized organizations to handle certain kinds of calculations for enterprises. In the original design for the State Network of Computer Centers, the backbone of OGAS, it had been envisioned that 200 large Collective Use Computer Centers (VTsKP) would be needed for the intermediate level OGAS.[39] These centers would connect to regional and branch systems above them, as well as to enterprise systems below them.

The computerization of the TsSU has proceeded rather slowly. By 1980 only 60 percent of all calculations performed at all levels of the TsSU had been transferred to the computer.[40] The data imply that only about 2.6 percent of the calculations could be computerized per annum, leading to the conclusion that it will be the year 2000 before TsSU has totally switched over to automation. The TsSU carries out calculations for 90,000 organizations and operates many of the 30 to 40 VTsKPs that have been created.

In evaluating the potential for OGAS and networking, it is important to distinguish between the kinds of computations done by ASUs on the one hand and those done by the TsSU on the other. ASUs carry out the full range of calculations for functions including planning, inventory, production scheduling, accounting, product and process design, and shipping. Most TsSU computer centers carry out a limited set of computations that are designed to produce the external accounting information collected by the TsSU for itself and various other bodies. Only a small number of ASUs have been implemented at VTsKPs and KVTs.[41] If OGAS is to have access to the most detailed information, it cannot be limited to the traditional accounting data collected by the TsSU.

Furthermore, it must have data in machine-readable form. All the rest of the calculations are carried out by the enterprises themselves. They often use abacuses, electromechanical calculators, pocket calculators, punch card machines, or accounting machines that are geared toward the output of specific forms. All of these devices share one thing in common: the information entered is used for the immediate computation and then discarded. When the time comes to compare monthly results, the preceding month's must be re-entered.

The slow absorption of computer-based management information systems by the Soviet economy has so far precluded the possibility of complete centralization envisioned by Glushkov. The concept of OGAS has gradually evolved, so that a statement from the State Committee on Science and Technology in 1983 noted the following:

> OGAS is not a "superstructure" above existing management agencies and is not a new economic agency, but a mechanism supporting the joint operation of many ASUs. OGAS will allow all state institutions to receive and send in an automated fashion through the computer centers of their ASUs the information needed in considering inter-branch and inter-departmental problems.[42]

However, the goal of optimization has not been abandoned. The Automated System for Planning Calculations of the State Committee for Planning (Gosplan) has taken over the central role as the system that will use the data collected through OGAS to make the economy run better. The ASPR is the command center of OGAS.

Gosplan's ASPR. Gosplan began the development of ASPR in 1967, although a design for the overall system did not emerge until about 1972. The design process bogged down when it became clear that the use of optimization models would require significant changes in planning methodology.[43] Software designers were charged with reforming the planning system itself. It was difficult to capture the informal methods used by the planners, let alone come up with an entirely new planning methodology. It became necessary, for example, to create a classification system that covered a tremendous range of products throughout the entire economy. Detailed planning also required detailed norms for inputs. By 1982 the database of norms contained over 300,000 entries.[44]

From the start it was necessary to make compromises because of the available hardware. Gosplan initially used an imported ICL machine, but continued ASPR development during the mid-1970s with existing second-generation computers.[45] In the late 1970s and early 1980s, the transition was made to Unified System computers, but even with these machines the amount of interactive processing remained small. Later the ASPR had to grapple with the poor suitability of Unified System machines for interactive processing and the small capacities of the SM minicomputers and Iskra-226 microcomputers that were adopted for local processing tasks.[46]

More than 140 organizations were involved in the design of ASPR for Gosplan and republic level Gosplan ASPR systems.[47] By 1977 enough individual data processing applications had been established to say that the "first stage" of ASPR was complete. These tasks encompassed planning at three levels: the summary balances for the economy; calculations dealing with major areas such as labor, finance, and costs; and subsystems devoted to planning for specific ministries.[48] Although a significant goal of ASPR had been to carry out optimization, the bulk of the tasks still performed routine calculations that simply replaced the use of calculators by clerks and planners. Most of the optimization tasks were for long-range planning and five-years plans, and were used in an advisory fashion only. Many of the tasks were built on a stand-alone basis, unable to share data with other tasks; no centralized database had been created. A new design for ASPR was approved in 1977.[49]

During the 1978 to 1985 period, the number of individual calculating tasks performed within ASPR grew at a rapid rate. By 1982 over 4,000 of them were being performed at the USSR Gosplan level, with an additional 8,000 being used by republic Gosplan organizations. The RSFSR became a leader in adopting minicomputers for interactive use by planners. Not surprisingly, the republican Gosplan systems turned out to be partially incompatible with the system of the USSR Gosplan. The design of ASPR was again updated in 1983.[50]

In USSR Gosplan, some departments enthusiastically embraced ASPR, whereas others actively resisted it. Lower level personnel made use of the computer, whereas the higher-level decision makers continued to apply the old methods. The number of optimization tasks being solved was still called much too low.[51] Next on the agenda came development of a "central complex of tasks" that would unify the disparate calculations and bring about the optimization that had been a principal reason for developing ASPR. Some of the work of integrating the interbranch calculations got underway during the 1981 to 1985 period, although considerable theoretical work remains to be done in order to complete these models. One of the most pressing problems continues to involve development of accurate norms.

Although the goal of connecting ASPR with other state-level ASUs and with branch ASUs had been articulated practically from the start of its development,[52] little progress has been made. One would expect to find that all the data flows among branch ASUs, the TsSU, the republic Gosplans, and USSR Gosplan were at least being carried out in machine-readable form, but this is not yet the case. During 1982, for example, only 20 percent of the planning forms created by the Ukrainian Gosplan were sent to the USSR Gosplan in this way.[53] The general transfer of information in machine-readable form has been delayed until the 1986 to 1990 timeframe.[54] The head of the main computer center of Gosplan, V. B. Bezrukov, wrote in 1987 that

> It is necessary to provide for the further improvement of the system of collecting normative data and to clean up the document exchanges between USSR Gosplan, ministries, departments, and union republic Gosplans. For this it is necessary, in the first place, to bring about the reception of all source information in machine-readable form . . .[55]

Bezrukov went on to note that the completion of a computer network for ASPR has been postponed until the year 2000.

Why Are There So Few Networks?

The state of the ASPR is representative of failure to bring about the massive introduction of networking envisioned by OGAS. Because ASPR itself has failed to transform the manner in which centralized planning takes place, direct connections to other organizations are not a pressing concern. Given the small number of enterprise-level ASUs, it is not surprising that few ministries have built networks. Where links between ministries and enterprises exist, they tend to be hierarchical and use part of the SNA protocols.

Some full-fledged networks have been built. For instance, the Sirena ticketing system in 1985 comprised eight SM-2M hosts servicing about 1,000 terminals through a packet-switched, Elektronika-60 based subnetwork.[56] Some important ministries in the energy field have contracted with the Hungarians to build networks for them.[57] The only evidence that suggests that there may be more networking than is known abroad are the numerous complaints about "illegal reporting" and the amount of data collected through the OASUs.[58] The Minsk Tractor Plant, whose ASUP has received extensive publicity over the years, is an example. It supplies five times as much data as remains approved by the TsSU. Most of this data, however, is probably transmitted over telegraph lines, in the form of magnetic tapes created at the enterprise, or as traditional reports that are keypunched into the computer by the ministry. Existing networks apparently are grossly underutilized.[59]

Some of the reasons for this are purely technical. For instance, a special front-end processor is necessary to run the IBM SNA software. Bulgarian and Polish versions of this machine had apparently been debugged by 1982.[60] Supplying a machine of this class is part of a new networking agreement that the Soviets have signed with the Hungarians, and the East Germans apparently are working on a microprocessor version.[61] However, the availability of SM or other minicomputers and the very limited availability of machines from this class has led to the development of a variety of different networking solutions involving other machines in the front-end-processing role. Computer centers tend to have more than one mainframe, and these machines are often being run with different operating systems on a stand-alone basis. They need to be tied together before it makes sense to use them in a network, because the USSR's Unified System machines are not particularly well suited for networking.[62]

Second, it is doubtful that enterprises desire that ministries dispose of networks that allow the latter to query enterprise databases. This was proposed during 1985 in Gosplan's house journal, *Planovoe khoziaistvo*. The primary justification was that "under the conditions of the economic experiment," it is necessary to have more accurate data.[63] However, enterprises that give more accurate data to their ministries are likely to be worse off in the long run.[64]

Finally, there exist organizational barriers. Networks cut across organizations, so it is difficult to assign responsibility for them in a country that is notorious for departmentalism. The difficulties of running networks that cross organizational boundaries are recounted by Boris Pan'shin of the Institute of Cybernetics of the Ukrainian Academy of Sciences:

> The territorial distribution of data processing nodes, the necessity of providing contacts of various groups of specialists from different organizations and departments, the difficulties of the legal status of access to collectively used computing and information resources, the problems of joint expenditures between organizations which are taking part in the network—these and other difficulties with the actual operation of a computer network may take on a global nature, that is, may make the normal functioning of the network impossible. Consequently, it is necessary to clarify these complications in advance and work out methods for eliminating them before the beginning of the real operation of the network, that is, at the design stage. In our country the system of external management of computer networks

has traditionally been developed in the form of information dispatcher services, intended for the organization of inter-branch redistribution of computing resources in regions (cities, oblasts) and in the future—for the management of the resources of the State Network of Computer Centers. The first stage was the creation of regional informational dispatcher points, which were organized in cities with large concentrations of computers.[65]

Ultimately, Pan'shin envisions a situation in which anyone seeking computing services can connect to them through the State Network of Computer Centers. In Kiev and a few other cities, these "dispatcher" services have been set up, although machines are not connected in a network. At most there is dial-up access to some of them.[66] In any case, regional dispatcher points are far removed from integrated networks.

It is ironic that the Soviets, who created the first plan for a truly national computer network, should now have so few networks. The gap with the United States is particularly large in this area. During 1986 American industry spent almost $17 billion on telecommunications, about half of this for private branch exchanges. In 1986–87 almost $5 billion worth of networking equipment was slated to be shipped. A 1987 survey of data communications sophistication in twelve industry groups found that about one-third of the surveyed organizations have terminals connected to local computer hosts and use telex or facsimile. Another 14 percent have workstations connected to remote hosts and PBX or LAN routing of data. Almost 45 percent have significant data communications traffic on long-distance lines, remote terminals linked to host computers, and workstations accessing remote hosts via leased lines. The remaining 9 percent use a variety of the most sophisticated networking techniques, including digital transmission. About 78 percent of the Fortune 1,000 companies have installed IBM's SNA, some 23 percent DEC's DECNET, and 17 percent networks by other vendors.[67]

The results of a poll of attendees at the International Communications Association conference in New Orleans points toward greater sophistication within corporations represented there. One-third of them have worldwide networks in place, and almost three-fourths have domestic networks. About 85 percent will use local area networks by 1988, and 75 percent all-digital T1 lines. Some 83 percent will have electronic mail and 75 percent voice mail.[68] The Goodman pervasiveness scale for business applications of wide area and local area networking would show the Soviets somewhere between levels two and three, whereas the United

States is approaching level five in some industries and is at a solid level four in general.

Networking and the Free Flow of Information

In the United States the proliferation of the personal computer has been largely responsible for the change from terminal-to-computer configurations to local area networks and more sophisticated file transfer capabilities. Since 1981 about 16 million microcomputers have been installed in business, science, and educational facilities. Three-quarters of the microcomputers used in the Fortune 1,000 companies are equipped with file transfer software. It is estimated that during 1987–88, another 10 million microcomputers will be shipped in four major machines classes.[69] By 1991 the number of personal computers in business is expected to total 22.5 million.

These personal computers have made possible explosive growth in electronic mail. By the end of 1988 more than four-fifths of American companies will have internal electronic mail systems in place. During 1986–87 about 900 million electronic messages were sent via four main channels: service bureaus (such as MCI Mail), telex, integrated office systems, and personal computer local area networks. There are now more than three million active users of electronic mail, and this number is expected to be 40 million by 1991. During that year the public mail services may deliver as many as one to ten billion messages that originate on in-house systems. By 1987 almost 3,500 databases and more than 650 bulletin board systems were accessible in the United States to users with personal computers and modems.[70]

As Stapleton and Goodman have argued in Chapter 5, the question of allowing individuals to have access to electronic mail, external databases, and bulletin boards via personal computers (PCs) in the USSR has been, for all practical purposes, a moot point. Whether or not the leadership fears a challenge to its hegemony if PCs fall into the hands of dissidents has almost been academic as well. Very few have been sold to the general public, and those that have been produced have gone to high-priority applications such as office automation in ministries, workstations for computer-aided design, and education.[71]

Despite the scarcity of personal computers, some advances have been made in networking that have a bearing on the flow of information in society. One of the most important developments is Akademset', the net-work for the Academy of Sciences.[72] During 1986 the first phase of Aka-demset' was accepted by a governmental commission. It consists of a backbone packet-switching network, with switching centers in nine major cities. Each of the switching nodes is to be connected to a regional local area network. In Leningrad and Novosibirsk, extensive regional networks have already been implemented. In 1984 there existed 46 remote termi-nals used for job submission in the Leningrad network; around 30,000 hours of machine time were rented by remote users. During the summer of 1986, users totaled about 100.

Akademset' has been inhibited by the networking infrastructure out-lined at the beginning of this chapter. In 1985 the links only functioned at 300 bits per second, although plans existed to upgrade. There were shortages of terminal equipment and trained personnel at Academy in-stitutions. So far, there is little indication that Akademset' is being used much. The main use it has received so far has been in permitting access to computing resources within local regions.

Another purpose of Akademset' has been to provide access to data bases. Several very large computerized data bases are being established in the Soviet Union, and it appears that on-line access to them is now becoming available to a certain extent. Several years ago, the All-Union Institute of Scientific and Technical Information (VINITI) began to establish a State Automated System of Scientific Technical Information (GASNTI). VINITI is one of a number of institutes throughout the country that are tasked with providing bibliographical services to the scientific and re-search communities. VINITI's Centralized Database System of Scientific Technical Information has been in operation since 1983, giving access to almost four million document references in data bases on various topics. More than 40 sites are being connected directly to VINITI in Moscow. Throughout the entire system of computerized data bases that is being constructed, about two million references per year are being added. Other databases with limited on-line access are being created by the State Com-mittee for Science and Technology, the Institute of Scientific Information on the Social Sciences, and various libraries. A fairly large number of information retrieval systems exist in ministries; some have remote ac-cess.

Through a gateway at the All-Union Scientific Research Institute for Applied Automated Systems (VNIIPAS), there is some access to Western networks and data bases. The director, O. L. Smirnov, says that he main-tains links to the largest Western data bases and that VNIIPAS has been actively promoting their use. The low bandwidth of the connection, difficulties in arranging payment, and the small number of users who have access to this gateway all suggest that the amount of data being transferred cannot be great. The fact that VNIIPAS is the "window" suggests that the party leadership is concerned about potential problems that might arise given unchecked computer-based communication with the West.

Although there have been positive discussions of electronic mail in the Soviet press,[73] it is difficult to find any implementation. It exists on a few of the local area networks, which have been built in scientific research institutes, but most evidence so far indicates that electronic mail is not a part of Akademset'. VNIIPAS has run an experimental computer-based teleconference involving 12 Soviet participants and guests from 16 other countries; according to Smirnov, more than 100 messages were exchanged each day of the conference. Smirnov even raises the possibility of teleconferencing with participants from the United States and allowing foreigners to have access to USSR databases.

Thus the Soviets are pressing ahead with some forms of remote access to information. Stressing such access to scientific and technical information as well as remote computing resources makes perfect sense for a country that needs to do much better designing of world-class products and has limited high-end computing resources. The situation described in the quotation at the beginning of this chapter, which came from an interview with Oleg Smirnov, involves access to information without making a commitment for two-way communications. Institutional access to data bases does not require the same telecommunications infrastructure that widespread home use of personal computers would, although given the extent to which the entire networking infrastructure has to be developed, it is unlikely that the USSR will come close to this vision for quite some time.

In any case, there is little to fear from electronic mail. In the past, it was impossible for the KGB to monitor more than a fraction of the telephone calls made. With official networks, users would put their electronic messages in machine-readable form themselves, so it will be possible to scan every message for key words, to keep track of communications patterns, and in subtle ways inform users that their messages are being watched. Undoubtedly the KGB will not pass up the opportunity to off-load all the messages onto tape for future reference, if necessary. The telecommunications infrastructure will serve to inhibit those who would create unofficial networks using ordinary switched lines. Americans take aggressive communication for granted. Their Soviet counterparts are likely to

view electronic mail with considerable suspicion, although using it will
be a sign of prestige. Most who enjoy this privilege will not want to
jeopardize it by sending questionable messages. Substantial individual
benefits can be gained by exchanging business- or research-oriented messages.

If the slogans of glasnost', perestroika, and *demokratizatsiia* are genuine, then the reformers may embrace electronic mail as a way to foster
independence among junior workers and encourage more participatory
management. More important than the threat of dissident collusion is the
gradual erosion of control from above, as traditional hierarchical information flows are subverted. In addition, electronic mail communication
with foreigners will permit many Soviets to gain a greatly enhanced picture of the West. This would be perceived as a powerful sign that glasnost' is more than the dissemination of carefully selected critical information. There is now a worldwide community of electronic mail users.
A survey of major research, computer corporations, and cooperative networks found that near the end of 1986, more than 30,000 host computers
were already connected to representative networks in their classes.[74] Most
major universities in the United States have access to one or more of these
networks. Provided appropriate equipment existed on the USSR side, it
would be possible to link Soviet academics, researchers, and practitioners
to the rest of the world overnight.

Conclusion: The June Plenum

Networking is not a technology that merits a good deal of attention unless
there are computerized devices that need to be connected together. If networking is a quintessential symbol of the information revolution in the
West, then the absence of networking applications in the Soviet Union
shows just how far it must go before an "information society" can become
a reality.

Sweeping changes in the economic system were approved at the June
1987 Central Committee plenum.[75] If the reformers succeed in carrying
through the plans that have been outlined, enterprises will gain a large
degree of autonomy and will be allowed to fail if they perform poorly;
centralized planning will assume an advisory nature only; the state's influence on production will be reduced through set orders that must be
filled first and certain other normatives; and enterprises will agree with
their counterparts on prices and goods to be shipped. It is unlikely that

all of these changes will be fully functional by 1991, as Gorbachev hopes. Most interest groups in society, and in particular the bureaucracy, have strong reasons to oppose them.[76]

One of the chief ways that the bureaucrats exert control from the center is by collecting detailed information about the operations of the enterprises subordinate to them. Over the past 20 years, the USSR has spent billions of rubles to set up a national system (OGAS) for collecting and processing these data. If the traditional information flows remain intact, this will be a signal that Gorbachev is not winning his war against the bureaucrats. The June 1987 plenum should be seen as a deliberate repudiation of the idea that computing can "save" centralized planning. If OGAS had delivered on its promises, there would have been no need to risk tremendous social upheaval in order to clean up the Soviet economic mess.

If Gorbachev does manage to reduce substantially the influence of the center, enterprises will need to use computers much more effectively than they do now. The focus of enterprise systems will turn away from the reporting needs of external agencies toward productivity-enhancing uses of the computer: forecasting, scheduling, order entry, computer-aided design, office automation, and so on. As the corresponding devices to which networks can be connected are installed in USSR enterprises, the demand for local area networks both for production and office automation will increase substantially. Newly formed interbranch production associations will need to be tied together, but the demand for wide area networking will be somewhat less than that originally envisioned by the OGAS plan. Networking will finally become an integral part of daily management, which is built as needed from the bottom up, rather than an appendage screwed on from above.

This cheerful picture of increased demand must be mitigated by the real possibility that things will become worse before they get better.[77] Computing applications are intimately tied to the organizational structures and tasks that give rise to them. Whenever those structures and tasks change, computer systems must also change or they will fall into disuse. At least the Brezhnev "stagnation" provided a stable, if not particularly nurturing, climate for OGAS. The Soviet software infrastructure is not prepared to deal with rapid changes in computer system requirements. Most USSR enterprises have a tremendous amount of learning to do before they will be able to make effective use of computers in a new competitive environment.

For at least the past two decades, demand for computing applications has been blunted for a host of reasons, including the very nature of the Stalinist centralized planning system. If the new reforms are successful, enterprises will finally have strong incentives to make extensive use of computers, including networking. In this case, it is almost inconceivable that the USSR will not be able significantly to improve the performance of its computing infrastructure. If the reforms are only partially implemented and the center continues to maintain a considerable amount of control, the Soviets may have the worst of both worlds. An ambiguous attitude towards centralization will remain, so that on the one hand, the "hypercentralization" envisioned by OGAS will be insufficient to permit centrally directed optimization, and on the other, decentralization will not go far enough to provoke extensive computerization by enterprises. Developments in networking will be one indicator of how the reforms are going.

Notes

1. *Ekonomicheskaia gazeta,* no. 13 (March 1987), p. 9.
2. The five stages include: "1. An experimental rarity, often an entrepreneurial or laboratory discovery; 2. An exotic tool or toy used by a small group of experts; 3. Products that are well known and manufactured in modest quantity, but direct use is limited to a small fraction of industrial or other environments; 4. Wide-spread production and availability, with direct use requiring little or modest training in a broad domain by a sizeable minority of the population; and 5. The technology has become part of the fabric and infrastructure of daily life, and its absence is often more noticeable than its presence." See chapter 2 by Seymour Goodman in this book.
3. Ironically, one of the greatest proponents of the information revolution in Japan, Yoneji Masuda, has described an electronic "withering away" of the state, which resembles the communism described by Lenin in *State and Revolution,* in which the population itself administers most state functions. This will be made possible by globally conscious, electronically connected, voluntary communities that will supplant private enterprise. Although few would share Masuda's extreme vision of a new theocracy founded on a computerbased, man-nature synergy, the popular conception of an information society in the West starts with the personal computer and leads directly to computer networks. See Yoneji Masuda, *The Information Society (as Post-Industrial Society)* (Tokyo: Institute for the Information Society, 1980) and "Computopia," Chapter 14 in Tom Forester (ed.), *The Information Technology Revolution,* (Cambridge: MIT Press, 1985), pp. 620–34. See also Alfred B. Evans, "Rereading Lenin's *State and Revolution,*" *Slavic Review,* 46, no. 1 (Spring 1987), pp. 1–19.
4. This section is based on R. W. Campbell, "Current Party Plans for De-

veloping Telecommunications," presented at the IREX/USIA Conference on Communications and Control in the USSR (Washington, DC, September 17, 1986); Robert Campbell, Richard W. Judy, and Hans J. Heymann, "The Implications of the Information Revolution for Soviet Society," first draft of the Phase I Report (February 12, 1987); McHenry, "Computer Networks in the Soviet Scientific Community," in Craig Sinclair (ed.), *The Status of Soviet Civil Science* (Dordrecht: Martinus Nijhoff, 1987), pp. 151–176; Central Intelligence Agency, Directorate of Intelligence, *Enterprise Level Computing in the Soviet Economy,* (August 1987), SOV C 87-10043.

5. A. A. Aleshin, "Future Telephone Network Plans Outlined," *Foreign Broadcast Information Service,* 3, no. 53 (March 17, 1985), p. U2; "Deputy Minister and Official on Telephone Prospects," *BBC Summary of World Broadcasts, Part 1: The USSR, Weekly Economic Report,* W1331/B/1 (March 22, 1985), London.

6. *Izvestiia* (September 3, 1985), p. 2.

7. Campbell et al., "Implications of the Information Revolution."

8. M. Sh. Levin and D. B. Magidson, "Vybor kanalov sviazi pri proektirovanii otraslevoi avtomatizirovannoi sistemy nauchno-tekhnicheskoi informatsii, "*Nauchno-tekhnicheskaia informatsiia, Seriia 2: Informatsionnye protsessy i sistemy,* no. 3 (March 1985), pp. 8–11; A. I Mikhailov, I. A. Boloshin, and B. A. Kuznetsov, "Nauchnye problemy sozdaniia raspredelennogo banka dannykh SATsNTI," in *Perspektivy razvitiia avtomatizirovannykh sistem upravleniia proektirovaniia i informatsii* (Novosibirsk: Nauka, Sibirskoe Otdelenie, 1986), pp. 65–74.

9. "Data View: Data Communications," *Computerworld* (June 1, 1987), p. 47.

10. Levin and Magidson, "Vybor kanalov."

11. Iu. Nesterikhin, "EVM: vozmozhnosti i problemy," *Trud* (January 20, 1984), p. 2.

12. L. I. Gusiatinskii and O. A. Artemenko, "Usloviia organizatsii baz danykh v seti VTsKP proektnykh institutov," *Upravliaiushchie sistemy i mashiny,* no. 2 (March-April 1986), pp. 64–67.

13. *Vestnik sviazi,* no. 11 (November 1982), pp. 37–38; V. S. Mikhalevich and Iu. M. Kanigin, "Informatika: pora stanovleniia," *Pravda* (July 31, 1984), p. 2; V. N. Kvasnitskii et al., *Vychislitel'nye tsentry kollektivnogo pol'zovaniia* (Moscow: Finansy i statistika, 1982); B. I. Tverdov, M. I. Oksman, V. T. Sivakov, *Telegrafnaia i faksimil'naia apparatura: spravochnik* (Moscow: Radio i sviaz', 1986); *Trud* (June 21, 1986), p. 2; McHenry, "Computer Networks"; Mikhailov et al. "Scientific Problems."

14. Campbell, "Current Party Plans."

15. I. V. Sitniakovskii, O. N. Porokhov and A. L. Nekhaev, *Tsifrovye sistemy peredachi abonentskikh linii* (Moscow: Radio i sviaz', 1987).

16. John S. Quarterman and Josiah C. Hoskins, "Notable Computer Networks," *Communications of the Association for Computing Machinery,* no. 10 (October 1986), pp. 932–71.

17. A. S. Kazak in "Tekhnologiia fuktsionirovaniia ASU," *Pribory i sistemy upravleniia,* no. 4 (April 1986), pp. 11–14.

18. For example, L. Ia. Zamanskii et al., "Programmnoe obespechenie ostraslevoi vychislitel'noi seti," *Pribory i sistemy upravleniia*, no. 4 (July–August 1986), pp. 84–89.

19. P. Belianin, "Gibkaia avtomatizatsiia mashinostroeniia: sostoianie, trudnosti, problemy," *Planovoe khoziaistvo*, no. 7 (August 1985), pp. 19–25; John Mark Dolan, "The Soviet Robotics Program," in Jack Baranson (ed.), *Soviet Automation: Perspectives and Prospects* (Mt. Airy, MD: Lomond, 1987), pp. 57–76; "Organizacja przed technika," *Export-import politika*, no. 3 (February 1986), p. 16, Warsaw; V. Kalashnichenko and T. Konik in "Dinamika proizvodstva osnovnykh vidov produktsii mashinostroeniia," *Planovoe khoziastvo*, no. 11 (November 1986), pp. 99–103; G. Stroganov, "Osnovnye tendentsii razvitiia mashinostroeniia," *Planovoe khoziastvo*, no. 6 (June 1985), pp. 5–13; D. Palterovich, "Organizatsionno-ekonomicheskie problemy razvitiia gibkoi avtomatizatsii," *Planovoe khoziastvo*, no. 12 (December 1985), pp. 43–53.

20. Belianin, "Gibkaia avtomatizatsiia."

21. *Ekonomicheskoe sotrudnichestvo stran-chlenov SEV*, no. 2 (February 1985), p. 46; G. Stroganov, "G. Stroganov: novyi etap avtomatizatsii proizvodstva," *Planovoe khoziaistvo*, no. 5 (May 1986), pp. 9–23.

22. P. N. Belianin, "Avtomatizatsiia i elektronizatsiia proizvodstva v mashinostroenii," *Vestnik Akademii Nauk SSSR*, no. 3 (March 1987), pp. 23–32; McHenry, "Computer Networks."

23. Hungarians actually have done considerably more work in this area than the Soviets. See *Szamitastechnika*, no. 3 (March 1986), pp. 10–11, Budapest.

24. *Avtomatika i vychislitel'naia tekhnika*, 4 (1985), pp. 61–64; private communication with Peter Wolcott (October 1987).

25. Belianin, "Gibkaia avtomatizatsiia," p. 23.

26. N. Panichev, A. Komin, and I. Mitiashin, "O razrabotke i ispol'zovanii gibkikh proizvodstvennykh sistem," *Planovoe khoziaistvo*, no. 7 (August 1986), pp. 126–128.

27. Belianin, "Avtomatizatsiia i elektronizatsiia." In cases where the Elektronika-60 is used at the bottom level of the hierarchy and is tied to a DEC-like SM minicomputer, DECNET software may be available as part of the OS RV operating system. We have no indication that this is used widely in FMS. See V. O. Azbel et al., *Gibkye avtomatizirovannye sistemy*, 2nd ed. (Leningrad: Izdatel'stvo Mashinostroenie, 1985). The Japanese, who also include somewhat less sophisticated machines in their definition of robots, have made fewer strides toward connecting their machines than one would expect. Robert Poe, "Inflexible Manufacturing," *Datamation* (June 1, 1987), pp. 63–66.

28. Private communication with Greg Kinsey (October 19, 1987).

29. G. Kulagin, "Rabochie usloviia robota," *Sovetskaia Rossiia* (February 26, 1985), p. 1; Kulagin, "Ob nekotorykh usloviiakh intensifikatsii mashinostroitel'nogo proizvodstva," *Planovoe khoziaistvo*, no. 6 (July 1985), pp. 25–29; McHenry, "The Application of Computer Aided Design at Soviet Enterprises: An Overview," Chapter 3 in Jack Baranson (ed.), *Soviet Automation: Perspectives and Prospects* (Mt. Airy, MD: Lomond, 1987), pp. 57–76; McHenry, "The Integration of Management Information Systems in Soviet Enterprises," U.S. Congress Joint Economic Committee, *Gorbachev's Economic Plans*, vol. 2. John

Hardt (ed.), 1987, pp. 185–199; Dolan, "Soviet Robotics"; Palterovich, "Organizatsionno-ekonomicheskie problemy."

30. Arthur J. Critchlow, *Introduction to Robotics* (New York: Macmillan, 1985); Bruce Hoard, "Study: 80% of Manufacturers Use or Plan DP," *Computerworld* (April 27, 1981), p. 10; Mickey Williamson, "In Pursuit of Integration," *Computerworld* (July 6, 1987), pp. S1–S6; Kathy Chin Leong, "MAP Users Group Lays Down Law," *Computerworld* (September 28, 1987), pp. 1,8.

31. V. Vasil'ev "Gibkie proizvodstvennye sistemy," *Planovoe khoziaistvo*, no. 12 (December 1984), pp. 19–30.

32. V. Kashitsin, "Elektronnaia biblioteka," *Sovetskaia Rossiia* (June 21, 1985), p. 4.

33. The Central Statistical Administration (TsSU) has been renamed State Committee on Statistics. In this chapter, we continue to refer to it by the old acronym.

34. Kathryn M. Bartol, "Soviet Computer Centres: Network or Tangle?" *Soviet Studies*, 23, no. 4 (April 1972), pp. 608–18; V. I. Maksimenko, "Osnovnye polozhenie gosudarstvennoi seti vychislitel'nykh tsentrov," in V. V. Malekhenkov (ed.), *Gosudarstvennaia set' vychislitel'nykh tsentrov*, pamphlet No. 12 (Moscow: Znanie, December 1982), pp. 5–18.

35. Martin Cave, *Computers and Economic Planning: The Soviet Experience* (Cambridge: Cambridge University Press, 1980); William J. Conyngham, "Technology and Decision Making: Some Aspects of the Development of OGAS," *Slavic Review*, 39, no. 3 (Fall 1980), pp. 426–45; McHenry and Goodman, "MIS in USSR Industrial Enterprises: The Limits of Reform from Above," *Communications of the Association for Computing Machinery*, 29, no. 11 (November 1986), pp. 1034–43.

36. V. M. Glushkov and V. Ia. Valakh, *Chto takoe OGAS?* (Moscow: Nauka, 1981), p. 7.

37. Fyodor I. Kushnirsky, *Soviet Economic Planning: 1965–1980* (Boulder, CO: Westview Press, 1982).

38. Conyngham, "Technology and Decision Making."

39. Maksimenko, "Osnovnye polozhenie."

40. N. Gorbatov, "Nekotorye itogi raboty vychislitel'noi sistemy TsSU SSSR" *Vestnik statistiki*, no. 3 (March 1981), pp. 25–31.

41. McHenry, "The Absorption of Computerized Management Information Systems in Soviet Enterprises," Ph.D. dissertation, University of Arizona, 1985.

42. "Ot mikroprotsessorov do OGAS," *Ekonomicheskaia gazeta*, no. 13 (March 1983), pp. 2,3.

43. "Napravleniia proektirovaniia ASPR," *Planovoe khoziaistvo*, no. 5 (May 1976), pp. 3–7.

44. N. P. Lebedinskii in "Itogi i perspektivy razvitiia ASPR," *Planovoe khoziaistvo*, no. 3 (March 1982), pp. 31–34.

45. V. Bezrukov and V. Shekhovstov, "Rol' ASPR i ASU v sovershenstvovanii planirovaniia," *Voprosy ekonomiki*, no. 3 (March 1975), pp. 107–16.

46. Lebedinskii, "Itogi i perspektivy."

47. V. B. Bezrukov, "Organizatsiia rabot po sozdaniiu i vnedreniiu ASPR," *Planovoe khoziaistvo*, no. 5 (May 1977), pp. 41–48.

48. N. P. Lebedinskii, "ASPR—vazhnii instrument planirovaniia," *Planovoe khoziaistvo*, no. 8 (August 1976), pp. 8–17.

49. N. P . Lebedinskii, V. B. Bezrukov, B. A. Raizberg, V. F. Soskov, B. I. Tikhomirov, Ia. M. Urinson, and O. M. Yun', *Avtomatizirovannaia sistema planovykh raschetov* (Moscow: Ekonomika, 1980); I. Romanov, "O primenenii optimal'nykh ekonomiko-ekonomicheskikh modelei v ASPR," *Planovoe khoziaistvo*, no. 10 (October 1978), pp. 49–56; Lebedinskii, "Itogi i perspektivy."

50. V. B. Bezrukov, "Razvitie avtomatizironvannoi sistemy planovykh raschetov," *Planovoe khoziaistvo*, no. 5 (May 1983), pp. 67–73; "V Gosplane SSSR," *Planovoe khoziaistvo*, no. 5 (May 1984), p. 126; B. Volchkov, "ASPR Gosplana RSFSR: itogi vnedreniia i perspektivy razvitiia," *Planovoe khoziaistvo*, no. 10 (October 1984), pp. 53–58.

51. V. B. Bezrukov, "Razvitie avtomatizirovannoi sistemy planovykh raschetov," *Planovoe khoziaistvo* no. 4 (April 1987), pp. 58–68; "Kruglyi stol redaktsii: problemy i perspektivy razvitiia avtomatizirovannykh sistem upravleniia (prodolzhenie)," *Ekonomika i matematicheskie metody*, 21, no. 4 (July–August 1985), pp. 740–54; Lebedinskii, "Itogi i perspektivy."

52. N. Kononov, "Vzaimodeistvie avtomatizirovannoi sistemy gosudarstvennoi statistiki i ASPR," *Planovoe khoziaistvo*, no. 3 (March 1975), pp. 68–73.

53. V. N. Khalapsin, "Pomogaet planirovat' komp'iuter," *Rabochaia gazeta* (September 23, 1982), p. 3.

54. Lebedinskii, "Itogi i perspektivy."

55. Bezrukov, "Razvitie avtomatizirovannoi sistemy."

56. T. K. Pestvenidze, "Zadachi setemetrii i ee realizatsiia vo vsesoiuznoi seti EMV bronirovaniia mest i prodazhi aviabiletov 'Sirena'," *Desiataia vsesoiuznaia shkola-seminar po vychislitel'nym setiam: Tezisy dokladov, Chast' 3* (Moscow-Tbilisi: AN SSSR Scientific Council on Cybernetics and AN GSSR IVM, 1985), pp. 305–10; V. A. Zhozhikashvili and V. M. Vishnevskii, "Set' EVM 'Sirena': Proektirovanie i analiz," *Desiataia vsesoiuznaia shkola-seminar po vychislitel'nym setiam i Tezisy dokladov, Chast' 3* (Moscow-Tbilisi: AN SSSR Scientific Council on Cybernetic and AN GSSR IVM, 1985), pp. 377–381.

57. *Muszaki Elet* (August 17, 1985), p. 3; Budapest.

58. P. Guzhvin, "Statistiki na sluzhbe uskoreniia," *Vestnik statistiki*, no. 6 (June 1986), pp. 3–11; M. Korolev, "XXVII s"ezd KPSS," *Vestnik statistiki*, no. 4 (April 1986), pp. 4–13; "Delo statistiki—na kachestvenno novyi uroven'," *Vestnik statistiki*, pp. 29–36; "V tsentral'nom komitete KPSS," *Vestnik statistiki*, no. 7 (July 1986), pp. 3–4; "V kollegii TsSU SSSR," *Vestnik statistiki*, no. 10 (October 1986), pp. 19–22.

59. B. Melik-Shakhnazarov, "Informatiki na starte," *Kommunist* (August 19, 1986), p. 4; Erevan.

60. Kvasnitskii et al., *Vychislitel'nie tsentry*.

61. *Muszaki Elet* (August 17, 1985), p. 3; *Leningradskaia pravda* (September 7, 1985), p. 2.

62. Kazak, "Tekhnologiia."

63. V. Andreiev, V. Vasil'ev and V. Smirtiukov, "Vychislitel'nii tsentr i nepriryvnost' planirovaniia," *Planovoe khoziaistvo*, no. 8 (August 1985), pp. 115–16.

64. "Kruglyi stol redaktsii: problemy i perspektivy razvitiia avtomatizirovan-

nykh sistem upravleniia" *Ekonomika i matematicheskie metody,* 21, no. 3 (May-June 1985), pp. 542–56; McHenry, "Absorption."

65. B. N. Pan'shin, "Problemy sozdaniia i razvitiia regional'nykh dispetch-erskikh sluzhb VTs," *Upravliaiushchiie sistemy i mashiny,* no. 1 (January–February 1987), pp. 14–18.

66. McHenry, "Absorption."

67. "Data View: 1986 Telecommunications Equipment Budget," *Computer-world* (April 27, 1987), p. 41; Elisabeth Horwitt, "Survey: DEC Still Can't Topple SNA," *Computerworld* (August 3, 1987), pp. 35,40; "Stats: Sophistication of Data Communications Activity," *PC Week* (August 18, 1987), p. C/34; "Data View: Data Communications," *Computerworld* (June 1, 1987), p. 47.

68. T1 lines are able to transmit data at 1.544 million bits per second versus ordinary telephone lines, which can handle at most 9,600 bits per second. The former are equivalent to 24 voice-grade lines. See Susan Kerr, "T1 Networks Are Hot Now, But Could Cool Off by '89," *Datamation* (July 1, 1987), pp. 32,37. The conference is discussed in Donna Raimondi, "Nets on the Rise, ISDN on Hold," *Computerworld* (June 1, 1987), pp. 51,55.

69. These four classes include the 16-bit Intel 8088/86 and 80286 machines as well as the 32-bit 80386 and 68000 machines.

70. *Directory of Online Databases,* vol. 8, no. 3 (New York: Cuadra/Elsevier, 1987); Donna Raimondi, "PC Use Up, Standards Needed," *Computerworld* (May 18, 1987), pp. 45–46; also her "E-mail to Grow Rapidly Through '91," *Computerworld* (June 22, 1987), pp. 43,46; Walter Ulrich, "Electronic Mail: What's Happening?" presentation at IRMCO 87, the Information Resources Management Conference (September 9–11, 1987) in Richmond, VA; also his "Sorting Out E-mail Issues," *Computerworld* (September 7, 1987), pp. 41,45; Mike Cane, *The Computer Phone Book Directory of Online Systems* (New York: Plume, 1986). "Active" electronic mail users send at least five messages per week. There are now a total of five million American users.

71. Not enough information is available to permit comments about military uses of personal computers.

72. The discussions of Akademset', data bases, and electronic mail are based on McHenry "Computer Networks."

73. Richard Baum, "Dos ex Machina: The Microelectronic Ghost in China's Modernization Machine" (Los Angeles: UCLA Department of Political Science, December 1986).

74. Quarterman and Hoskins, "Networks."

75. "Osnovnye polozheniia korennoi perestroika upravleniia ekonomikoi," *Pravda* (June 27, 1987), pp. 2–3.

76. From the Politburo on down, support for Gorbachev's plans remains mixed. There is no interest group, with the possible exception of the *intelligentsiia,* which is firmly in favor of the reform. See Timothy J. Colton, "Approaches to the Politics of Systematic Economic Reform in the Soviet Union," *Soviet Economy,* 3, no. 2 (April–June 1987), pp. 145–70; "Prepared Statement of Professor emeritus Joseph S. Berliner of Brandeis University and the Russian Research Center at Harvard University for the U.S. Congress, Joint Economic Committee (September 4, 1987), forthcoming.

77. Berliner, "Prepared Statement."

7

COMPUTER SIMULATION AND *PERESTROIKA*

Thomas H. Naylor

When Soviet leader Mikhail S. Gorbachev repeatedly called for "radical economic reform" in his February 25, 1986 speech to the 27th CPSU Congress in Moscow, few USSR citizens realized that this direct assault on the centrally planned economy had been the subject of countless computer simulation experiments involving several hundred economists and management scientists for over a decade. Not many Americans were aware of the fact that literally all of Gorbachev's reforms had been subjected to extensive computer simulation analysis long before being introduced into the Soviet economy. Although it was not politically feasible to implement radical economic and political reforms in the 1970s under aging Leonid I. Brezhnev, it was possible to simulate the effects that such reforms might have on the economy.

My first direct contact with the USSR was in 1972 when I visited mathematician Dr. Alexander Schmidt of the Central Computer Center of the Academy of Sciences in Moscow. At that time it was very difficult for an American to visit the Central Computer Center. I was only allowed to drive by in a taxi and not go inside.

Over lunch the conversation with Dr. Schmidt moved quickly to economic reform—a subject about which he had obviously given considerable thought. We then began to speculate on how computer simulation models might be used to evaluate the effect of alternative economic reforms on the overall performance of the Soviet economy.

Two years later, as a result of Schmidt's efforts, my book *Computer Simulation Experiments with Models of Economic Systems*[1] was translated into Russian and Polish. On my next trip to Moscow in 1982, I learned that 10,000 copies had been sold in the USSR—twice as many as in the United States. The truly amazing part of this story is that literally all of the computer simulation models included in my book were based entirely on a free-market economy, since that was the only type of economic system with which I was familiar.

As a result of my book having been published in the Soviet Union and Eastern Europe, I began receiving numerous visitors from that part of the world who wanted to discuss computer simulation methodology. Although some of my visitors from the USSR alluded to the use of computer simulation to evaluate the effects of "changing the economic mechanism" in the Soviet Union, their descriptions of this research were often vague and unclear. I learned little about the actual thinking of these economists during the 1970s.

But all of this took a dramatic change for the better in December 1980, when I was visited by Dr. Vassili Presniakov, a junior-level economist with the Central Mathematical Economics Institute of the USSR Academy of Sciences. During his six-week stay at Duke University, Dr. Presniakov explained in considerable detail the fascinating research that he and his colleagues were doing back in Moscow. What he described was a wide variety of computer-based planning models, all aimed at evaluating the effects on the Soviet economy of introducing decentralized, market-oriented planning and management into the economic system. Presniakov's models were technically quite sophisticated and incorporated state-of-the-art management science techniques. For me, the USSR economy, about which I previously had little or no interest, suddenly took on an entirely new perspective. Presniakov went on to say that this research had been going on for a number of years in Moscow and Novosibirsk and involved several hundred Soviet economists and management scientists.

Taking note of my strong interest in his research, Presniakov asked me whether I would like to visit Moscow again to observe this work at close range. Because of the deterioration in U.S.-Soviet relations, I was not able to go to the USSR until May 1982—six months before the death of Brezhnev.

My host for that visit was academician Nikolai Fedorenko, director of the Central Mathematical Economics Institute (TsEMI). During my seven-day trip I visited ten major research institutes spread over the Academy of Sciences, the state planning agency Gosplan, and Moscow State University. I interacted with over 250 economists, management scientists, and computer scientists who were using a variety of state-of-the-art management science and computer modeling techniques on IBM 360-vintage computers—easily ten years behind the computer hardware and software technology of the West. Their research agenda, however, was always the same: evaluating the effects of introducing decentralized planning and marketing, flexible prices and wages, profits and incentives, and credit and banking.

Among the analytical tools used by the Soviets were microeconomics, macroeconomics, econometrics, linear programming, input-output analysis, computer simulation, and computer gaming. These scientists seemed to be technically quite sophisticated and very enthusiastic about their work. The quality of their research was at least equal to that being produced by leading American corporations and graduate schools of business. It was apparent that the United States need not fear that the USSR might try to steal our management science technology. They had already developed their own technology, and some of it could prove quite useful to American corporations.

One of the most interesting projects was a computer-based management game to show the effects of flexible wages and incentives on worker productivity and absenteeism. Another involved real-world experiments combined with simulation experiments, with a sample of industries to study the effects of alternative management systems and price-formation mechanisms on Soviet enterprises.

These 1982 research efforts appeared to go well beyond reforms of the 1960s that consisted of isolated and abortive attempts to introduce market-oriented techniques. First, the work observed in Moscow had moved far beyond that of a few isolated economists. It was widespread throughout the USSR and other Eastern European countries, including Hungary and Poland. Second, this work was being done with the full knowledge of the Soviet government. Indeed, Gosplan was one of the sponsors. Upon my return to the United States, I responded to cynics who claimed that none of this was new in an article published by the *New York Times* in which I said, "it appears that someone in Moscow is listening to what these Soviet economists are saying. Maybe we should, too."[2] It was not until my next visit to Moscow in May 1985 that I learned who, in fact, had been listening to these economists—Iuri V. Andropov and Mikhail S. Gorbachev.

In response to my query as to why these economists were engaged in this challenging research, they responded, "We have very big economic problems in the USSR." They then proceeded to define some of these problems, including economic stagnation, low productivity, shortages of food and consumer goods, poor morale on the part of managers and workers, and a serious technological gap with the West. They also acknowledged serious shortages of raw materials and energy that gave rise to production imbalances, unfilled production quotas, the need for imports from the West, rising costs, and foreign currency shortages. Their objective was to use computer simulation models to convince Brezhnev's successors of the merits of emulating the Hungarian and Chinese experiences with decentralized market-oriented planning and management. Just as American managers use computer-based planning models to make the case to their bosses that their favorite projects should be supported, so, too, were these economists using computer models to convince their political leaders that the only way to rejuvenate the USSR economy was by introducing radical economic reform.

Through computer simulation experiments with their economic models, they could demonstrate that partial economic reform would never work. They were able to show the communist party bureaucrats that everything is related to everything else in the USSR economic system. Fixing one part of the system may very well aggravate other parts of the system. They also demonstrated the virtual impossibility of central planners attempting to anticipate all of the possible consequences of a series of small changes in the economy.

In summary, the message from these nonideological technocrats to their party bosses was very clear. Unless the Soviet leaders were willing to consider major structural changes in the economic mechanism similar to those implemented by China and Hungary, then the economy was likely to continue to stagnate. Anything short of the Hungarian type of market-oriented socialism would be inadequate to deal with the myriad of economic problems faced by the USSR.

The computer simulation experiments I observed in Moscow in 1982 were by no means restricted to economic problems. There were also simulation models dealing with a number of significant social problems, including alcoholism, high death rates, high infant mortality rates, low birth rates, and alienation. There was no single integrated model attempting to treat all of these socioeconomic problems simultaneously, but rather a series of problem-specific models. Inadequate computer software was one reason why it proved difficult to link very many of these different models. However, in one way or another, Soviet social scientists were analyzing all of the socioeconomic problems that are currently the subject of Gorbachev's policies of *glasnost'* (openness) and *perestroika* (restructuring).

Thus on July 26, 1983, when Iuri V. Andropov announced a package of "economic experiments," with the objective of introducing decentralized, flexible planning in all of the enterprises belonging to five USSR industrial ministries, there was a solid scientific basis justifying these experiments. The five ministries selected to implement the new ideas included two national ministries—heavy electrical equipment and transportation machinery—and three regional ministries—the food industry in the Ukraine, light industry of Belorussia, and local industry in Lithuania. Under the decree from the Central Committee of the CPSU, which established these experiments, plant managers were given wider authority over budgets, with greater discretion in matters of investment, wages, bonuses, and retained earnings, all of which had been tightly controlled by the supervisory ministries and Gosplan in the past.

The Andropov experiments began on schedule on January 1, 1984. One month later Andropov died, and Konstantin V. Chernenko presided over their implementation until his death in March 1985. Although the Soviet press had a great deal to say about these experiments throughout 1984, its American counterpart virtually ignored them until the latter part of 1985, after Mikhail S. Gorbachev had taken control of the party and government. Most American experts on the Soviet economy scoffed at them as merely cosmetic changes rather than much-needed structural changes.

These experiments were the logical consequence of nearly 20 years of scientific research by such well-known Soviet economists as V. S. Nemchinov, L. V. Kantorovich, Nikolai Fedorenko, and Abel G. Aganbegian. Indeed, Aganbegian, who is considered to be Gorbachev's principal economic advisor, was one of the most active economists involved in developing computer-based planning models to simulate the introduction of Hungarian-like economic reforms in the USSR.

Although Chernenko had little to say about these experiments during his year in power, he did nothing to impede their progress. However, he did introduce an important reform in foreign trade practices, which helped pave the way for the more sweeping foreign trade reforms announced by Gorbachev in 1986. For the first time, Soviet managers were permitted to trade directly with their counterparts in enterprises in other CMEA countries without having to go through the USSR Foreign Trade Ministry. This was an important step toward the decentralization of foreign trade.

In May 1985, six weeks after Gorbachev came to power, I met with enterprise managers and government officials involved with the economic reforms in Moscow, Leningrad, and Tbilisi. By that time the number of ministries participating in the economic experiments initiated by Andropov had been increased from five to 21—one-third of all USSR ministries. When asked why the experiments had been extended to include all of the enterprises in 16 additional ministries, Soviet officials indicated that the experiments had been extremely successful. Enterprise managers who participated in the experiments reported increased output and efficiency, reduced production lead time, lower costs, higher profits, increased benefits and wages, and significantly improved employee morale. Not bad for the first year, by almost any standards.

How was this accomplished? Enterprise managers were given the freedom to determine prices, output, product mix, new product development strategies, domestic marketing strategies, and even international marketing strategies with CMEA countries. The ministries to whom the enterprises reported still retained control of technology and funding. More recently, some enterprises have developed their own technology, now trade directly with Western companies, and have become self-financing.

Gorbachev understands the futility of attempting to manage the production and distribution of 24 million different types of items through Gosplan and a handful of highly centralized government ministries. Today the emphasis on enterprise plans is focused on qualitative indicators reflecting efficiency in the use of resources, rates of plant modernization, and the growth of labor productivity through the achievements of science and technology. Government ministries now set efficiency targets and cost reduction rates. The rigid centrally planned targets and controls of the past are being replaced by more flexible, bottom-up, enterprise planning. The role of Gosplan is being redefined along the lines of the Hungarian state planning office as one of providing guidelines and long-term forecasts. All of this is rationalized by Soviet ideologists as "the extension of the rights of economic enterprises and broadening the participation of employees in the management of these enterprises."

The use of computer simulation models to support the underlying principles of perestroika has accelerated under Gorbachev both in economic research institutes and in individual enterprises. The Central Mathematical Economics Institute (TsEMI) and its offspring, the Institute for Economic Forecasting of Scientific and Technical Progress, as well as Aganbegian's former center, the Institute for Economics and Organization of Industrial Production in Novosibirsk, are among the most active ones working with computer-based planning models. Since May 1, 1987, it has been legally possible for economists and management scientists from these centers to work as private management consultants for state-owned enterprises. This development, combined with the advent of the personal computer in the Soviet Union, has created considerable interest at the enterprise level. For example, the MC Men's Shirt Shop in Moscow uses computer models to forecast demand. Computer-based planning models were introduced at the Vladimir Tractor Company by economists from TsEMI, who helped design the plan for restructuring the company.

To help him de-Stalinize the USSR and open the closed society, Gorbachev has turned to a sophisticated team of five high-level economic strategists headed by Abel G. Aganbegian. Their strategy calls for nothing less than dismantling the centrally planned economy and a frontal assault on the communist party, the government bureaucracy, the military, and the KGB. As one member of the team said to me, "The only way to save socialism is to abolish Gosplan."

These strategists and their respective economic research institutes played a major role in laying the groundwork for the additional reforms announced by Gorbachev at the Central Committee plenum held in June of 1987. All of the radical reforms included in the new enterprise law, which went into effect on January 1, 1988, were based on further simulation studies conducted by the aforementioned research institutes.

Under this new enterprise law, 60 percent of the Soviet Union's 48,000 industrial companies are required by law to be financially self-sufficient. No longer will Gosbank (the central bank) extend credit to companies that are unprofitable, have huge unsold inventories, or make poor quality products.

In addition, under the new system of cost accounting called *khozraschet,* local managers have been given a great deal more decision-making freedom than was the case in the past. Under khozraschet, the Soviets are also experimenting with forms of workplace democracy, similar to those that have been adopted in Sweden, West Germany, Hungary, and Japan.

To obtain hard currency needed to pay for the importation of food, technology, and consumer goods from the West, the USSR is placing much more emphasis on bilateral trade with Western Europe, Japan, and the United States. In no area are Gorbachev's reforms more radical than in the field of international trade. The power of the world marketplace is one of Gorbachev's most important instruments of change.

The Soviets have also announced their intentions to begin introducing Hungarian and Chinese financial and banking reforms in 1988. These will be spread over a three-year period and will include creation of new financial institutions, introduction of capital markets, application for membership in the World Bank and the International Monetary Fund, cooperation with the Federal Reserve Bank, and eventually introduction of flexible exchange rates. Within the not-too-distant future, USSR firms will have access to a number of alternative sources of capital, and corporate finance is likely to take on a whole new meaning.

Gorbachev's strategy team works closely with the new rector of the Academy for the National Economy, Evgenii K. Smirnitskii, to re-orient senior level bureaucrats to the new way of thinking. Ministers, deputy ministers, and heads of the largest enterprises are brought to the Academy for an intensive executive development program of seminars, small group experiences, role playing, computer gaming, and private consultation with the architects of the economic reforms. The methods being used to retrain Soviet managers are identical to those being taught in the very best American graduate schools of business.

As I reflect back on my 1982 trip to Moscow as well as my 1985 and 1987 visits to the Soviet Union, it is clear that virtually all of Gorbachev's reforms have been the subject of intense simulation analysis for a long period of time—including foreign trade reform, monetary and banking reform, and khozraschet, to mention only a few.

When American sovietologists suggest that there is no clearly defined strategy underlying Gorbachev's perestroika, they are essentially denying the relevance of nearly two decades of management science research on which perestroika is firmly grounded. Indeed, there is substantial evidence to suggest that perestroika may be the most comprehensive, in-depth management science project ever implanted anywhere in the world.

Based on Gorbachev's actions and words during his first three years in office, as well as the extensive computer simulation studies I have observed in Moscow since 1982, it appears that USSR strategy rests on ten fundamental objectives:[3]

1. Economy: To strengthen the economy and make significant improvements in the quality of life of the people.
2. Agriculture: To become self-sufficient in agricultural products and foodstuffs.
3. Technology: To reduce the technological gap between the USSR and the West—particularly with regard to computers, automatic machines, and robotics.
4. Consumption: To produce world-class consumer goods for domestic consumption and export abroad.

5. International trade: To integrate the Soviet economy into the global economy.
6. Democratization: To encourage democratic principles and socialist self-government in the USSR and Eastern Europe.
7. Foreign policy: To strengthen the Soviet Union's political and economic relations with such countries as West Germany, Japan, China, Israel, India, Mexico, Argentina, and Brazil.
8. Third World: To reduce the cost to the USSR of its relations with Third World states such as Afghanistan, Ethiopia, Angola, Mozambique, and Cuba.
9. Arms control: To reduce the level of tension between the Soviet Union and the United States and negotiate a major arms control agreement by 1990 covering conventional forces, strategic nuclear forces, and space weapons.
10. Culture: To change the culture of the USSR in such a manner that, in exchange for more personal freedom, individual citizens will be encouraged to assume more risk and responsibility for their individual lives.

Before Andropov and Gorbachev came to power, through the use of exhaustive computer simulation studies, most Soviet social scientists had become convinced that the only viable way to turn the USSR around was through a strategy of radical economic, political, cultural, and foreign policy reform. Even before the first Andropov economic experiments were introduced in 1984, simulation studies provided substantial evidence that anything short of radical reform was doomed to failure. Among the strategies rejected by most sophisticated Soviet economists were strategies based purely on discipline and partial reform.

Under a conservative strategy based primarily on discipline, the Soviet economy would continue to be highly centralized, rigid, and tightly controlled. The state would own the means of production and all property income would revert to the state. Since private enterprise would not be permitted, individual income would be limited to wages and salaries. Economic administration would continue to be hierarchical, with decision making centralized at the top in Moscow. The production and distribution of goods and services would be planned in detail by Gosplan.

Those who argue that Gorbachev is following a conservative strategy also claim that his ambitious economic objectives are unattainable with such a strategy. Does this mean that Gorbachev has deliberately developed a strategy that is doomed to failure at the outset? Or is he simply stupid or perhaps a pathological liar?

Even today, despite considerable evidence to the contrary, most sovietologists still claim that Gorbachev will pursue a liberal strategy based on partial reform. According to this scenario, he would not only make personnel changes and stress discipline, but he would implement a limited number of organizational and policy changes as well. Under a liberal strategy, the overall economic and political system would still remain virtually intact.

A strategy based on partial reform assumes that if a single part of the system is fixed, then the entire system will benefit as well. But everything is related to everything else in the USSR economy. With computer simulation models, it is rather easy to demonstrate that fixing one part of the system may very well aggravate other parts of the economy. It is virtually impossible for central planning to anticipate all of the possible consequences of a series of small changes. Cynics are understandably pessimistic about the likelihood that partial reforms will produce any significant long-term benefits to the Soviet economy.

To achieve his overall objective of making the USSR a more open society, Gorbachev has formulated and is in the process of implementing a strategy of radical reform consisting of ten specific strategies:[4]

1. Economy: Decentralization of decision making by state-owned enterprises including such decisions as product mix, prices, output, wages, employment, investment, research and development, domestic and international sales and marketing, and incentives. Creation of new financial institutions to finance the expansion of Soviet enterprises. Authorization of private enterprises in the service sector of the economy.

2. Agriculture: Decentralization of state-owned farms and strengthening of agricultural cooperatives. Greater use of market incentives and an increase in the number of private farms.

3. Technology: A substantial increase in the commitment of resources to education and research and development in high technology fields—computers, process controls, robotics, genetic engineering, space research, and so on. Creation of joint ventures with Western high-tech companies. Increased purchases of Western technology from such countries as West Germany, Japan, Israel, and Brazil.

4. Consumption: Increased investment in the manufacturing of con-

sumer goods. Importation of high-quality consumer goods from the West.

5. International trade: Decentralization of foreign trade to individual enterprises and the authority to trade directly with Western companies. Encouragement of joint ventures with the West. Participation in international trade and financial institutions.

6. Democratization: Decentralization of the communist party, the government, and the economy. Increased democracy in the workplace. Greater freedom of political dissent. Improved possibilities to emigrate from the USSR.

7. Foreign policy: Encouragement of increased political independence for Eastern Europe. A major effort to increase bilateral trade with Japan and China. The establishment of diplomatic relations with Israel.

8. Third World: Development of a face-saving strategy to withdraw from Afghanistan. Concentration of political and economic relations on the more affluent Third World countries that offer the greatest promise for trade and technology.

9. Arms control: Reduction in the level of anti-American rhetoric and pursuit of a strategy aimed at signing a major arms control agreement with the United States by 1990.

10. Culture: Increased freedom of expression in speech, the press, literature, art, drama, movies, and religion. Permission for firms to go bankrupt and to dismiss incompetent employees. Tough disciplinary actions for alcohol and drug abuse, bribery, theft, and corruption.

Not only have all of these strategies been subjected to repeated simulation analyses by Soviet social scientists over the years, but they continue to be the subject of ongoing research as well. However, these social scientists now enjoy a major advantage that was not available to their counterparts in the 1970s and early 1980s. They now have over four years of empirical data on the actual results of economic reform going back to the initial Andropov experiments, which began in 1984. Computer simulation becomes a much more powerful analytical tool when simulated results can be compared against actual real world results. It is impossible to validate simulation models, when there is no empirical data with which to compare simulated results. Until the death of Brezhnev in late 1982, there was no meaningful empirical data base that could realistically be used by Soviet economists to validate their simulation models.

It is no longer business as usual in Moscow, and computer simulation models have played an important role in helping shape the nature of the business in which the USSR will be in the 1990s. Perhaps it is time to reprogram some of the American computer simulation models, for they may be based on obsolete assumptions about the Soviet Union. As political scientist Bruce W. Jentleson has said, "Policies predicted on yesterday's realities stand little chance of succeeding in tomorrow's world."[5]

Notes

1. Thomas H. Naylor, *Computer Simulation Experiments with Models of Economic Systems* (New York: John Wiley, 1971), translated into Russian and Polish.

2. Naylor, "A Menu of Options by Soviet Economists," *The New York Times,* October 16, 1982.

3. Naylor, *The Gorbachev Strategy: Opening the Closed Society* (Lexington, MA: Lexington Books, 1988), pp. 43–44.

4. *Ibid.,* pp. 48–49.

5. Bruce W. Jentleson, *Pipeline Politics* (Ithaca, NY: Cornell University Press, 1986), p. 246.

8

COMPUTER-INTEGRATED MANUFACTURING

*Richard W. Judy**

The official communist party (CPSU) newspaper announced that the Politburo had "considered and basically approved a state-wide program to establish and develop the production and effective utilization of computer technology and automated systems up to the year 2000."[1] Raising economic productivity and efficiency by accelerating scientific and technical progress, particularly in machine building and electronics, was claimed to be the overarching objective of this new program.

General Secretary M. S. Gorbachev, reporting to the Central Committee six months later, put the matter in the following words:

> Machine building plays the dominant, key role in carrying out the scientific and technological revolution . . . Microelectronics, computer technology, instrument making and the entire informatics industry are the catalyst of progress. They require accelerated development.[2]

The new informatics program, which has not been publicly disseminated, is said to call for acceleration of production, improved quality, and the introduction of new models of computer equipment.[3] Application of informatics technology, especially computers and microprocessors, and automation are to lead to a "comprehensive intensification of the national

---

*The views expressed in this chapter are those of the author alone, who expresses his gratitude to the National Council for Soviet and East European Research for its financial sponsorship of the research upon which this work is based.

economy." The machine-building sector was one of five named as main foci for the new technology.[4]

The 12th Five Year Plan (FYP) targets for the machine-building sector are highly ambitious. In addition to approving output targets for the sector, the 27th CPSU Congress approved a "restructuring" of the sector's investment and structural policies. Investment in civilian machine building was slated to approximately double in comparison with the previous FYP.[5] Between 10 and 12 percent of the "active part" of capital stock in the machine-building sector was targeted for annual replacement. The annual rate of replacement of the sector's capital stock was scheduled to grow from only 4.5 percent in 1985 to 13 percent in 1990 and, in total, over half of the capital stock was to be replaced during the current FYP. Output of machine building was supposed to increase nearly twice as fast as that for industry as a whole. Within that sector, the production of instruments, computer technology, electronics, and related machines was scheduled to increase from 1.3 to 1.6 times faster than the sector as a whole.[6]

Quantitative indices were not the only ones scheduled to improve during the 12th FYP. The time required to develop and introduce new technology was to be cut one-third or a quarter of its previous length. All newly introduced technology was to raise productivity no less than by 150 to 200 percent compared to items previously produced. Labor productivity in machine building was to increase by 39 to 43 percent; total unit costs were to decline by 9 to 11 percent.

How were all of these ambitious targets to be attained? According to academician K. Frolov, the decreed acceleration of the machine-building sector is possible only on the basis of widespread introduction of FMS, CAD, CAM, CNC, and robotics.[7] In other words, the USSR is hoping to produce a technological revolution from above in the key machine-building sector by force feeding it with the set of technologies that comprise what Westerners call computer-integrated manufacturing, or CIM.

What is Computer-Integrated Manufacturing?

By CIM, we mean a set of four computer-based technological innovations that involve the automation of physical labor and/or information processing in manufacturing organizations. Over the last two decades, these innovations have evolved and now hold the promise of revolutionizing manufacturing. In various degrees and differing combinations, they are now being adopted in all the major industrialized nations of the world.[8] The four components of CIM are shown in Figure 8.1.

Computer-integrated manufacturing is a whole that is greater than the sum of its parts. The history of recent years has been one of ever higher levels of integration of new but disparate manufacturing technologies under computer control. The various technologies, that is, CAD, CAM, CAPP, and MRP, developed more or less independently and, when implemented, have constituted "islands of automation." The CIM factory of the future, examples of which already exist, will connect these four technologies in two basic ways: (1) technically, they will be connected by means of a distributed information processing network, which will link and coordinate the computers that control the various subsystems, and (2) logically, they will be connected by organized information exchanges, concepts, algorithms, simulation models, and management subsystems, such as JIT order and inventory management, GT data organization, CPT/SLAM, which are methods for bottleneck elimination, and "manufacturability," which is a discipline that CIM forces on the designer by the CAD-designed object manufacturable by a CAM production process.[9]

Western Literature about Soviet CIM

Despite the potentially profound implications of CIM and the evident intent of the Soviet leadership to pursue it, the topic has received surprisingly little attention in Western literature. A welcome exception is a recently published book on Soviet automation.[10]

Soviet discussions of new manufacturing technology rarely take the integrated point of view of CIM. Instead, the component technologies (CAD, FMS, etc.) are usually addressed individually. This disintegrated approach in itself is significant, because it indicates continuation of a piecemeal approach to the subject.

The purpose of this chapter is to examine recent Soviet plans, progress, and problems in CAD and CAM, two of the key technologies that together make up CIM.

Computer-Assisted Design in the USSR

CIM begins with CAD, so that makes it a logical place to begin this survey. First, we look at Soviet motivations for introducing CAD and a

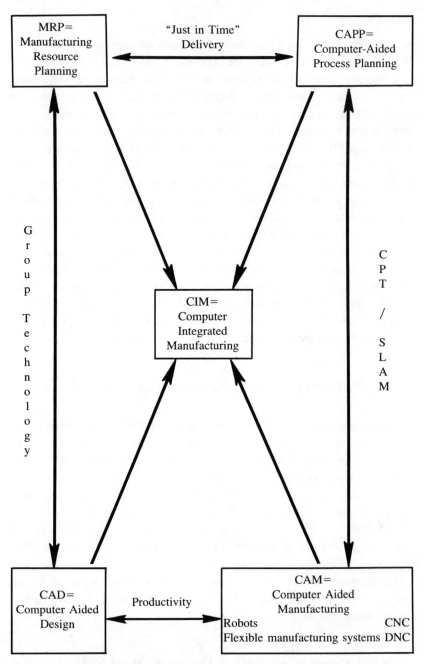

Figure 8.1. Computer-integrated Manufacturing. (Source: Adapted from Gerald I. Susman & Richard B. Chase, "A Sociotechnical Analysis of the Integrated Factory," *Journal of Applied Behavioral Science,* 22:3, p. 258.)

sample of results. Next we attempt to piece together the CAD components of the unpublished 15-year informatics plan and to evaluate these in light of reports on the plan's implementation. This section concludes with some observations on the computing environment for CAD in the USSR.

Enthusiasm for CAD is keen. An important source of this attitude is in the deep dissatisfaction with the quality of Soviet design work that is felt at many levels in the politico-economic apparatus. It has been argued recently that design is the bottleneck preventing new technology from being introduced by industry.

> . . . the creation of new technology is retarded not by the absence of scientific ideas and engineering solutions, but by long design periods and sometimes unsatisfactory quality in design and technological development of innovations.[11]

A recent article points up serious problems in the design of industrial construction. Many projects are put into the plan before their designs are finished and documented. That impedes organization of construction activity, determination of input requirements, supply, and so on. The poor quality of designs, their rapid obsolescence, and the absence of working documentation turns the project site into a *dolgostroi* [protracted construction project], and produces overruns of materials, labor, and money.[12]

A survey of construction project designs in a number of USSR ministries indicated that only about half of the designs were up-to-date. The matter apparently is even worse, because many ministries define "up-to-date" very liberally. According to data of Stroibank SSSR, about 25 percent of all construction projects in the 12th FYP, which their ministries claim to be of "modern" design, were, in fact, designed 10 to 20 years ago. For example, in 1985 the Ministry of Non-Ferrous Metallurgy approved some 69 projects that were designed in 1965–75, Minavtoprom-20, and Minstankprom-18.[13]

CAD is regarded by many Soviet observers as a key to improving the work of their design organizations. The specific advantages anticipated include:

Reducing time for design completion.
Improving quality of designs and documentation.
Lowering cost of design, manufacturing, and construction.
Permitting flexible manufacturing.

Reducing routine work of engineers.
Encouraging engineers to be more creative.

To what extent have these sought-after benefits been achieved? Unfortunately, a satisfactory answer to that question cannot be given. No systematic treatment of either the costs or benefits of CAD is to be found in the Soviet literature, although ad hoc accounts are plentiful. The following examples are illustrative:

Miasnikov states that design times at the Leningrad Elektrosila were cut by 12 percent, materials required by 6 percent, and reliability increased by 25 percent. He also claims that the use of CAD in electrical machine design economized 1,000 tons of materials and 150 million kilowatt hours annually.[14]

Maksimenko asserts that the use of CAD resulted in 2.6 million rubles of savings in the construction of facilities in Western Siberian oil fields. Another 200,000 to 300,000 rubles were saved by CAD by Mingasprom in the design of gas refineries.[15]

The use of CAD in production engineering is said by Mozhaeva to raise engineer's productivity by four to six times, to raise the quality of technological documentation, to diminish the time for the preparation of routings by 10 percent to 15 percent, and to produce an annual payoff in the range from 100,000 to 450,000 rubles.[16]

The use of CAD for the logical design of printed circuit boards is said to quadruple the productivity of designers. The design of modern integrated circuits would be "unthinkable" without the use of CAD.[17]

Both before and after the advent of *glasnost'*, the Soviets published their plans for CAD in bits and pieces with few of the details and explanations needed to fully understand them. In an early step, the State Committee on Science and Technology launched a CAD program during the 9th FYP (1971–75), with the intention of establishing 40 systems. Some 47 CAD systems were to be deployed during the 10th FYP (1976–80).[18] From the skimpy evidence available, it would seem that most of these early CAD installations were intended for the design of military and quasimilitary equipment, primarily aerospace systems.

After those slow beginnings, CAD was declared to be a high priority for the 11th Five-Year Plan (1981–85), and the program of the State Committee on Science and Technology called for the development of 23 CAD installations in various industrial organizations, 41 in construction organizations, and 27 CAD research installations in various institutions of higher education.[19] By 1985 only 24 CAD systems were working in the electrotechnical industry, whereas the instrument-building industry could boast 40.[20] Such modest numbers hardly evince a dynamic program.

Only in the 12th FYP does the Soviet CAD program begin to show evidence that it has been accorded real priority. According to Politburo member L. N. Zaikov, some 2,500 CAD installations with 10,000 workstations are to be introduced during 1986–90.[21] This is supposed to permit from 25 to 40 percent of design work to become "automated."[22] The fact that only 249 CAD systems were installed during 1986 indicates that, if the plan is to be fulfilled, most of the CAD systems will have to be installed during the end years of the current plan period.[23]

Soviet Hardware for CAD

The supporting hardware for early Soviet CAD applications consisted of general purpose mainframes such as the BESM-6 and, later, various models of the Riad family of IBM compatibles. The main memories of these machines were small, and so were their disk storage capabilities. Their computational speeds remained slow. Graphics capabilities were first nonexistent and then poor. Time-sharing became available in the decade of the 1970s but remained very limited. Interactive graphics was nonexistent.

The appearance of the 16-bit SM-3 and SM-4 minicomputers in the late 1970s opened a second line of development for Soviet CAD.[24] By 1980 two CAD workstations were being serially produced. These systems were designated the ARM-R for radio-electronic designers and ARM-M for designers in machine building.[25] Both were based on the SM-3 and SM-4 minicomputers and were configured with tape or small disk external memory, a graphics input device, a graphics display, and a plotter.

Software for the ARM-R and ARM-M was extremely limited and consisted only of an operating system, the usual language (e.g., FORTRAN), and a graphics package. The ARM-M also had a routine that produced code for numerically controlled machine tools. Beyond this, the user was expected to produce his or her own software or otherwise acquire it.

Due to their modest computational and graphics capabilities, small main memory and auxiliary storage, frequent unavailability of appropriate peripheral devices, and paucity of CAD software, these early ARMs were of limited usefulness for design work. Their applications essentially were restricted to tasks requiring relatively simple computations or data manipulation, especially when graphics results were to be produced. The design of shop floors, printed circuit boards, block diagrams, and other layout problems were within the power of the ARMs. Beyond that, they were useful for limited text processing, redrafting of drawings to reflect minor changes in specifications, and writing programs for numerically controlled machine tools.

In the early 1980s, Minpribor (see Note 21) began to produce "second-generation" upgrades of the ARM workstations called ARM2. Like their predecessors, the ARM2 workstations were based on the SM-4 minicomputer. These systems were normally configured with two to four graphics displays and digitizers, sharing an SM-4 minicomputer with a magnetic disk storage unit and plotter. Maximum internal storage was 256K bytes, and disk storage consisted of up to two ES-5061 drives with 29 megabyte capacity each. The main distinction between the "second-generation" ARM2 and the "first-generation" ARMs lay in certain improvements in their peripheral equipment.

The ARM2 is known to be serially produced in two versions: the ARM2-01 for use in mechanical and electrical design problems, and the ARM2-05 for programming and testing microprograms for digital systems based on microprocessors. In 1985 the ARM2 was being manufactured in plants under four ministries. "Large quantities" are produced only at the Gomel Factory of Radio and Technological Equipment, which also was the first Soviet factory to produce the CAD workstations.

In 1983 Minpribor produced 14 CAD systems, presumably comprised of ARM-2 workstations. The number installed in 1984 was to have doubled. The 11th FYP called for some 120 CAD systems to be introduced within the ministry. Beginning in 1984, Minpribor was to begin production of the ARM-2 for users outside the ministry. Versions for both mechanical and electrical design were to become available. By 1986 some ARM-2 workstations were being introduced with the improved SM-1420 in place of the venerable SM-4.[26]

CAD workstations based on various Soviet microcomputers have appeared in very recent years. One, based on the Iskra-226, was intended for developing code for numerically controlled machine tools.[27] Owing to the tardy development of personal computers in the USSR, the development of CAD applications for this class of machines was only in its early stages by 1986.

The most recent and potentially most significant addition to Soviet CAD hardware capabilities is the SM-1700, which is a 32-bit super minicomputer that may be comparable to the VAX.[28] Shkabardnia, the minister of Minpribor, stated that models of the SM-1700 had been developed and furnished with "a powerful operating system and highly developed software for CAD in machine building."[29] A new series of CAD workstations called Aftograf has appeared, and it may be based on the SM-1700. The Aftograf series is said to be the basis for CAD in machine building during the 12th FYP. Until more research is done, it will be difficult to evaluate the significance of this new generation of Soviet CAD hardware.

The last years of the 11th FYP saw completion of design work on a number of peripheral devices sorely needed by Soviet CAD. These included graphic displays, memory devices, digitalizers, plotters, and other devices. More research is required to determine the contribution that this new technology may make to Soviet CAD.

Soviet CAD Software

The development of Soviet CAD software work has proceeded along two lines.

1. Most early Soviet software consisted essentially of individual subprograms that could be accessed by FORTRAN or ALGOL main programs. These packages, such as GRAFOR, GRAFOL, and ALGRAF, owed a heavy debt to Western predecessors produced by firms like Calcomp. Their contribution lay in their ability to perform graphic representation, compute strength of materials, and do limited modeling. They suffered the serious disadvantage that they were not integrated and were able to share data only in cumbersome ways that were very memory intensive.

2. In the mid-1970s, specifications were drawn up for an integrated, interactive CAD software system. Formulation of these specifications was "guided" by software produced by a number of Western developers, especially by Applicon and Siemens. Additional research is needed to determine the degree of similarity of the resulting Soviet CAD to Western models.

An example of Soviet integrated, interactive CAD software is a package called GRAFIKA-81, which was developed by the Institute of Control Problems in Moscow. This package reportedly had been well developed as of 1986 and was intended for design work in machine building, radio electronics, architecture, and construction. The system is said to consist of the following components and capabilities:

1. A CAD system generator capable of producing a CAD package for a target computing system. The generator is said to link required applications software subsystems, graphics and other peripheral drives, and data base files. "International standards" are claimed to be observed.

2. A capability that permits nonprogrammer designers to describe the object to be designed in a language that is "close to natural." The basis of this capability is a graphics language for modeling two- and three-dimensional objects.

3. Programming tools, consisting of a selection of modules, said to be capable of solving many design problems including production documentation and codes for numerically programmed machine tools. Operation in both batch and interactive modes is claimed. The base language is FORTRAN IV.

4. Portability to a variety of computer configurations from minis to large systems equipped with a wide selection of peripheral devices, including intelligent terminals, graphics devices, production equipment such as numerically controlled machine tools. The system is said to run on a wide range of computers, including the Riad, M-6000, SM-2, SM-3, and SM-4, as well as foreign and domestic systems that are compatible with them.

It is difficult, without more research, to judge the real, as distinct from the claimed, capabilities of GRAFIKA-81. How does it compare with the Western CAD software? Is it "vaporware," or a piece of practical operating software? Academician V. A. Trapeznikov, director of the Institute of Control Problems, recently indicated that more powerful graphics display units would be necessary before GRAFIKA-81 could be "serially produced."[30] Since Trapeznikov's institute is known for its Military Industry Commission (VPK) work and connections, it may be that the recently intercepted large order of highly sophisticated Tektronix graphics workstations were destined for use with GRAFIKA-81.

Another recent addition to the battery of Soviet CAD software is the set of application programs known as ARM-PLAT. This system, which operates on the ARM2-01, serves the needs of designers of printed circuit boards. It is said to be superior to other Soviet packages of similar type.

Still another recent package is KAPRI, an integrated, interactive CAD/CAM system for designing products and processes in a flexible manufacturing system or computer-integrated manufacturing environment. This sytem was designed by the Kurchatov Institute of Nuclear Energy and the Keldysh Institute of Applied Mathematics for the design and fabrication of small-lot and experimental machine building. It operates in a multilevel environment with an ES-1045 at the center, supporting four ARM-M workstations.

The 12th FYP calls for serial production of hardware and software for CAD workstations at three levels; that of super computers and large mainframes (e.g., Elbrus-2, ES-1065), of minicomputers (e.g., SM-1420, SM-1700), and of personal computers (e.g., ES-1840, Elektronika MS-1212). Multilevel CAD systems operating on local area networks are said to be in the offing.[31] On the software side, Soviet CAD is said to be moving toward integration, better graphics, use of data base management systems, and artificial intelligence.[32]

Soviet Applications of CAD: Examples

In the USSR, CAD has found its heaviest use in the computer industry both because of the complexity of the design problems and because the engineers are accustomed to computers and their use.

In the early 1980s a three-level CAD system was being used by the Ministry of the Electronics Industry (Minelektronprom) for designing integrated circuits.[33] At the top level, the system's main computing power is provided by a troika of linked BESM-6 mainframes. At the bottom are interactive graphics workstations of the Elektronika 100-25 and M-6000 types, of which 16 may operate simultaneously in a time-sharing mode with an average two-second delay for access to the mainframes. The system accommodates a maximum of 48 workstations. FORTRAN is the system's basic language and a variety of specialized subsystems provide the capability for logical design, chip layout, testing, lead placement, and photocomposition. System output is the photographic template for chip production.

Soviet CAD software for the IBM-compatible Riad computers included packages named RAPIRA and PRAM. These packages were not integrated CAD systems, but, rather, collections of individual routines and subsystems that could be used by electronics designers. A minimum computer configuration of 512K bytes of main memory and plotter was required by these packages. Their main usage was macro level of design, for example, main logic design, circuit board layout, and preparation of design documentation.

In 1983 G. Lopato, director of the Scientific Research Institute for Computers (NII EVM), reported that his institute had developed and introduced a CAD system for computer design.[34] The system reportedly was used in the design and manufacture of several models of the Riad-2 computer and its peripherals, for example, the ES-1055 and ES-1060. Development of this system apparently has continued within NII EVM and includes manufacture of more than ten types of specialized equipment for the encoding and editing of graphics information and the fabrication of photographic templates, as well as drilling holes in printed circuit boards and performing certain quality control operations. The system reportedly has reduced development time by a factor of two to three times.

CAD in the USSR: Problems and Resistance

Soviet attempts to implement and use CAD have encountered an impressive array of difficulties. Some of these have much in common with difficulties met everywhere. Others are occasioned by one or another aspect of the Soviet politico-socioeconomic system and are basically unique to the USSR. What follows is a partial list of both types of difficulties.

Inadequate graphics displays. Without fast, interactive color graphics, CAD is more promise than reality. Soviet CAD workstations have traditionally been weak in this vital department. They have been slow and monochromatic, with poor resolution. Academician Andrei Ershov, a senior Soviet computer specialist, stated that no other aspect of his recent three-week tour of American computer facilities, impressed him so much as the graphics capability he saw on Apollo CAD workstations.[35]

Inadequate memory and processing power. Modern CAD systems lay heavy demands on both memory and processing power. Soviet CAD has relied mainly on older, slower computer designs such as the BESM-6, Riad-2, SM-4, and Iskra-226. The technology and capabilities of these machines date to the early 1970s or before. The RAM and disk storage capabilities available to these machines are woefully short of those required to support sophisticated CAD and computer-aided engineering.

Other hardware deficiencies. Even when the technology is available, users complain of its unreliability, poor manufacturer support, and lack of spare parts.

Inadequate CAD software. CAD software has suffered the same defect of arrested development that has plagued other software in the Soviet Union. Designers with CAD workstations faced the choice of using generally available but poorly supported subroutines or of developing their own software. Only a handful of organizations were engaged in CAD software development, and few incentives encouraged them to polish and support packages for widespread use. By contrast, about 200 American companies were offering CAD/CAE software in 1986 for the Apollo system.[36]

Insufficient data bases. To be fruitful, CAD must assist the designer by rendering quick and easy access to large libraries of engineering and design information. Soviet CAD users frequently complain of the lack of this vital data.

Improper incentives. Conservative resistance is not uncommon among designers everywhere. American engineers have expressed considerable opposition to the introduction of interactive computer graphics and manufacturing data bases.[37] Soviet CAD must contend not only with this "normal" conservatism but also with systemic disincentives to use the technology. In construction design, for example, payment to the design organization is a positive function of the cost of the project. CAD, to the extent that it fulfills its promise to optimize the use of materials, reduces the cost of the project and thus also the payment to the design organization, which, therefore, has little incentive to use it.

Lack of trained personnel. The Soviet educational establishment has been slow to produce engineers with qualifications in CAD/CAE. The reason for this is twofold: (1) few institutions have taken the initiative to put such CAD training into their curricula, and (2) the shortage of CAD workstations has hindered even that initiative. Technicians to support CAD workstations are also in short supply.

High cost of CAD workstations. An ARM2 workstation is said to cost some 600,000 rubles.[38] It is not known if this includes the 11 technical

persons specified to support and maintain the system. Software costs also
are very high; CAD software for ship design is said to have required 600
man-years.

Computer-Assisted Manufacturing in the USSR

Production automation has been a Soviet holy grail for many years. Official data on the production and installation of sophisticated manufacturing gear in recent years seem to tell an impressive story. Planned targets for the 12th FYP and beyond are even more ambitious. Quite another,
less flattering story emerges from Soviet reports on how this equipment
actually works on the factory floor.

Production of *NC machine tools* began in the late 1960s and comprised
about 2.5 percent of all machine tools built in the USSR during the 9th
and 10th FYP (1971–80). Annual growth rates of NC machine tools during the 11th FYP exceeded 20 percent and production reached 17,700
units in 1985. In 1986 the value of NC machine tools comprised 45 percent of the value of all machine tools produced in the Soviet Union.[39]
The 12th FYP calls for a 90-percent expansion in the production of NC
machine tools and, by 1990, the target is to produce 34,200 units.[40] These
numbers compare with a total of 2,286 machine tools shipped in the United
States during 1985.[41]

The impressive Soviet production and installation data for NC machine
tools clash jarringly with the sketchy information on how these machines
are being used. In small-run serial production shops, where the majority
of them are employed, it turns out that NC and CNC machine tools stand
idle 90 percent of the time. This dismal performance is attributed by one
author to "a traditional approach to the use of a radically new technology." More specifically, it arises from the poor reliability of the machines, shortages of spare parts, and an absence of organized maintenance
services for smaller enterprises, as well as a lack of personnel qualified
to install, program, operate, and maintain the equipment.[42]

Soviet *industrial robotics* began in the 1960s with the rather primitive
UM-1, Universal 50, and UPK-1 devices. Pieces of a technological base
for robotics production were put into place during the 1971–80 period.
In the last five years of this period, over 100 models were built and about
1,000 industrial robots reportedly were deployed, mainly in the machine-
building industry.

According to official Soviet statistics, some 40,000 robots were produced during the 11th FYP (1981–85).[43] Between 1980 and 1986, the annual output of robots in the USSR increased on the order of ten times to 15,000 units. Despite rapid gains in the Soviet production of robots, the annual output plan was underfulfilled by 7 percent in 1986.[44] The 12th FYP calls for the annual production of industrial robots to grow to 28,600 by 1990 and for a total of about 100,000 robots to be installed by that year. In the city of Moscow, the plan calls for nine plant-level CAD implementations, 12 at the shop level, 900 sections and lines using over 10,600 industrial robots, manipulators, and transfer arms by 1990.[45]

Some international data provide a rough standard for comparison. In 1982 Japan claimed nearly 32,000 installed robots; France, about 10,000; and the United States, 6,300.[46] The total number of robots shipped in the United States during 1985 (the last year for which data are available) was 5,796.[47] It seems probable that the Soviets are currently producing approximately three times as many robots of all kinds and about ten times as many CNC machine tools as in the United States. Because of non-congruence of definitions, however, these comparisons must be taken only as approximate.

The Soviets, like the Japanese and French, produce a much larger proportion of simple robots than the Americans. The vast majority, at least 95 percent, of USSR industrial robots produced in the 11th FYP were unsophisticated, "first-generation" materials handling devices with "hard-wired" controls. Most were of the so-called pick-and-place variety that performed rather simple materials movements.[48]

The Soviet Union also has imported a significant number of robots from its CMEA trading partners; East Germany was and is an extremely important source, and Bulgaria supplied over 1,000 robots to the USSR during the 11th FYP. In 1985 Eastern Europe provided over one billion rubles worth of machine tools to the USSR.[49] The applications of these robots were in such basic industrial operations as loading and unloading, goods movement, and some painting and welding.

The Soviet *Flexible Manufacturing Systems (FMS)* terminology may be explained as follows. The counterpart to FMS is GAP (*gibkoe avtomatizirovannoe proizvodstvo,* or flexible automated production). This category is subdivided into:

1. GPM (*gibkii proizvodstvennyi modul',* or flexible production module). Normally, a module (cell) consists of one piece of equipment (e.g., a CNC machine tool or other metal fabrication device) operating under program control.

2. Several modules (GPMs) operating in concert under computer control comprise a GAL (*gibkaia avtomatizirovannaia liniia*—flexible automated line) or a GAU (*gibkii avtomatizirovannyi uchastok*—flexible automated section). A section (GAU) differs from a line (GAL) in that the former permits changes in the sequence of technological operations being performed by the various pieces of equipment. In both, the modules are served by a materials handling and transport system, as well as warehousing systems for materials and/or finished work. These two categories appear to correspond to the American term "FMS cell."

3. A collection of sections (GAU) or lines (GAL) may comprise a GATs (*gibkii avtomatizirovannyi tsekh,* or flexible automated shop).

4. GAZ (*gibkii avtomatizirovannyi zavod,* or flexible automated factory). This concept corresponds to the American CIM plant.

Work on FMS (GAP in Soviet parlance) in the USSR is said to have been underway since the early 1970s.[50] Some 13 reportedly were installed in the period 1971–80 and 40 more during 1981–83. By 1985 about 60 FMS were reported to be at work in the Soviet Union.[51] Soviet data claim that more than 200 FMS of all types were deployed in 1986.[52]

The 12th FYP calls for the widespread introduction of "second-generation" robots as well as continued use of earlier models, and their application in more sophisticated manufacturing assembly operations. It also calls for the production of 546 FMS by 1990.[53] The number of flexible production systems is to grow to about 2,000 by 1990.[54] Juxtaposing these Soviet plans with market forecasts in the United States, we note that the Yankee Group of Boston estimates that the number of installed FMS in the United States will grow from 50 at the end of 1985 to approximately 280 in 1990.[55]

As is also true with CAD, the role of East Germany as an exporter of advanced manufacturing technology to the USSR cannot be overlooked. The GDR has become one of the world's largest machine tool exporters, and the share of those exports going to the Soviet Union is estimated to exceed 75 percent. East German robotics and electronics are finding places in top-priority Soviet CAM applications, where quality and precision requirements are high. Soviet efforts to harness East European manufacturing technology have intensified in recent years. In June 1985 a general CMEA agreement on multilateral cooperation in the design, production, and implementation of FMS in machine building was signed.[56]

The technological level of Soviet CAM equipment historically has lagged significantly behind analogous equipment manufactured in the West and

Japan. The "brains" of Soviet CAM applications, to the extent that they were not "hard wired," during the first half of the 1980s were serially produced devices such as the Elektronika-60, NTs-31, NTs-80-31, and SM-3 microcomputers, and the KR580 family of microprocessors, all of which embody technology of the early 1970s. The Elektronika systems are rather slow 16-bit machines with small memory that are software compatible with the SM-4 and, hence, with the PDP-11, which was first shipped by Digital Equipment Corporation in 1970. The KR580 is a Soviet version of the 8-bit Intel 8080, MS UVT B7, and KTS-LIUS-2, which are used in Soviet CAM installations.

Soviet Applications of CAM: Some Examples

It was noted earlier that the number of "flexible production systems" that the Soviets claim to have in operation has grown from about 13 in 1980, over 50 in 1985, to as many as 200 in 1986.[57] The available evidence suggests that most of these are working in the machine-building industries. There is strong reason to suspect that the bulk of Soviet CAM applications are in the military industrial complex (VPK) industries.[58]

What follows are a few details of several Soviet CAM complexes and implementations. The purpose is to illustrate the general picture by way of a few specifics, not to exhaustively list the type and locations of these implementations.

The Ivanovsk Machine Tool Combine *imeni 50-letiia SSSR* appears to be a flagship organization in the manufacture and installation of FMS. More than any other, it is cited with pride by Soviet authors when discussing FMS. But the Ivanovsk factory is not the only place where CAM systems are being developed. Other enterprises are also involved, for example, the Moscow *Krasnyi Proletarii* and the Riazan machine tool factory are to produce lathe FMS modules, the Kosior factory in Khar'khov is to produce grinding modules, and the Gor'kii works are to make milling modules.

The ASK-20 is a flexible automated section (GAU), manufactured by the Ivanovsk machine-building combine that reportedly was brought on-stream in 1982.[59] It is controlled by an SM-2 minicomputer and consists of five numerically controlled machine tools and an automated materials handling system. The frame size is 800 × 800 × 630 millimeters. The cell is said to have freed 16 workers.

The ASVP-01 is a flexible automated line (GAL), manufactured by the same Ivanovsk machine-building organization, The line, which is used in rotary machining, consists of one MMRG-79 and two 1B732 machine tools, one UM-160 industrial robot. The line turns objects weighing up to 150 kg. It reportedly has freed four workers and five machine tools.

The Dnepropetrovsk electric locomotive plant has a flexible automated shop (GATs) consisting of 33 numerically controlled machine tools, one universal machine tool, on ORG-4 materials handling system with two STAS-3 stockage points or warehouses, a robotized transport device, and so on. Its computerized control system is based on an M-6000 computer and embraces subsystems for production scheduling, materials and product routing, and equipment control. It reportedly manages the manufacture of about 400 items. It is said to have proven its worth particularly on short runs, that is, those of from one to 100 units, where labor productivity reportedly rose 330 percent, machine tool utilization increased to 75 percent, plant output rose by 20 percent, while 83 men were released, the number of machine tools reduced by 53 units, and floor space decreased by 630 square meters, or 40 percent.

A flexible automated shop (GATs) has been manufactured and installed at unknown places. The cells consist of 16K20 and 16B16 lathes operating under a 2C85-63 CNC controller. Up to six CNC controllers are controlled by an Elektronika-60 node controller. Another Elektronika-60 controls a RSK50LT warehousing systems and self-propelled trolley with on-board NTs-80 computer. An SM-4 "Dispatcher" controls the Elektronika-60s.

The Gor'kii Automobile Factory has an FMS based on an SM-2 minicomputer.

The Riazan Machine Tool Combine has FMS sections called ASV-30 and ASV-31. They include eight CNC machine tools.

A computer-integrated manufacturing system (CIM) with the acronym KAPRI has been developed by the Kurchatov Institute of Nuclear Energy and the Keldysh Institute of Applied Mathematics.[60] The system includes subsystems for CAD, CAE, and CAM in small-run machine building. KAPRI operates on a multitiered LAN incorporating a high performance mainframe (about two MOPS, two to four Mbytes RAM, one to two gigabytes external memory) at its apex, microcomputer workstations, and minicomputer controllers.

Most Soviet FMS are used in metal forming applications, with an unknown proportion being supported by materials handling and warehousing capabilities. Outside machine building and the automotive industries, other enterprises mentioned as leaders in the use of robots and FMS have been the Smolensk *NIItekhnopribor* and the Vladimir Electrical Motor works. The literature as of the mid-1980s leaves the impression that such technological leaders were quite the exception rather than the rule.[61]

CAM in the USSR: Problems and Resistance

Western authors have given mixed signals concerning the *technological level and quality* of Soviet CAM equipment. Writing in 1976, Berry and Cooper concluded that the technological level of Soviet NC machine tools lagged behind that of Western models but by less than in the 1960s. Their final words were: "This case study indicates that in the conditions of the Soviet economy technological lags can be very quickly narrowed and overcome once their existence has been acknowledged and priority granted to their elimination."[62]

In his 1979 article, Grant arrives at much less sanguine conclusions about the quality and technological level of Soviet machine tools. He found that: "In the most advanced areas of machine tool technology the USSR has made little progress and lags far behind the West . . . There is no evidence that the Soviets have developed or produced FMS systems." He attributed the Soviet technological lag to three factors: (1) an emphasis on standardization and mass production rather than custom design and manufacture of machine tools; (2) a poor industrial supply system in which ". . . the supply of components and parts to manufacturers of NC machine tools is frequently chaotic"; and (3) inappropriate success criteria for machine tool producers that discourage efforts to improve quality and to innovate technologically.[63]

Hill and McKay, writing in 1985, arrive at conclusions closer, although less pessimistic, to those of Grant. They note that empirical studies ". . . revealed certain shortcomings in the design and manufacture of those machines which subsequently affected their working speeds, continued accuracy, reliability, and down-times; even though the initial tolerances as specified in the state standards, and achieved in the alignment tests, were reasonably satisfactory.[64]

Dolan, in his 1985 summary of Soviet robotics, found a technological and quality lag behind American and Japanese equipment, but places greater stress on organizational problems and perverse incentives as factors retarding the diffusion of this technology in the USSR.

Recent Soviet literature clearly indicates that the quality and technological level of CAM equipment have caught the attention of engineers, planners, and political leaders. It is now fully recognized, for example, that a sine qua non for CAM is high reliability of all components of the systems since a highly integrated system is only as strong as its weakest link. This poses severe problems for Soviet industry where the mean time between failure (MTBF) of many numerically controlled machine tools is 35 hours or less, intolerably low for FMS equipment. Targets for the 12th FYP call for a new generation of computer-controlled machine tools to be manufactured by Minpribor, with MTBF of about 5,000 hours. By 1995 plans call for MTBFs to be in the 8,000- to 10,000-hour range even in conditions of multishift operation. Given the Soviet track record in quality control and equipment reliability, a certain skepticism about these targets is difficult to suppress.

A second requirement for broad-scale CAM is the convenient availability of a wide variety of instruments and devices for measurement, control, and so on. Since the technological base for providing these components does not yet exist in the USSR, the 12th FYP was written to contain ambitious targets for its creation. Plan fulfillment reports indicate that considerable difficulties have been encountered in meeting the planned goals.

If the Soviets are to achieve the CAM breakthrough that they seek, they must make major advances in their robotics technology. Until very recently, many Soviet specialists considered industrial robotics to be basically materials handling devices, for example, inserting sheet metal in die-stamping presses and later extracting the shaped parts. Modern CAM, however, assigns many more functions to automated equipment, for example, processing, welding, fastening, assembling, spraying, and other basic manufacturing operations. For these functions, the Soviets are attempting to create a new set of robots controlled by microprocessors and capable of a wide range of operations.

The introduction of "second-generation" robots has been retarded because of the insufficient number and variety of sensors and other components required for their employment. A shortage of analog to digital converters has also been noted. Soviet observers have complained about the lack of standardization in the design of robots and their attachments. Robotics engineers work in a variety of enterprises subordinated to several ministries, each producing its own series of robots. Some 128 different models of programmable materials handlers were manufactured in the CMEA countries during 1986.

Soviet microprocessor and microcomputer technology needs to progress further so as to better serve the needs of CAM. The strides are needed at least in the software field as in that of hardware. Data bases, communications protocols, and languages for systems design need to be created or improved.

Still another necessary condition for successful and widespread application of CAM is a new and strong emphasis on CAD and on *manufacturability* in product design. Most products currently manufactured in the USSR were designed with no thought of their manufacture by robots and other devices of CAM systems. The implication is that a massive product redesign effort faces Soviet engineers before CAM can be used efficiently. The traditional modus operandi of USSR design organizations has been to design products with scant concern about their manufacturability.

The *human factor* is a key ingredient of CAM. With its traditionally narrow focus, Soviet engineering training has not produced designers with the broad spectrum of competencies required to implement CIM on a grand scale. Many managers also lack the breadth of outlook necessary to perceive the possibilities of CIM. Belianin put it as follows:

> The question of supplying skilled personnel to flexible automation is also extremely important. Many machine building enterprises suffer from what might be called a "critical technological deficiency." The existing situation must be rectified, the more so since the role of technologists in creating and introducing products that can compete on the market has dramatically increased. As quickly as possible, we must train and retrain a large number of skilled personnel to design and operate FMS. For example, the traditional designer cannot cope with the demands of flexible automation; a designer-technologist is required who is also a production engineer. To achieve effective exploitation of FMS, we need systems engineers, mathematicians, programmers, electronics specialists, debuggers, etc. I submit that vigorous action in this dimension is one of the most important items on the agenda for achieving more effective manufacturing.[65]

Also on the human level is the decreased job safety noted in some Soviet plants, where automated devices have not been surrounded by the proper protective equipment. Hazardous operation has been reported to be characteristic of several first-generation Soviet robots.

As of early 1987, the Soviets had not solved the problem of providing maintenance and support service to enterprises with CNC machine tools and other advanced manufacturing technology. Those enterprises or combines large enough to staff and train their own maintenance departments were in a much more favorable position than smaller enterprises forced to depend on outside service organizations. Since a majority of machine-building enterprises are of medium or small size, the unavailability of satisfactory service, so long as it persists, will be a serious drag on their willingness to "gamble" on this new technology. Recent attempts to rationalize the informatics service sector have been weakened by strife among the ministries and state committees concerned.[66]

Not least important as a retardant to the introduction and effective use of all parts of CIM are managerial incentives and attitudes toward new technology and innovation. An American magazine cited a Gosplan report, which stated that half of the 5,000 robots produced from 1976 to 1980 remained for a protracted period in warehouses at the factories to which they had been delivered.[67] Plant managers were reluctant to interrupt current production and install the new technology because of their concern not to jeopardize fulfillment of their annual output plan.

The new manufacturing technologies, if their potentials are to be realized, greatly elevate the requirement for integration and communication among engineering, production, and managerial divisions within manufacturing organizations. This heightened degree of coordination is not easy to achieve and attain, and for the Soviets with their proclivity toward departmental parochialism, it may be especially difficult.

CAM can be tremendously disruptive to organizations. Factory floors are totally redesigned and in a state of turmoil until the new system is installed. Workers may become redundant or require fundamental retraining. Their responsibilities are likely to be completely redefined. Managers, especially at middle levels, also may become redundant and/or find that their roles have been drastically changed. A period of chaos is not unusual as the new system is brought on line and its bugs are eliminated. The payoffs may indeed be great, but the path toward them is anything but easy.

Payoffs of Soviet CAM: Anticipated and Actual

Soviet claims for FMS in machine building are stout. Makarov[68] states that, in comparison to traditional manufacturing equipment, FMS results in the following reductions:

Quantity of equipment by 50 to 75 percent.
Personnel numbers up to 80 percent.
Unit labor costs by approximately 25 percent.

Production costs by about 55 percent.

Overhead and auxiliary expenses by about 87 percent.

The production cycle, that is, time from order to output of finished goods, by five to six times.

As noted above, utilization of numerically controlled machine tools in the USSR traditionally has been low due to their poor reliability. Looking to the future, the Soviets hope that FMS will improve equipment utilization, but his may prove to be a chimera. Unless the reliability of the individual machines is greatly improved, linking them together can be devastating for total system performance since a single malfunctioning machine can cause the entire system to malperform or even halt.

The Soviets hope to realize substantial finished goods inventory savings from their FMS. Whereas many runs of small scale, serially produced machines result in production of six months demand, they look to reduce this to only two weeks demand as they move to their own version of JIT (Just In Time) inventory management. They hope to reduce average finished goods inventories to a quarter or tenth of traditional levels. But until and unless the entire Soviet system of industrial supply is massively improved, it is difficult to imagine that bufferless JIT inventory management could possibly work.

Where Will Soviet CAM Be Employed?

In mass production industries, such as automobile, agricultural machinery, ball bearing, timepiece, and electronic component production, some degree of automation is said to affect 60 to 85 percent of output. But mass production now accounts for only about a quarter of all Soviet machine building. The remaining three-quarters are job shop, individual, or small-scale serial production. This type of production is typical of ship building, machine-tool building, construction equipment, chemical equipment building, and various other types of machine building. Here the runs are short and the degree of automation traditionally has been low, and it is precisely here that the Soviets hope to realize great gains from CAM.

Prospects for Soviet CAD and CAM

In attempting a top-down technological revolution in factory automation, Soviet leaders and their machine-building industry have undertaken a daunting task. Their goal is to pull the industry up by its bootstraps over the course of the next six or seven years and, by the early 1990s, to make it a real competitor on the world scene. CIM based on microprocessor technology is one of the chief means that they have chosen to reach this goal. One cannot help but be impressed by both their ambition and the difficulty of the challenge that they have undertaken. Two facets of that challenge merit final comment.

A dramatic improvement in the *quality and technological level* of CAD and CAM hardware and software is a necessary condition for the realization of Soviet plans. That fact is clearly understood by the current leadership. The 12th FYP calls for 80 to 95 percent of the "basic types of production" to meet world quality levels, and for "practically all" newly introduced products to do so. New state acceptance standards (*gospriemka*) were established in 1987 for many products marketed by machine-building enterprises. Many of the latter were hard pressed to meet 1987 marketing plans, because a high proportion of their output failed to meet the new standards. Only time will tell whether these will be consistently enforced and finally will induce greater concern for quality among Soviet industrial enterprises.

Higher levels of quality and technology are a necessary but not sufficient condition to accomplish the top-down technological revolution that the Kremlin seeks in machine building. For this to happen, a basic restructuring of Soviet industrial organization must occur. The restructuring must greatly enhance managerial incentives to install and effectively use new technology. It must also promote the development of a professional service infrastructure to support such installation and use. Professional services for software development, engineering design, system integration, and maintenance are sadly lacking in the USSR, especially for the job-shop and small-scale serial production enterprises that bulk so importantly in the Soviet machine tool industry. Sporadic attempts to provide such services via centralized organizations have failed to solve the problem. A decentralized approach is almost certainly necessary. Whether a professional services infrastructure will emerge from Gorbachev's perestroika remains to be seen.

It seems likely that Soviet political leaders regard CIM as a kind of technological fix that can win them relatively quick gains. It also seems likely that they underestimate the preconditions for and difficulties of successfully implementing CIM. If so, they are certain to be disappointed. Nevertheless, it is very important that the West should have an accurate and up-to-date picture of Soviet CAM. If, despite all the difficulties, the

USSR should succeed in some substantial measure, the economic and military implications could be profound.

Notes

1. *Pravda* (January 4, 1985).
2. *Ibid.* (June 12, 1985), p. 2.
3. V. Vinokurov and K. Zuev, "Aktual'nye problemy razvitiia vychislitel'noi tekhniki," *Kommunist*, no. 5 (1985), pp. 18–29.
4. The remaining four are scientific research, metallurgy, power engineering, and natural resource exploration. Military applications were presumably covered in a "series of other" but unnamed sectors.
5. K. Frolov, "Mashinostroenie i nauka v strategii uskoreniia," *Kommunist*, no. 6 (April 1986), pp. 36–47.
6. *Ibid.*, pp. 37–38.
7. *Ibid.*, pp. 38,41. "FMS" means Flexible Manufacturing Systems, "CAD" means Computer Aided Design, "CAM" means Computer Aided Manufacturing, "CNC" means Computer Numerically Controlled machine tools. Each is explained later in this chapter.
8. See "Emerging Worldwide Trends: Industrial Adoption of Advanced Manufacturing Techniques," a set of papers prepared for a conference at the Center for Research on Industrial Strategy and Policy, Illinois Institute of Technology (October 15–17, 1985).
9. OPT are the initials for Optimized Production Technology and SLAM derives from Simulation Language for Alternative Modeling. See M. E. Goldratt and J. J. Cox, *The Goal: Excellence in Manufacturing*, Creative Output, The Netherlands, 1984; and A. A. B. Pritsker, *Introduction to Simulation* (New York: Halstead Press, 1979).
10. J. Baranson (ed.), *Soviet Automation: Perspectives and Prospects* (Mt. Airy, MD: Lomond, 1987).
11. E. Krukovskii, "We Discuss pre-congress documents," *Sovetskaia Latvia* (January 23, 1986), p. 2.
12. *Ekonomicheskaia gazeta*, no. 34 (August 1986), p. 6. The Russian word *dolgostroi* is a satirical paraphrase of a typical Soviet construction firm name, except that it means "protracted construction company."
13. *Ibid.* Minavtoprom is the acronym for Ministry of Automobile Industry, Minstankprom for Ministry of Machine Building.
14. V. A. Miasnikov, "EVM i mikroprotsessory," *ELORG informiruet*, no. 6 (1983), pp. 5–6.
15. V. I. Maksimenko, "Effektivnost' primeniia vychislitel'noi tekhniki v narodnom khoziaistve," *Vychislitel'naia tekhnika sotsialisticheskikh stran*, no. 16 (1984), pp. 86–94. Mingasprom means Ministry of Natural Gas Industry.
16. N. B. Mozhaeva, "Mekhanizatsiia i avtomatizatsiia vychislitel'nykh rabot," *Pribory i sistemy upravleniia*, no. 2 (1983), p. 41.

17. V. A. Maslov and Sh. S. Muladzhanov, *Roboto-tekhnika beret start* (1986), p. 56.

18. W. K. McHenry, "The Application of Computer Aided Design at Soviet Enterprises: An Overview," in Baranson, *Soviet Automation*, p. 58.

19. Miasnikov, "EVM."

20. Maslov and Muladzhanov, "Roboto."

21. *Pravda* (August 9, 1986), p. 2. Data on the distribution of these CAD systems by ministry are scarce, but Minpribor, a machine-building ministry, is scheduled to receive about 100 of the new systems, whereas the electrotechnical industry reportedly will obtain 15 of them. Maslov and Muladzhanov, "Roboto."

22. N. I. Ryzhkov, "Po gosudarstvennom plane ekonomicheskogo i sotsial'nogo razvitiia SSSR na 1986–1990 gody," *Pravda* (June 16, 1986).

23. *Ekonomicheskaia gazeta*, no. 5 (1987), p. 10.

24. The SM-3 and SM-4 were PDP-11 compatible systems.

25. The acronum ARM stands for *avtomatizirovannoe rabochoe mesto* or automated work station.

26. The SM-1420 is a 16-bit computer, software compatible with the ancient PDP-11; it is more than twice as fast as the SM-4 and offers up to two megabytes of main memory, eight times that of the SM-4. The SM-1420 is said to be in serial production at the Kiev Elektronmash plant. It was designed jointly by Elektronmash and the Institute of Electronic Control Machines. According to Shkirikova (1983) and TASS (July 7, 1984; 1245 CMT), the SM-1420 entered serial production in 1983. Another report, that of Rilskii (1985), indicates that it entered serial production in 1985. Either Rilskii is in error or the SM-1420 met with formidable production difficulties.

27. The Iskra-226 is an 8-bit system, based on a Soviet version of the Intel-8080 microprocessor.

28. Zavartseva and Ivanova (1986) state that the architecture and systems interface of SM-1700 is compatible with the SM-4.

29. M. S. Shkabardnia, "Razvitie otrasli i nauchnotekhnicheskii progress," *Pribory i sistemy upravleniia*, no. 2 (1986), pp. 1–4.

30. V. A. Trapeznikov, "Nekotorye voprosy metodologii SAPR," *Pribory i sistemy upravleniia*, no. 3 (1986), pp. 1–3.

31. V. A. Miasnikov, "ASU tekhnologicheskimi protsessami" *Ekonomicheskaia gazeta*, no. 4 (January 1986), p. 14.

32. I. P. Norenkov, "Printsipy prostroeniia i struktura," *SAPR: Sistemy avtomatizirovannogo proektirovaniia* no. 1 (1986), pp. 111–12.

33. A. A. Vasenkov and Ia. A. Fedotov (eds.), *Mikroelektronika i poluprovodnikovye pribory*, Nov. 9, 1984, Moscow, Radio i sviaz', 304 pp.

34. G. Lopato, "The Heart of the System is the Data Bank," *Promyshlennost' Belorussi*, no. 3 (1983), pp. 67–69.

35. Personal communication to the author.

36. R. L. West et al., "The computer-aided design and engineering facility, *Johns Hopkins APL Technical Digest*, July–September 1986, vol. 7, no. 3, pp. 244–249.

37. L. M. Salerno, "What happened to the computer revolution?" *Harvard Business Review*, November–December 1985, vol. 63, no. 6, pp. 129–138.

38. V. Ponomarev, "Computer-aided workplace of a designer today and tomorrow," *Narodnoe khoziaistvo Belorussi*, January 1986, pp. 14–15.

39. *Ekonomicheskaia gazeta*, no. 5 (1987), p. 11, and annual plan fulfillment reports for previous years.

40. Ryzhkov, "Po gosudarstvennom plane," p. 15.

41. *Statistical Abstract of the United States* (1987), p. 745.

42. Maslov and Muladzhanov, "Roboto," p. 8. Also see J. Grant, "Soviet Machine Tools: Lagging Technology and Rising Imports," in *Soviet Economy in a Time of Change*, 1, (Washington, D.C.: Joint Economic Committee of the U.S. Congress, GPO, 1979), pp. 566–72.

43. Maslov and Muladzhanov, "Roboto," pp. 11–20. In their statistics, the Soviets employ a very catholic definition of *robot*. The word is used to mean everything from very simple to very sophisticated devices. For this reason, international comparisons are hazardous.

44. *Pravda*, January 18, 1987.

45. E. K. Smirnitskii, *Dvenadtsataia piatiletka 1986–1990*, 1986, Moscow, pp. 66; A. M. Vpichinskii, N. I. Didenko, and V. P. Luzin, *Gibkie avtomatizirovannye proizvodstva*, 1987, Moscow, p. 10.

46. *Japan 1984, An International Comparison* (Tokyo: Japan Institute for Social and Economic Affairs, 1984), p. 29.

47. *Statistical Abstract of the United States* (1986), pp. 765–66.

48. Dolan, in Baranson, *Soviet Automation*, p. 43.

49. G. W. Simmons, M. H. Soule, H. L. Rees, H. Z. Shaffer, and W. J. Kelly, "The Eastern European Contribution to Soviet Industrial Automation: The Role of Machine Tools," a paper presented to the Midwest Slavic Conference (April 24, 1987) in Ann Arbor, MI.

50. Unfortunately, no indication is given in the Soviet source for these statistics of the proportion that each FMS type comprises of the total. That obviously becomes a serious impediment to meaningful interpretation of the numbers; the apples of "modules" are added to the oranges of "sections," the bananas of "lines," the peaches of "shops," and the watermelons of "factories." When attempting to make comparisons over time within the USSR or comparisons with other countries, it is hard to make sense of this fruit salad.

51. Maslov and Muladzhanov, "Roboto," p. 58.

52. *Ekonomicheskaia gazeta*, no. 5 (1987), p. 10. In *Izvestiia* (January 28, 1987), p. 2, Gorbachev stated that "integrated production modules" were up 120 percent, but failed to specify the base. "Integrated machine systems" were said to have increased by 40 percent, although the definition of this category is unclear.

53. E. K. Smirnitskii, *"Dvenadtsataia,"* p. 66.

54. L. Yelin, "Robots at Work," *New Times*, no. 32 (1986), pp. 25–26. When contemplating this figure, it is well to remember that the Soviets lump everything from relatively unsophisticated "modules" (GPM) to complete "factories" (GAZ) under the term "flexible production system" (GPS).

55. Without further investigation, it is difficult to say how comparable the Soviet and American definitions of FMS may be.

56. G. W. Simmons et al., "Eastern European Contribution."

57. Strong grounds exist for suspecting that the Soviet definition of the statistical category being reported has been changed.

58. Despite the significantly large numbers of FMS reportedly installed, only a handful are discussed in the open literature. Indeed, the same few examples are cited repeatedly. Several interpretations of this fact are possible and reality may be a blend of all three. Perhaps they do not have as many implementations as they report. Another possibility is that the literature is slow to report details and descriptions of the actual implementations. A third interpretation is that many of the implementations are only dubiously successful and not the kind that can be pointed to with pride. Finally, it seems very likely that many of these FMS installations, like others falling under the CAM rubric, are disproportionately in the Military Industrial Commission (VPK).

59. The Soviets use the term *uchastok* where Western usage would be "cell."

60. KAPRI stands for *Kompleksnaia Avtomatizatsiia Proektirovaniia, Razrabotki i Izgotovleniia* (complex automation of design, engineering, and manufacturing).

61. See, for example, *Izvestiia* (December 1, 1984), p. 1.

62. M. J. Berry and J. Cooper, "Machine Tools," in R. Amman, J. M. Cooper, and R. W. Davies, *The Technological Level of Soviet Industry* (New Haven: Yale University Press, 1977), p. 199.

63. Grant, "Soviet Machine Tools," pp. 571–71.

64. M. R. Hill and R. McKay, "Soviet Product Quality, State Standards, and Technical Progress," in R. Amann and J. Cooper, *Technical Progress and Soviet Economic Development,* (London: Basil Blackwell, 1986), p. 96.

65. P. Belianin, "Puti povysheniia effektivnosti mashinostroeniia," *Kommunist,* no. 13 (September 1986), pp. 20–31.

66. For an account of these struggles, see the letter from E. Mironenko in *Ekonomicheskaia gazeta,* no. 2 (January 1987), p. 10.

67. *Business Week* (August 17, 1981).

68. I. M. Makarov, *Sistemnye printsipy sozdaniia gibkikh avtomatizirovannykh proizvodstv,* vol. 1 in the nine-volume series of books by I. M. Makarov (ed.), *Robototekhnika i gibkie avtomatizirovannye proizvodstva,* Moscow, Vysshaia shkola, 1986, p. 45.

9

SOVIET SCIENTIFIC–TECHNICAL PERFORMANCE: A FRAMEWORK FOR THE USSR'S INFORMATION REVOLUTION

*John R. Thomas**

To assess the impact of an information revolution on the USSR and the chances for its achievement, we must consider the following: the larger systemic goals and societal forces that have and will drive the direction and efforts of the Soviet science and technology (S&T) community, which must carry out that revolution; the obstacles that stand in the way of success; and the currently proposed measures and remedies to mitigate or remove those obstacles. (In Chapter 2, Seymour Goodman examines the specific technical factors applicable in the USSR's efforts to transform itself into an "information society.")

The basic question is: Does the Soviet S&T community have the ability to meet national requirements? The answer? To date, the S&T community has been unable to meet effectively both civilian and military needs of the USSR. The reasons for this failure are found in the factors examined below.

---

*The views expressed in this chapter are those of the author and do not necessarily represent the official position of the U.S. government.

Factors Affecting Soviet S&T Performance

Systemic

The most basic factor affecting S&T performance is inherent in the Soviet system itself: the pervasive communist party control over all elite groups (military, governmental bureaucracy, industrial production managers, arts and literature community, and the S&T community). The party's perseverance and overall inflexibility in exercising such control is heavily reinforced by a selection process—through the *nomenklatura*—that assures continuity in office of an elite that is unyieldingly bent on preserving power even at the expense of modernizing the economy and the S&T components or increasing overall efficiency. This situation exists because the party itself was not modernized after Stalin's death. Khrushchev tried unsuccessfully to do so with his proposed reforms in the early 1960s; even though these were designed to affect only the middle and lower levels of the apparatus, not the very top (such as the Politburo), his proposals aroused such widespread opposition that they were largely responsible for his downfall in mid-October 1964.

Organizational

The S&T community also suffers from perennial organizational deficiencies that affect its ability to perform productively. Ironically, in a highly politicized and centralized system, the S&T community is severely affected by a key fact of not having a "command center" for coordinating efficient R&D or production. On the contrary, duplication and counterproductive rivalries exist among and are fostered by the major S&T agencies: the USSR Academy of Sciences and the 14 republic academies, about 50 production ministries, and the State Committee for Science and Technology (GKNT).

Thus the fragmented S&T community is currently plagued by three major problems. First, there are jurisdictional disputes between the Academy of Sciences and the GKNT that arose from the Academy's loss of its monopoly over (1) establishing and maintaining contacts with foreign science communities, and (2) providing the main guidance for the development of Soviet science. It lost this monopoly after the forerunner of the GKNT was formed in 1961 because of Khrushchev's dissatisfaction with Academy performance.

Second, there are problems between the Academy and some 50 production ministries over the issue of basic versus applied science. Traditionally, the Academy has wanted to engage in basic research; the ministries, however, want the Academy's help on the applied side because of their need to meet production goals. Since the mid-1970s, frictions have increased because the Academy no longer receives all of its funds from the state budget, as was the case earlier, but only about 85 percent of the funds it needs from this source. Therefore, Academy research institutes must make up the funding shortfalls by obtaining contract work from production ministries; this allows the latter to exert pressure on the Academy to work on applied research problems. In turn, this situation creates still another negative reaction: many Academy scientists on assignment (*kommandirovka*) to ministry enterprises are extremely unhappy because they have to be away from their prestigious institutes to work on what many consider less challenging and interesting "nuts-and-bolts" production tasks.

Finally, there are problems between the GKNT and the production ministries. The GKNT is charged with identifying foreign technology and having it introduced into the ministry production process. But the ministries resist this effort to impose new technology, because no allowance is made for the downtime involved in installing new equipment and retraining workers; such an allowance is important since the interruption of production involved in downtime can result in not meeting annual production goals, which, in turn, affects bonuses and promotion. Consequently, the ministries and plants resist innovation, even though over the long run it would lead to greater and more efficient output.

Cultural/Historical

Cultural and historical factors also play a role in the quality of S&T performance. The Academy, representing the leading edge of science, dates its founding back to 1724 under Peter the Great. It was originally based on West European models; the latter were highly academic with little relevance to applied science and virtually none to production. A heavy residue of the academic approach remains in the USSR Academy of Sciences, successor to the Russian Academy, despite the regime's efforts since the 1920s to bring the Academy's research institutes closer to application and production.[1] (Because of the Academy's major role in S&T, it is discussed in greater detail below.)

Then, too, even though statistically the population is heavily urban, in reality it still retains psychologically a highly rural mentality, particularly in regard to time and labor discipline. This can be seen most prominently among Soviet workers outside the main centers of Moscow and Leningrad; although called on to run modern machinery or work in advanced laboratories, many workers still have the outlook of the *derevnia* (a relaxed rural attitude) toward industrial production and discipline. This cultural/technological lag affects work in both manufacturing and science research.

Other Factors

Other factors also bear adversely on S&T performance, creating a need for Western technology. Thus the Soviets do not have the necessary *supporting infrastructure* for efficient S&T development; for example, they lack the many small supply companies that exist in the United States to provide instrumentation, Bunsen burners and test tubes, chemicals, and other common supplies required to conduct experiments and testing. Therefore, many Soviet scientific institutes must divert personnel and time to obtaining, or themselves making, such equipment and supplies. This inefficient situation is due mainly to the traditional priority placed on military and heavy industry production, at the expense of balanced economic development, including an appropriate supporting infrastructure to meet the needs of the civilian economy and S&T community.

Also, the S&T approach (in philosophy, organization, and policy) differs significantly from that of the United States. This affects S&T performance and has implications for the USSR entry into the information era. The following differences can be noted illustratively. Frequently, Soviet S&T policy tackles problems in a narrow context. This often involves, for example, establishment of separate institutes with massive funds and personnel focused narrowly on specialized S&T tasks, whereas U.S. R&D addresses questions over a broader scientific range. Then, too, Soviet S&T funding plans are laid out for a number of years; this can be a strength in terms of providing continuity in efforts to score breakthroughs but a weakness in terms of continuing to expend funding on work that may be irrelevant to current needs.

Similarly, the USSR educational system dictates where its S&T graduates will work on completion of their education. This is an advantage in terms of planning to meet the economy's needs, as *perceived* by Soviet leaders, but is a disadvantage in misdirecting manpower resources, arising from party command, instead of scientific-technical judgments at top levels. The political judgments may not be alert to or comprehend the significance of the latest S&T trends and, therefore, may lock highly trained manpower into work that is no longer on the leading edge of S&T developments. In effect, this misdirection of manpower wastes skills and dampens enthusiasm as well as initiative. This factor is particularly relevant and critical to the fast-moving information revolution, for example, to be locked in with a surplus of mechanical engineers when the need is for electronic specialists.

Next, the party control structure, imbedded in the S&T community (similar to the parallel party structure in the military, namely, the Main Political Administration), can be a strength in terms of imposing the party's will on the S&T community to meet the leadership's priorities. But the situation also constitutes a weakness when it results in political hacks substituting their ill-informed judgment for those who are more familiar with S&T trends and who could anticipate and meet official requirements more productively.

At the same time, the S&T community is politicized (and thereby rendered less effective), not only because of the party's pervasive controls, but also because it is subjected to an organizational straightjacket: it is totally a part of the state framework. (This contrasts with the American S&T community, which is divided among government, academia, and private industry.) As a result, the "all-state" context frequently does not allow for alternative or creative exploration of S&T problems. Yet, such exploration is likely to produce better results—as it has in the United States—than a monopolistic, state-directed S&T effort, afflicted by indifferent, insensitive, or illiterate judgments of the governmental bureaucracy, comparable to those of the party *apparat*.

Moreover, as part of party and state control over travel and contacts of citizens, the access of scientists and technologists to foreign S&T communities is highly controlled and limited. This prevents greater and freer interaction between foreign and Soviet S&T communities that could serve as a stimulus to better S&T results. (This contrasts with unrestricted access by U.S. scientists and technologists to their counterparts abroad.)

Then, too, the Soviet S&T community itself, like the system as a whole, is highly centralized within each of the major components that make up that community—the USSR Academy of Sciences, GKNT, and the production ministries. This creates the problem of "The Center" versus *mest-nykh* ("the locals"), that is, the strains between the scientific-technolog-ical hierarchy or research organizations in Moscow and the S&T communities elsewhere in the 15 Soviet republics. Regional communities consider the "Muscovites" to be overbearing in their direction and oversight of local S&T work. In the 1970s this was reflected during U.S.-Soviet S&T interaction: Moscow research institutes took over from local institutes outside the capital cooperative activities with American scien-tists even though the local institute had worked out the original arrange-ments. (Again, this overcentralized approach contrasts with the relatively decentralized process in the United States.)

Finally, a relevant problem affecting S&T performance stems from domination of the Soviet S&T community by Great Russians versus the many other nationalities that make up the USSR. This situation, again, parallels the same domination of the political system, and contrasts with the U.S. "melting pot" approach—especially in science—that reduces majority versus minority strains. The domination of Soviet S&T by ethnic Russians has reduced the ability of other talented scientists to work on the frontiers of science, to the detriment of the USSR.

The Academy's Role and Implications for the Information Era

In spite of systemic, organizational, and other problems noted above, the USSR Academy of Sciences is the most creative part of Soviet S&T and, more than other sectors, works on the leading edge of science, particu-larly on the information era technologies. For example, the Lebedev Physics Institute leads the research effort in fiber optics and has produced two Nobel Prize winners. Therefore, success in the information revolution will depend heavily on the Academy's scientific breakthroughs. For this reason, its role must be considered in more detail.

Compounding organizational fragmentation and lack of a unifying, co-ordinating mechanism noted earlier, in the 1960s the Academy lost its decisive role in science and accompanying influence. In this connection, we should note an overriding political fact: Soviet science, and the Acad-emy as its leading institution, has never had a member on the Politburo. (By contrast, the military, the KGB, and even the foreign ministry do have—even if on and off—representation on this top ruling body.) Whereas, currently, Academy Vice President Evgenii Velikhov is apparently Gorbachev's science adviser, he has no direct voice in top decision making. Then, too, the GKNT has moved from an initial role in the 1960s of overseeing technology to also currently monitoring and coordinating applied science. Since the line between basic and applied science is already fuzzy in many areas, the Academy is suffering erosion of its leading role not only to the GKNT, but also to several production ministries, even in the area of the Academy's supposed primacy—basic sciences.

The Academy's position in the recent past has been weakened further. It is one of the last, if not the only, major institution with some autonomy in the Soviet Union: its members are elected by secret ballot. During the 1970s, the Academy provoked the party, particularly the powerful old ideologue Mikhail Suslov, when it resisted election of party hacks (for example, S. P. Trapeznikov) as Academy members: these much sought after memberships are prestigious, even if not significant politically. The party's negative attitude was further heightened by growing dissidence in scientific ranks, symbolized by academician Andrei Sakharov and the Academy's refusal to expel him at the height of embarrassment for the Soviet regime in the 1970s and 1980s. This demonstration of independence only increased the pressure within the Soviet leadership to bring the Academy to heel. This was highlighted by Suslov's several unprecedented appearances at the Academy in the early 1980s to deliver in person the party's stern message on adhering to the line. (The erosion of academic freedom was best illustrated earlier by the regime's abrupt postponement of the Academy's 250th anniversary celebration from 1974 to 1975; this caused much embarrassment to the Soviet science community, since it had issued invitations to foreign guests and arranged elaborate commemorative ceremonies and events.) Then, too, party membership has become a sine qua non for election to the Academy and promotion in the S&T hierarchy. Such party membership subjects an Academy member not only to normal administrative control but also to party discipline.

Equally important, the Soviet leadership's growing stress on applied science in order to improve and increase production has further decreased the Academy's influence. In the face of current and projected poor economic performance, manpower shortages, systemic problems (for example, party control at the expense of efficiency) and other difficulties, the Academy stands to lose even more of its influence, particularly if it continues to advocate work on basic research as its prime interest.[2]

But any decrease in the Academy's role and capabilities has a direct bearing on long-term development and productivity of science. Diminishing that institution's capabilities would negatively affect scientific achievements since the Academy represents the most vital and creative part of the S&T community. Then, too, since it has been oriented heavily toward fundamental research, reducing its role in this area would affect the quality of basic research with ensuing implications for future S&T development, including the information revolution. In the recent past, the Academy's first rate basic science work impressed the West. Thus in the 1970s, the United States entered into cooperation with the USSR because it benefited from the Academy's advanced fundamental research in areas such as theoretical physics and mathematics. Consequently, any marked shift by the Academy to applied research where achievements on the whole have been meager could make the United States and others in the West, now leading in information technology, less interested in joint activities. This could significantly delay the USSR's entry into the information era, because it has benefited more than the West from the bilateral S&T exchanges.

Militarization of the Academy

The Academy's lead within the S&T community at home and ability to interact with foreign scientists on equal terms may be increasingly affected (to the detriment of prestige) by its "militarization"—direct or indirect involvement of Academy personnel in military-related work, from basic research to the development of applied military technologies. Indeed, the militarization of the Academy will increase even more in coming years, given the Soviet regime's growing requirements for advanced military systems and weaponry, particularly if the American SDI program proceeds at an accelerating pace and on a large scale.

Such a diversion of the Academy from basic research would not be new. After 1917 it underwent a process of "politicization, industrialization, and militarization" intended to increase its contribution to industrial and military modernization. In this context, the Academy's personnel have been responsible for many of the USSR's most important military breakthroughs, including atomic and hydrogen bombs as well as intercontinental ballistic missiles. All were developed much earlier than the United States had expected, and most American experts were unaware until the mid-1960s that the Academy was so heavily involved in these and other military projects.

Evidence for this militarization is abundant. For example, all Academy presidents since World War II have been specialists in defense-related sciences and involved in military work. Academy personnel also are often members of various weapons advisory councils. Indeed, some conduct both defense and nondefense work, as did Andrei Sakharov (commonly credited with developing the Soviet hydrogen bomb), and some Academy members hold high military rank. In addition, defense ministry representatives (*voenpredy*) are involved in the Academy's work in an oversight capacity, just as they are at defense production facilities. Likewise, some Academy scientists are assigned to those facilities outside of their own institutes. Finally, the USSR Academy of Sciences maintains a section devoted to "applied problems" that serves as the interface between the Academy's work in basic research and the development of military technologies. Military related work has become so extensive that Academy leaders openly proclaim their contribution to the "Motherland's defense capabilities."

Moreover, the Academy's autonomy has been affected by "purse string" changes. Until the mid-1970s, the institution received its entire funding from the state, which has consistently devoted over 3 percent of the gross national product (GNP) to research and development. (By contrast, the United States erratically devotes less than 2 percent of the GNP to research and development.) Today, however, more than 15 percent of the Academy's budget comes from various industry contracts, including those with military production facilities and the defense ministry. This margin provides critically effective leverage on the Academy, which has been under increasing political pressure to focus more on concrete problems and less on basic research. Consequently, the militarization of the Academy is accelerating because of its growing dependence on industry funding.

But not only are the Academy's major departments involved in military work; many of the republic academies are increasingly being drawn into military research and development. This suggests that the USSR Academy's 250 institutes and 160,000 scientists cannot handle all the work required by Soviet leaders. Nevertheless, as the country continues its efforts to develop sophisticated military technologies such as those for space weapons, advanced conventional and information-related command and control systems, Academy scientists—some of the best minds in the USSR—will have to become increasingly involved in military projects out of necessity, if not because of patriotic duty.[3]

Proposed Solutions to win the Information Revolution

In order to alleviate the problems noted above and lay the conditions for carrying out the information revolution, the Gorbachev leadership is undertaking numerous reforms. The most important are examined below. Whether these go far enough and are implemented will determine the success of the information revolution in the USSR.

"Reform" of Party Control

On the central issue of party control, Gorbachev has as yet proposed no basic reform. Indeed, in describing himself as a true Leninist (who views the party as the vanguard of the proletariat), he has focused not on easing the party's hold, but only improving its performance. Thus, as a key aspect of perestroika, he says that "it is important now through the work of local Party organs" to regain touch with the Soviet work force.[4] This sounds like familiar declarations from the past. Nowhere has Gorbachev suggested that the party's role should be reduced, much less restructured to remove it from clogging the Soviet economy. He has not, for example, proposed (as has Deng Hsiao-ping in China) the formal separation of party from government responsibilities, to curtail party cadres' interference in scientific research and production management.[5] On the contrary, Gorbachev has stated the need for enhanced party role in perestroika, and according to him, the party's potential influence and impact have not yet been fully reached.[6]

Given the foregoing, it can be said that Gorbachev has not even reached the reform level of Khrushchev, when the latter tried to break the power of local bosses by reorganizing the party along industry and agricultural, instead of geographical, lines; the latter allowed *mestnichestvo* (localism), including intrusion by the all-pervasive local party apparatus, to prevent efficient performance by local plants and research institutes.

It is true that Gorbachev has caused a turnover of over 40 percent among local party secretaries. Instead of fundamental political reform, however, this change can be viewed simply as the replacement of Brezhnevites with Gorbachev loyalists, with little effect on that traditional structure of party dominance over industry and the S&T community; but this relationship has been and is greatly responsible for lagging economic performance.

Yet *Pravda* reasserted, in good Leninist fashion, that politics must stay in command of economics; it did so even as it argued the need for new information technology and declared that the introduction of such technology into Soviet society would mark a new stage of the scientific-technical revolution. To underscore the proper priorities, the newspaper approvingly cited Lenin: "Politics must take precedence over economics. To think differently is to forget the basics of Marxism."[7]

The foregoing priority dominates the strategy of the current Soviet leadership, including Gorbachev: to retain centralized *political* control, even as it tries to decentralize *administratively,* by devolving control, now exercised by ministries in Moscow, to local enterprises and scientific institutes. This order of priorities and approach raises the most fundamental question of whether the Soviet system can, without being modernized and reformed at the highest policy command levels, provide the proper political setting for S&T achievements that match the vast material and human investment already made by the Soviet regime. Only basic political reform would provide the tolerance of alternative views and approaches, required by scientists to explore various hypotheses that could lead to research breakthroughs. This is even more critical in the accelerating information revolution.

Autarchy versus Interdependence

The future direction and capability of Soviet S&T will also be affected by how the difference of views between the recent president of the Academy of Sciences, A. P. Aleksandrov, and his successor, G. I. Marchuk, are finally resolved. Aleksandrov advocates S&T self-sufficiency and self-reliance so that, for example, the USSR should produce its own quality equipment and instrumentation instead of importing them from the West. By contrast, Marchuk—as a former participant in joint exchanges with the United States in the 1970s—advocates cooperation with the United States to enable the Soviet Union to obtain access to the latest and more advanced S&T. Such access, in Marchuk's view, would prevent the USSR from lagging too far behind the West; by contrast, Aleksandrov's self-reliance attitude, without Western input and cooperation, could leave the Soviet Union even further behind than it is at present in the absence of fundamental systemic/political reform.

With regard to the Academy itself, replacement of Aleksandrov as president in 1986 suggests that Marchuk's policy of interdependence had won

Gorbachev's approval. Therefore, the Academy will presumably be allowed more freely to interact with American S&T communities, to forestall the lag that developed under Stalin and probably would occur under the autarchical policy advocated by Aleksandrov.

Transfer of Experience from Military Production to Civilian Industry

Another solution to lagging civilian S&T currently being applied is the transfer of Soviet managers with heavy industry and military production experience to civilian tasks. This is exemplified by the appointment of Boris Tolstykh in early 1987 as chairman of the State Committee for Science and Technology, replacing Marchuk. The former came to GKNT with management experience in the Sverdlovsk heavy industry-military complex.

Because of his production successes there, Soviet leaders apparently assume that managers like Tolstykh can improve civilian output. In this context, Soviet consumers are not being given (at least on paper) the equivalent of rights enjoyed by the military, through the *voenpredy* (military representatives), namely, the power to reject poor quality production. Thus the *Gospriemka* (state agency to oversee quality output and deliveries) is now being introduced to civilian enterprises with the power to reject poor output. But this organizational innovation is now causing new problems; since consumer production plants, unlike the military, do not get high priority and guaranteed timely deliveries of raw materials and other resources needed for high quality output, they may still fail to produce such output despite Gospriemka. Therefore, this "transfer-of-experience" reform will work only if the former military production managers in new civilian posts receive the high political priority, streamlined organizational decision making, and vast and timely resource allocations that they enjoyed in their heavy industry and military production posts. But we can be sure that any significant reallocation of priority and resources from military to consumer goods production will be opposed in both civilian and military ranks of the Soviet government. Some evidence suggests this is already occurring: Gorbachev has fired some military leaders who have resisted or been unenthusiastic about perestroika. Whether he can make these changes stick and dampen even greater opposition in the future will depend on whether he can engage the full support of the larger Soviet elite.

Organizational Changes

It is ironic that, in a system touted for its rationality and planning, the establishing of GKNT and the subsequent reorganization of the USSR Academy of Sciences, including the transfer of some Academy research institutes to the jurisdiction of production ministries, have led to greater inefficiency and organizational problems instead of the intended streamlining and responsiveness to economic needs. In particular, this applies to the gap between research and application. In an effort to increase productivity in general, and information technology breakthroughs in particular, the Soviets are once again embarked on extensive organizational changes, some predating Gorbachev, but most since his accession to power.

Thus a new organizational form, combining Academy research institutes and industry plants (interbranch S&T complexes, or MNTKs), was introduced several years ago to solve the largest traditional problem— translating laboratory results into production. This problem has often seen brilliant Soviet pioneering research not carried through to application. For example, it was the Soviets who originally made a nuclear fusion breakthrough (via *Tokamak*), only to see the U.S. application superiority produce the first effective output by the Tokamak process. Since the MNTKs replaced an earlier organizational form, science-production combination (NPOs), it remains to be seen whether the MNTKs will prove any more successful than the NPOs.

The Soviet regime is specifically engaged in organizational innovation in the information technology area. Thus a new Department for Informatics, Computers and Automation was recently established in the Academy of Sciences. Its importance was underscored by the appointment of academician Velikhov as head. Because of his authority within the science hierarchy as the Academy's vice president for S&T and his connections as Gorbachev's science adviser, information technology development will presumably receive the kind of priority that other S&T areas have not had. (For example, promising solar energy research, with its advantages over nuclear and other more hazardous forms, has withered on the vine because the relevant scientists cannot obtain the necessary funding and resource support.)

In any case, the "new" proposals and organizational forms under Gorbachev do not as yet address the overarching and pervasive bureaucratic problems among the Academy, GKNT, and the ministries. For example, Velikhov has not expressed the will or even the need to solve these problems, whether from political caution or from vested institutional interest in not wanting to see the Academy lose its traditional autonomy by being subordinated to others, for example, the GKNT. The danger of the Academy losing its autonomy could arise from being pressured even more to work on applied problems (as was noted earlier) and from GKNT's overall coordination role (nominal to date) being strengthened with the appointment of Tolstykh, an ex-manager of a heavy industry complex.[8]

Educational Effort in Information Technology

As discussed in Chapter 2 by Seymour Goodman, the Soviet regime has initiated a massive effort, headed by Velikhov, to train the population, starting in elementary schools, to operate in the new microelectronic and computer world. Even though this program started only recently, it is already threatened by failure because of the inability to produce *quality* computers and chips and in the *quantity* needed to propel the Soviet people into the information era. (An indication of how far the USSR lags behind the United States in information technology can be seen from children practicing on cardboard simulations of a computer keyboard instead of obtaining hands-on training on actual PCs.)

Civilian-Military Convergence and Foreign Technology Acquisition

Because of a convergence of views on information-technology needs, most civilian and military leaders agree on the need for Soviet acquisition of information technologies abroad until the day when their own S&T can produce these at home in required quality and quantity. Consequently, the USSR has launched a massive West-to-East technology transfer effort, both legal and illegal, overt and covert. Because this acquisition effort to date has been driven by military priorities, it will distort and frustrate a needed balance between civilian and military needs. The militarization of the Academy will drastically reinforce this counterproductive result.

Conclusions and Implications

The S&T community has been unable effectively to meet both civilian and military needs of the USSR. Because of this failure, the Gorbachev leadership has proposed numerous reforms. These solutions are likely to fail, however, in the absence of basic structural reforms—particularly in the *political* realm related to the party's overbearing role—and lacking a Soviet retrenchment in its activist foreign policy and accompanying heavy military requirements. As a substitute for genuine retrenchment, the USSR is and will engage in traditional *peredyshka*—a breathing period—during which it will exercise tactical restraint vis-a-vis the West; but over the long term, an activist policy, backed by a continuing military buildup far exceeding defense needs, will continue to prevent a much needed balanced approach to meeting civilian and defense requirements. In turn, this failure of the USSR will continue its need for foreign technology. Such a dependence will particularly apply to information technologies in which the Soviets already seriously lag behind the United States, Western Europe, and Japan. This disparity could become even larger without basic structural and economic reforms.

The information revolution (if defined as increased accumulation, storage, and dissemination of information and data affecting all aspects of society) can have profound implications for the Soviet system. The latter is based on highly centralized control with overarching societal, domestic, and foreign policy goals, shaped by history and ideology and defined and interpreted by a small group of decision makers (the Politburo). Therefore, the single most important development affecting the impact of the information revolution on the USSR relates to politics.

To date, Gorbachev has not proposed any fundamental structural political reform. Instead, he is pushing party "democratization." As effected up to now, this consists of elections to party posts at *lower* levels: members ostensibly have a genuine choice to vote for local party secretaries from among several candidates preselected from the *nomenklatura*. But since the latter is a tightly controlled list, its abolition would be a key to any genuine democratization of the party.

Another major characteristic of the Soviet system has been the tremendous upward flow of information to the party and its controlling center—the Politburo—with drastically less flow downward and with little revelation to the outside world of how the Politburo uses the incoming information in its decision making, much less of how it arrives at its decisions. As a pointed illustration, one need only note the following: even today—some 70 years after the Bolshevik Revolution and in the midst of an information explosion—we not only do not know how the Politburo reaches its decisions, but we have had no access to transcripts or minutes of its meetings since it began operating. We can only assume or guess how it conducts business from our own administrative procedures. Therefore, it is difficult in this ignorance to assess in specific terms the impact of the information revolution on the Soviet Union. But we can conclude in broader terms that, in the absence of basic political reform, any efficient acquisition and storage of information and data could help the party at all levels to maintain, if not strengthen, its grip over the system and economy. And we can further conclude—reasonably—that any failure to genuinely democratize the party and devolve some of its power to nonparty agencies, down to local S&T institutes and industrial enterprises, will frustrate the unleashing of inherent Soviet talent needed to make the information revolution breakthroughs.

And we can be more certain that the continuity of the "permanently operating factors" (to borrow Stalinist terminology) related to the USSR's geopolitical situation, strategic problems, and goals, and the influence of bureaucratic and organizational institutions and experience noted earlier, will affect and frustrate the innovations needed to realize the information revolution. Indeed the Soviets have already said that politics (domestic and foreign) must dominate the economic changes wrought by that revolution. For just as the USSR's defense needs governed and shaped the first, internal revolution, namely, the industrialization of the USSR carried out under Stalin, so will the current activist foreign policy, the resultant strategic-military problems and opportunities, and the primacy of party rule dominate the coming, second—the information—revolution.

To effect this revolution, in the face of the foregoing political priorities and strategic goals, Gorbachev faces several dilemmas. The first is to make his current reforms work, he really has to take on the bureaucracies (civilian and military), viz., to push the *civilian* (governmental) bureaucracies to give up centralized control over local scientific institutes and enterprises, and to push the *military* to adjust to smaller allocation of resources in the short run, so that a growing economy over a longer term can provide both "butter and guns."

But the harder Gorbachev pushes both bureaucracies, the more they will oppose him. They could even cause his downfall, as they did Khrushchev's in 1964 because of the latter's many reorganizations, including breaking up the party *apparat* into industrial and agriculture sections from the previous unitary regional (*oblast*) groupings. But the failure to solve the first dilemma will impact on Gorbachev's second dilemma.

To make his reforms work, Gorbachev needs the full support and unleashing of the talented S&T community, but he will not get such support until he proves to that community (which has been "bitten" before by the failure of Khrushchev's and Kosygin's reforms) that he can make his reforms work. This includes removing the heavy hand of the bureaucracies, as represented in his first dilemma.

Whether Gorbachev can solve the two dilemmas will determine whether his plans to modernize the USSR and propel it into the information era will succeed. Indeed, they could determine whether he will be around five years hence and not suffer the same drastic political fate as "the reformers" before him, for example, Khrushchev, or remain in power and still see his reforms fail because of party and bureaucratic inaction or sabotage, as occurred with Kosygin's reforms of the late 1960s.

Outcome of the Information Revolution

The following conclusions seem warranted about the outcome of the information revolution in the USSR:

1. Unless the activist *foreign policy* is modified, the S&T community will be under heavy pressure to meet both military and civilian requirements that may prove beyond its capabilities.
2. Unless the *systemic* problems are ameliorated (e.g., party rule loosened), and unless S&T policy and organizational shortcomings are corrected, Soviet S&T will not produce efficiently despite any continuing heavy investment in S&T by the regime.
3. Unless Gorbachev solves the *two dilemmas* (reduces the heavy hand of bureaucracies—military and civilian—and enlists the full support and creative talent of the S&T community), the USSR will not make significant progress in advanced areas such as information technologies.
4. Unless the above problems are solved in total, the USSR will continue to be *dependent on Western S&T,* including information technologies such as microelectronics and computers, with the relevant implications for the vitality of Soviet foreign policy, internal modernization, and political control.

Relevant Implications

From Soviet history, recent behavior, and current policies and actions, we can also infer the following implications relevant to the information revolution in the USSR:

1. Externally, current and projectable foreign policy goals and strategic requirements suggest that the information revolution will be used heavily, if not primarily, for strategic and military purposes.
2. Internally, the leadership will use information technologies primarily to maintain party control and state security over society and the system; this means that technologies contributing to those goals will be favored and developed, for example, supercomputers to be used for military operations (such as nuclear-missile simulations), science research, and industrial manufacturing, instead of developing individual PCs and software relevant to consumer needs. If so, this will not significantly improve the people's standard of living, as promised by Gorbachev.
3. Because current and future foreign policy and strategic priorities are likely to be directed toward undermining U.S./Western interests, the United States will have to consider how far it should respond to open Soviet commercial overtures for advanced dual-use technologies and how to combat covert or illegal USSR activities to acquire such technologies.
4. In response to the above-noted Soviet acquisition effort, the West will have to determine whether Gorbachev's current "democratization," perestroika, and *glasnost'* efforts are intended merely to modernize the USSR economy and make it more efficient, or whether such self-proclaimed reforms could lead to basic political restructuring (such as giving the people a real voice and laying the basis for a pluralistic society); in turn, whether these "reforms" will lead to a genuine "live-and-let-live" foreign policy, or whether these current measures (democratization, perestroika, glasnost'), combined with detentelike moves abroad, are merely in line with the traditional strategy of "peaceful coexistence" and peredyshka (the latter is designed as a tactical breathing space to allow the Soviets time to remedy domestic problems and revive their economic strength before resuming a more rigorous foreign policy that advances USSR interests around the globe at America's expense).
5. The development, introduction, and expanded use of costly information technologies will strain an already overburdened economy; this will, in turn, exacerbate Soviet *politico-military* relations over the allocation of scarce resources between meeting civilian and military requirements. To reduce the ability of the military to resist his reforms, Gorbachev could try to carry out radical defense reforms comparable to Khrushchev's in 1960, when over 250,000 officers

were retired, some literally put out to pasture on collective and state farms.

6. The information revolution will also create strains *within the Soviet military;* even though in the long run, the development, production, and deployment of advanced information technologies would strengthen the USSR's overall military capabilities, in the short run, a focus on such technologies, diverting scarce resources from other S&T areas, would be at the expense of conventional capabilities. This would make unhappy the many officers who still serve in the predominantly conventionally equipped army. (There already have been reported tensions within the armed forces, e.g., between strategic nuclear missile troops—chief users of advanced information technologies—and the ground forces.)

7. Finally, any failure of the S&T community—for the systemic, policy, and organizational reasons noted earlier—to close the information technologies gap with the West will affect the Soviet ability to carry on an expensive, activist foreign policy and meet related strategic-military requirements. In turn, this could adversely affect the USSR's superpower position and ability to influence global events, as it has since World War II when it acquired nuclear missile capabilities that revolutionized strategy and foreign policy in the last several decades. These capabilities, however, may become less relevant in the coming information era. The many social, ecological, and economic problems can be solved not by weaponry, but by the development of sophisticated information and communication technologies that may be beyond Soviet grasp because of overambitious foreign policy goals and distorted economic priorities imposed by an inflexible political system.

Notes

1. A significant exception to this situation is the Academy's heavy and increasing involvement in military research and development.

2. It remains to be seen whether Gorbachev will have a different attitude from his predecessors. It should be noted that the academician closest to him is Evgenii Velikhov, who is known for weapons research work and who may or may not stand up for retaining the Academy's autonomy and basic research. Gorbachev in any case has already said he expects the application of S&T to production to be the primary goal. This means that the Academy will have to adjust to Gor-

bachev's (and the party's) views of priority for applied science, and not vice versa.

3. For a detailed discussion of the Academy's increasing involvement in military research and development, see John R. Thomas, "Militarization of the Soviet Academy of Sciences," *Survey* (London), 1985.

4. Gorbachev asserted this view, for example, on his visit to the Baltic republics in February 1987. See *Tverdo idti dorogoi perestroiki i vglubleniia demokratii* (Moscow: Politizdat, 1987), p. 11.

5. For a description of Deng's political reforms, see *Christian Science Monitor*, September 3, 1987.

6. See Gorbachev's speech on November 2, 1987 on occasion of the 70th anniversary of the Bolshevik Revolution.

7. *Pravda* (January 23, 1987), pp. 2–3.

8. As far back as 1981 (see his *Literaturnaia gazeta* interview in September), Velikhov openly expressed opposition to overall coordination of the Academy, GKNT, and production ministries, needed to translate research results into production. On the one hand, he noted that the Academy did not have the personnel and other resources to provide such coordination and, on the other hand, there was no need for such coordination since the present system was working fine. Implicitly, he appeared to say that any other alternative would be worse. The appointment of Tolstykh as the new GKNT chairman, with his industrial production management experience, undoubtedly will reinforce GKNT's effort to reassert its dominant coordination role, which was lost somewhat by his predecessor, Marchuk, and for which the latter was criticized before his transfer to head the Academy. Whether a weakened Marchuk can restore the Academy's earlier autonomous role is open to question.

10

COMPUTER–ASSISTED THIRD INDUSTRIAL REVOLUTION IN THE USSR: POLICY IMPLICATIONS FOR THE SOVIET UNION AND THE UNITED STATES

John P. Hardt and Jean F. Boone

Having undergone the first Industrial Revolution in the late nineteenth century and the Second Industrial Revolution (intensification of production) since World War II, the Western advanced economies have now embarked on the Third Industrial Revolution, involving the utilization of computer and information technologies. Participation in this computer-assisted Third Industrial Revolution is important to the future economic superpower position of the USSR. Success in attaining the computer-assisted technological underpinning of a modern industrial society will determine whether the Soviet Union is to become a

- Technologically advanced economic power, able to use economic resources for national security and international power purposes.
- Modern, competitive economy better able to serve the needs of Soviet citizens.
- Participant that is influential in the world market in concert with the First World (the developed market economies).
- Model that is attractive for socialist economic development in the Second World (the centrally planned economies).
- A model for emulation by developing countries in the Third World.

Achieving a transformation (*perestroika*) of the Soviet economy and becoming competitive in the Third Industrial Revolution, at least by the end of the Fifteen-Year Plan (1986–2000), requires that the Soviet Union change its institutions and its cadre, and accept the "New Economic Thinking" on a broad basis—in fact, transform the psychology of the people, and engage as well in a Second Industrial Revolution—the shift from extensive to intensive growth.

Whereas some aspects of Gorbachev's economic strategies have been clearly stated and their implementation, especially since the June 1987 plenum, is underway, the strategy for undertaking the Third Industrial Revolution remains unclear and its implementation has not commenced. Also uncertain is how the attempt to engage in the Third Industrial Revolution will be related to USSR foreign economic policy. Therefore, in considering the options before the Soviet leadership and the implications for the United States, we must rely on identifying stated intentions, qualified judgments, and perceptions.

In general, Gorbachev's strategies for perestroika, as applied to technological change, remain Leninist in approach. The primary policy options for integrating computer technology through the Third Industrial Revolution are twofold: (1) continued centralization of both strategic planning and management—emulating the military approach, or (2) greater centralization of policy and guidance, with more decentralization of research management and application, drawing on the principle of the "commanding heights" from Lenin's New Economic Policy. The latter follows the structural change of perestroika in production; the former extends the relatively successful military R&D system to the economy as a whole. Can either of these systemic frameworks create the innovative, dynamic environment needed for rapid innovation and application, or are they contradictory to the requirements of an "information revolution"? The Western experience, based on an open system of scientific communications and a "marketplace of ideas," may not be effectively applied or tested in either the centrally planned military type strategy or the controlled Gorbachevian/Leninist strategy of change.

Besides these policy choices for stimulating domestic scientific and technological development, Gorbachev's policy regarding the Council for Mutual Economic Assistance (CMEA) and foreign technology transfer will play a critical role in determining Soviet success in the information and computer technologies revolution. In this area, three alternatives can be considered: a CMEA autarky approach, a Western strategy for CMEA based on bilateral interaction by each member country, or a Soviet-led, coordinated strategy for CMEA interdependence with the West. The Fifteen-Year Plan for CMEA stresses the self-sufficiency of technology within the Eastern economic bloc alliance as one option. This has the advantage of control and affordability, although it may not be sufficient for raising the technological level of the CMEA economies. The Western option—a second variant—is necessary to advance more rapidly in technology, and is probably favored by many in the East European countries, but may be less certain, controllable, and affordable, particularly given limitations on hard currency earnings. Western export controls, especially those of the United States, add uncertainty and constraints. The third approach might be seen as containing elements of the other two—incorporating greater interdependence with the West but through a coordinated effort in which the Soviet Union would dominate.

The choice among these options may be influenced by the fact that the United States and the Soviet Union each began to face in 1986–87 a rising need for global interdependence and trade-deficit management. Past policies of adopting unilateral superpower controls on East-West commerce have lost their effectiveness and may even be impairing each superpower's ability to be competitive in the world market. The United States, moving toward more limited export control lists in line with the Western alliance (the Coordinating Committee for Multilateral Export Controls—CoCom), has freed new grades of personal computers from controls and is keying multilateral controls to the general availability of computers in the world market. The Soviet Union has begun to implement reforms of its foreign trade mechanism that allow for more extensive and direct links with Western businesses.

In the process of superpower summitry, trade-related agreements may facilitate bilateral commerce through mechanisms such as joint ventures, renewed bilateral science and technology exchange, and the further reduction of controls placed on widely available computer equipment.

The Third Industrial Revolution in the Soviet Union

Gorbachev's *Perestroika*

General Secretary Mikhail Gorbachev, since coming to power in 1985, has clearly given first priority to the revival of Soviet economic performance and broad improvement in the quality of life. His long-term goals, as expressed in the Fifteen-Year Plan, provide the framework for projected growth in the quality and quantity of economic performance. This optimistic projection calls for a doubling of output by the year 2000, with a growth rate of 4 percent per annum in GNP—ambitious targets that may serve the political purpose of creating pressure and momentum for comprehensive change as much as representing real goals for economic achievement. Success may not be attainable in terms of the optimistic goal of 4 percent growth, twice the rate achieved under Gorbachev's predecessors. A lower growth with sharply improved efficiency and quality of output may represent even more success. A baseline projection of 2 to 3 percent, accepted by many Western specialists,[1] may be attainable and adequate politically to assure Gorbachev's maintenace of power. Even so, his course is dangerous as significant changes in the economic structure might lead not to rapid improvement but rather to slow growth and failure.

Despite the risks, Gorbachev has stressed the imperative of change— the restructuring, reforming, and reviving of the Soviet system—and to achieve it has adopted four general strategies:

1. Renewal of centralized planning and decentralization of management: reform of institutions and mobilization of cadres.
2. Intensification: achievement of a Soviet "economic miracle" through the Second Industrial Revolution.
3. Implementation of a technological-information revolution: the Third Industrial Revolution.
4. Creation of a more open and interdependent foreign economy.[2]

Each of these strategies is based on a fundamental shift in the allocation of responsibility for economic performance. As described by Gorbachev at the June 1987 Central Committee plenum and spelled out in the law on state enterprise, the system of planning will shift toward strategic centralization, whereas the system of management will be decentralized under a market-simulating economic mechanism in which the enterprise is expected to perform as a self-financing, self-managing unit.[3]

Although these strategies may be far-reaching, changes within the Leninist framework are not intended to bring about a free market economy or a Western-style democracy. Decentralization is to be accompanied by greater democratization and openness, in order to assure more responsibility and accountability of officials, but these changes are to occur in the context of democratic centralism. This approach does not suggest acceptance of Western political institutions, based on consent of the governed.

As Gorbachev embarks on the implementation of these new economic strategies, the key to his success is improvement in capital efficiency and in labor productivity (through his "human factor" policy). Prime Minister Nikolai Ryzhkov, speaking at the 27th Communist Party Congress, observed that the achievement of Soviet growth goals under the 12th Five-Year Plan (1986–90) would require the addition of 22 million individuals to the labor force if productivity remained at its then current level. With an expected increment to the labor force of only 3.2 million persons over the plan period, productivity must rise significantly if Soviet economic objectives are to be met. According to Ryzhkov, industrial labor productivity must increase from 3.1 percent annual growth during 1981–85 to 8.8 percent growth by the year 2000; two-thirds of this increase is to be generated by the introduction of new machinery and technology and the remaining one-third depends upon the "human factor."[4] A marked improvement in the capital stock of the Soviet economy turns on the successful simultaneous pursuit of the Second and Third Industrial revolutions, facilitated by improved interconnections with the technologically advanced Western industrial economies.

Central to this process of improved efficiency and productivity is the application of computer and information technologies. Stalin liked to refer to machinery as the heart (*serdtse*) of the first, his own industrial revolution; Gorbachev might refer to the computer as the heart of the Third Industrial Revolution. Its application will be integral to the effectiveness of perestroika as a whole and to the success of each of his strategies.

Integration of Computer Technology in Gorbachev's Plans

Computer applications, microelectronics, and the use of lasers and robotics are all part of the dramatic changes occurring in the economies of the Western industrial countries. Gorbachev has stressed again and again that the Soviet Union must not fall further behind in this new frontier of science, technology, and economic development. The technological message inherent in the Strategic Defense Initiative may be one motivating force behind the new determination to improve Soviet technological capability. Civilian technological dynamism drives the American SDI research programs and, regardless of whether the military defense vision of President Reagan is credible or attainable, the research and development effort behind SDI will result in technological components and spinoffs of broader applicability.

The technologies under development to support the United States SDI are creating a pool of innovative concepts that will have potential applicability to the U.S. defense industry in strong interaction with the civilian sector. For example, battle management/command, control, and communications requires the development of computer hardware and software on an unprecedented scale. Kinetic energy weapons systems require research on microelectronic controls, advanced infrared and radar sensors, compact chemical propulsion devices, and electromagnetic launchers, which could lead to advanced antitactical weapons and propulsion systems. Thus, the American SDI, by relying on and stimulating technological advancement with applications both in defense and throughout the economy, symbolizes a further potentially serious erosion of USSR claims to being an economic superpower. Because of its deteriorating economic base, the Soviet Union may become a more technologically inferior power, unable to make the leap necessary to compete economically, and thus militarily. As some observers conclude, "The [USSR military] analysts of future survivability of new arms technologies are seriously concerned about the adequacy of inputs from civilian R&D and the general receptiveness of production for innovations throughout Soviet industry in the long run."[5]

Considering not only the specter of SDI, but also the rapid development of computer technologies and applications in Japan and the newly industrialized countries (NICs) of Asia, it is not surprising that at the 27th Party Congress in 1986 the Soviet leadership already stressed the importance of computer and information technologies in future economic development. The automation and mechanization of industry was strongly emphasized in the discussion of the economy—the number of industrial robots is planned to treble during the 12th Five-Year Plan (1986–90), the use of "progressive technologies" is to increase by 50 to 100 percent, and "mass assimilation" of computer technology is to take place.[6]

In assessing these plans, however, many Western specialists emphasize the enormity of the task. As compared with the production and application of computer technologies in the West, Soviet efforts are seriously lagging. Despite, for example, 20 years of introducing automated management systems into enterprises, only 8.4 percent of the approximately 44,000 industrial enterprises in the USSR now have such systems.[7] The computer literacy program launched by the Soviet leadership also incorporates long lead times, taking into account the low levels of computer hardware production and lack of experience in development of software; in 1984 the Soviet press noted that the USSR computer industry meets only 5 percent of small computer needs.[8]

Whereas Gorbachev's plans grant high priority to computerization through, for example, the creation of a new State Committee for Computing and Informatics, specific programs for furthering the development and absorption of new technologies still seem to be lacking. Furthermore, certain conflicts may arise in the implementation of actual programs for economic restructuring related to computerization. Looking at the industrial application of computer and information technologies, Richard Judy notes that there may be a conflict between the goals of the Second Industrial Revolution—modernization—and those of the Third Industrial Revolution—application of information technologies:

> A serious contradiction exists between Gorbachev's push, on the one hand, to implement computer-based manufacturing technology and, on the other, his insistence that the thrust of investment should be in existing plants rather than new ones. However great may be their eventual payoffs, the implementation of flexible manufacturing systems (FMS) and computer integrated manufacturing (CIM) in the Soviet Union or anywhere else is extremely disruptive in the short run. We speak here of dismantling production lines, gutting shops or factories, lengthy retraining of many workers, and the redundancy of many former employees. These are wrenching changes in an established organization . . . The success of Gorbachev's drive to "intensify" Soviet industry by adding large catalytic doses of informatics thus hinges critically on his ability to implement fundamental reforms in Soviet industrial management.[9]

Gorbachev must also address the dilemma of how to allocate scarce R&D resources between the development of current applications of information technologies and the development of technologies at the cutting edge. As equipment slowly becomes available, through domestic production or imports, allocation decisions must be made particularly between application in the civilian versus the military sector.

The technological-information revolution is intended, through the development and utilization of new computer-based technologies, to lead to a quantum change in the effectiveness of the capital plant and infrastructure of the Soviet economy. If successful, when will its results begin to have an impact on the economy? Even if the effort is successful over time, will supply systems and institutions be burdened in the short run by costly change for potential benefits in the longer term?

Effectively initiating the Third Industrial Revolution may be possible during the 12th Five-Year Plan, but results will not likely be forthcoming until the 1990s. Even laying an effective groundwork for this revolutionary change will require not only an upgrading of resource priorities for civilian research—the cutting edge of effective change—but a merging, opening, and radical reform of the scientific and technological process. Scientific communications and effective transfer of basic to applied research require such a degree of openness and response to a marketlike incentive system that little short of drastic change in the traditional Soviet system of research and development may be adequate to lay an effective foundation for the Third Industrial Revolution.

Strategic Options for Achieving the Third Industrial Revolution

To accomplish the ambitious requirements for a Third Industrial Revolution in the Soviet economy, Gorbachev may face several fundamental policy choices in both the internal sphere and in external economic relations. Given the low level of production and application of computer and information technologies, the USSR leadership must not only spur domestic research, development, and utilization, but combine these improvements with a trade policy that will fill the gaps of domestic production. How will this be achieved? Several basic approaches to the problem may be considered.

Domestic Policy Options

Option 1: Maintain the centralized command economy for planning and maintain centralized management. Gorbachev may look to the military sector as a model for how new technology can be effectively integrated within a centralized framework. There are many indications that the Soviet leadership is looking to the defense industries for a model of planning and management that would effectively improve the scientific and technological base of civilian industry. Specific measures that reflect this approach, according to Paul Cocks, include:

1. Improving the effectiveness of bureaucratic levers—the party's sponsorship and oversight of new technology development, and strong centralized management—that have been generally weak in the civilian sphere but are crucial to military technology and defense modernization.
2. Strengthening the role of long-range scientific forecasting and technology assessment in economic planning—important management tools used in defense for decades.
3. Creating big, goal-oriented projects to accelerate the development of key technologies (laser, computers, robotics, biotechnology) modeled along the lines of the USSR's nuclear and missile programs.
4. Tasking the defense industries to help develop and apply new technology for critical civil sectors.
5. Organizing new superagencies at the Council of Ministers, led by deputy premiers and patterned on the Military-Industrial Commission, to oversee and coordinate the work of related ministries.
6. Introducing military-style quality control inspections at the most important nondefense industrial enterprises.
7. Moving top defense executives with experience in managing high technology into critical civilian jobs.[10]

Although the defense sector management techniques may be effective for mobilizing civilian industry in general, can a system characterized by control, secrecy, and centralization coexist with the necessary communications and innovation of the Third Revolution? An intellectually open, interconnected scientific research community is critical for indigenous development of the high technology tools of the Third Revolution; an unfettered, interconnected user community is critical for applying these tools, requiring computer education and information networks for industry, transportation, health care services, and other sectors.

A kind of futures contract may be required between the party, the military, and the police for this new technological revolution: in the current context, such an agreement might involve an opening of military R&D to a broader, more dynamic civilian-military research environment. The future mutual benefit of this restructuring would be a sharing of research and development between the civilian base of the technological information revolution and the SDI-type military requirements. A more open system in the sensitive areas of advanced research and technology would breach the security and secrecy shield traditional for these areas of national security. Furthermore, it could have other social implications—it is knowledge of outdated technologies and research processes that is purported to be the rationale for denial of exit visas to dissident scientist Andrei Sakharov and many hundreds of "refuseniks." The constraints on innovation posed by the continuation of this centralized approach accompanied by secrecy and control of information may make it necessary for Gorbachev to consider a riskier course, if he is to be successful.

Option 2: Adopt a more open system of scientific research and development, a "marketplace for ideas," within a centralized system of policymaking. In science and technology, as in production, the "commanding heights" approach of highly centralized science policy control and decentralized research and development may be an effective formula for change, but that remains to be demonstrated. Although Gorbachev may recognize the need for an open, dynamic, and innovative scientific and technological community—one that can see its fruits translated into operational systems—no concrete changes have been proposed that would encourage the development of a genuine scientific "marketplace of ideas."

This approach to reform of science and technology would take the Western system of management as its model and follow principles similar to those laid out in the Corson Report of the National Academy of Sciences.[11] The findings stressed that in the tradeoff between open scientific communication that generates innovation and new applications, and a policy of restricting the flow of ideas of strategic value, the tilt should be toward openness. Security, from this point of view, can be maintained through accomplishment, and "tall fences" should be built around only limited areas of greatest security sensitivity.

The arguments of the Corson Report, though they are directed to maintaining external, not internal, security, might to some degree be applied against the traditional, centralized Soviet system of overclassification and compartmentalization. USSR research institutes have difficulty developing scientific communications both at home and abroad. There is an absence of "invisible colleges" or peer group communication networks that in Western experience help to promote scientific and technological innovation. Whereas the policy of *glasnost'* (public disclosure) may help open the scientific journals and other channels of communication, the institutional and legal barriers remain formidable.[12]

Without such an opening to interaction, both within the Soviet Union among scientists and users and as part of the international scientific community, active participation in technological development will likely be sharply constrained. The recent scientific activity surrounding superconductivity demonstrates why. The superconductivity race has been advanced without even waiting for the formal publication of experiment results in scientific journals, but through direct communication among scientists on computer networks and in personal contacts, and through immediate reports of developments in national newspapers. Thus effective computer applications and a more open and flexible environment for scientists will be a necessary part of the "entrance fee" the USSR will have to pay to enter future scientific competitions.

Furthermore, entry into the technological competition with timely application of scientific developments to the production process will require reform at the enterprise level. To bridge the gap between scientific development and technical application, a competitive environment will be needed requiring, perhaps, the introduction of self-financing and self-management. The creation of joint ventures with foreign enterprises active in the world market might offer a more promising mechanism for technological change than the introduction of domestic incentives.

Foreign Economic Policy Options

In the absence of domestic technological development sufficient to bring about a Third Industrial Revolution, Gorbachev must look for external strategies as well. The Soviet leadership has placed great emphasis on the role of the CMEA and division of labor, as reflected in the Complex Program of Scientific-Technological Development of the CMEA Member Countries to the Year 2000. Views still differ, however, within CMEA and even within the USSR over how CMEA technological development might be most effectively achieved and what role trade with the West should play. As Soviet control over the countries of Eastern Europe has weakened over the past two decades, developing and maintaining a cooperative alliance policy on economic development have grown more difficult but more important. The major alternatives are: (1) reliance on CMEA integration and specialization, (2) increasing commercial interaction of CMEA countries with the West, pursued on a bilateral basis, and (3) increasing interdependence between the East and West, with the USSR taking the lead role.

The Socialist Alternative

From the point of view of those advocating a socialist alternative,[13] the tasks of the Fifteen-Year Plan for development of electronics, complex automation, atomic energy, new materials, and biotechnology may be attained within CMEA without exposure to the uncertainty of Western technology transfers. This approach would avoid the putative costs of possible embargoes, creation of a debt burden, and the negative implications of foreign dependency through reliance on indigenous science and technology—a form of scientific and technological autarky within CMEA.

Whereas the socialist alternative might have political benefits for the Soviet Union in terms of control, it raises a number of questions in terms of economic effectiveness. Would this strategy be sufficient to raise the USSR's technological level to the world standard? Does CMEA have the resources necessary to achieve a leap to the Third Industrial Revolution, without inputs from the West, producing both the quantity and *quality* of output that is needed? Furthermore, a strategy that creates new forms of dependency between the East European countries and the USSR may not be altogether positive for the latter's interests. The Soviets may be obligated to continue to purchase "second-best" goods, thereby "subsidizing" CMEA manufacturing and perpetuating low quality production.[14] As the Japanese "just-in-time" system of production management suggests, quality production cannot be achieved unless quality performance by all suppliers can be assured.

The Bilateral Western Alternative for CMEA

Others contend that if CMEA is to attain a world level of technology, productivity, and competitiveness—achievements deemed essential by the Soviet leadership—it will require increased and direct East European contacts with Western partners and increased Western technology transfers on a bilateral basis.[15] East European export strategies are keyed to a technological specialization program. For them to be effective, each country would need to link its export strategy to domestic restructuring and reform programs. A reduced defense burden among CMEA-Warsaw Pact members, including the Soviet Union, would represent another central ingredient in such a solution. Articulated particularly by Hungarian economists, this approach of bilateral interaction with the West may be the preferred policy of the East European countries.

Soviet-Dominant Western Alternative

Under this approach, the Soviet Union would take the lead in raising the technological level of the CMEA economies through more extensive economic interaction with the West, principally USSR-dominated joint ventures with Western firms. The role of East European producers in such a strategy would be to supply parts for Soviet-built products, such as trucks or cars, with access to the world market provided by the Western partner. In addition, Soviet import needs, such as materials, food, and less than world-level manufactures, might be met with CMEA goods in order to reduce any unnecessary hard currency drain. The efforts of the CMEA to initiate trade relations with the European Community (EC) also fit into this type of strategy of coordinated relations with the West.

Pursuit of this path, or the previous one—the bilateral Western alternative—would depend to some extent on a Soviet accommodation with the United States, possibly through the summit process, on the question of technology transfer and export controls. If the United States moves toward acceptance of multilateral controls as defined by CoCom, access to Western technology might be expanded. This might lead particularly to increases in Soviet manufactured goods trade with Japan and the Federal Republic of Germany.

In a broader context, how the United States decides to pursue its commercial relations with the East—whether to facilitate or restrict trade, whether to pursue trade on an economic basis or use it as a political lever—will affect Soviet choices. Furthermore, the interest of the USSR in using Western interaction not simply to substitute for domestic production but to assist in the development of an indigenous capability may raise other questions for U.S. policy. Some might suggest caution on this kind of technology transfer, pointing to the costs incurred by the United States in loss of domination over high technology development when it pursued close commercial and technological interaction with Japan.

Technology Transfer from the Western Perspective: U.S. Options

Gorbachev's interest in rapid modernization of the USSR economy and increased participation in the information technology age has led to heightened interest in expansion of commercial links with the West as at least part of his strategy for achieving these objectives. From the Western perspective, the Soviet movement toward greater interdependence with the world economy may be seen as coinciding with a general trend toward "globalization" of technological development. In light of these parallel developments, what are U.S. interests and options in technology transfer policy? On one of the central elements of the American approach to technology transfer to the East, export control policy, an active debate had been generated in the United States in the mid-1980s.

Dispersion of Technology and Economic Power throughout the World Economy

The current debate on export control reform is being shaped, to a large degree, by recognition of significant changes in the world economy that have reduced U.S. technological dominance and, with the growing trade deficit, appear to challenge American economic security. The 1987 study by the National Academy of Sciences on national security export controls made the following finding:

> Advanced technology has diffused widely throughout the industrialized countries and is becoming increasingly available in some of the more developed newly industrializing countries (NICs). As a result, U.S. control policies can no longer be based on the assumption that the United States holds a monopoly on nearly all dual use technologies essential to the most advanced weapons systems. The United States now must have the cooperation of other technologically advanced countries to succeed in blocking Soviet acquisition efforts.[16]

As noted by the Academy study, the emergence of new trends in technological development—products created through "global production" as well as the wide manufacture and use of "technological commodities"— has also contributed to a changed environment for consideration of U.S. policy toward export control and technology transfer. The rapid, international character of new scientific, technological developments can be seen in the current race to perfect superconducting materials. As soon as the first discovery was made of materials that are superconducting at temperatures much higher than previously known, scientists all over the world immediately joined the effort to be first in both scientific development and technological application. Each advanced country is faced with the dilemma of how best to support the required research and technology developments to ensure that this promise has the best chance of being fulfilled and to ensure that it does not lose any competitive advantage to a country whose industry responds more rapidly.[17]

For the United States, the dispersion of high technology development throughout the world has brought a loss of its leading role in advanced technology trade and increasing concern about maintaining U.S. international competitiveness. The unprecedented growth of the trade deficit—from $40 billion in 1981 to $170 billion in 1986—in combination with the transition from creditor to debtor nation, brought to the forefront the need for a review of trade policy, including the question of export control policy.

U.S. Control Policy

The dispersion of technological innovation implies that the United States can no longer effectively control technology transfer to the USSR on a unilateral basis and, by trying to cast an overly broad unilateral control net, may be losing markets in the Western countries. Thus, a basis of agreement must be found with the other members of the Coordinating Committee for Multilateral Export Control (CoCom) to establish multilateral consensus on what should be controlled and on how controls should be enforced.

The need for a newly defined consensus on appropriate measures to promote both military and economic national security was stressed by many as the debate over export control policy resumed in the 100th Congress. Given the interdependence of these twin objectives, the discussion has reflected increasing interest in focusing export controls more narrowly and achieving a stronger Western consensus on the scope of controls. Former Undersecretary of Commerce Lionel Olmer, clearly expressed these concerns:

> America's huge trade and current account deficits, and especially the precipitous decline of our surplus in high-tech trade, may not have a silver lining, but these facts have clearly reawakened the Administration and Congress to a basic reality—that the need to maintain U.S. technological preeminence is no less a fundamental national interest than is the effort to delay Soviet acquisition of Western defense-related technology. Revising the export control system to eliminate unnecessary and unworkable controls can contribute to both goals and should be the focal point of efforts to reform the export control system. I would argue that the first imperative is that the list of national security-controlled items be dramatically reduced

for the plain and simple reason that national security controls are not working: the U.S. monopoly on technological innovation has ended, and unless
irrelevant controls are eliminated—quickly—a further erosion in U.S. high-
tech capabilities is foreshadowed.[18]

These views correspond with those presented in the National Academy
study, which concluded that the export control regime, as currently administered, has imposed an economic cost of $9 billion and 188,000 jobs
a year as a result of the "de-Americanization" of products, lost markets,
and competitive disadvantages.[19] The Reagan Administration also has given
increased attention to this problem, as reflected in the presidential Competitiveness Initiative, announced in January 1987. Containing a section
on export control as an element of competitiveness, the president's initiative seeks to "level the competitive playing field while strengthening
multinational controls over products and technologies that can contribute
to Soviet military capabilities," and "decontrolling those technologies that
offer no serious threat to U.S. security."[20] Paul Freedenberg, Assistant
Secretary of Commerce for Trade Administration, articulated the administration's position in testimony before the House Foreign Affairs Committee, stating clearly the need for reform:

> We must stop subjecting to over-control and undue controls the very same
> private sector companies upon which we rely to keep us technologically
> superior to our adversaries. We must limit the role of government to doing
> only that which is truly necessary to protect national security . . . To re-
> main competitive without diminishing our security safeguards, we must
> decontrol non-strategic, non-critical goods and technology, retain flexibil-
> ity to deal with changing world situations, incorporate new generations of
> technology and applications without impeding legitimate trade, maintain a
> workable, multilateral effort, and reduce excess burdens on U.S. busi-
> ness.[21]

The U.S. interest in improving the effectiveness of control and in maintaining global competitiveness suggests a reconsideration of policy relat-
ing to technology transfer. In response to the growing debate, the om-
nibus trade legislation of the 100th Congress contains some provisions
designed to reduce unilateral and obsolete controls and to improve the
administration of the licensing process. To a large degree, success in making
the control system more effective will depend upon narrowing the list of
controlled technologies. This is necessary both because the current list is
too extensive to be efficiently and thoroughly administered, and because

effective control requires the agreement and cooperation of the CoCom allies, which can be more certainly secured through a focusing of controls on a narrow scope of militarily critical technologies. In a first step in this direction, the United States in August 1987 dropped its long-maintained objection in CoCom to the decontrol of certain personal computers for the Soviet Union.[22]

Prospects for Western Control Policy

In this increasingly complex commercial environment, unilateral policy has proven ineffective for controlling multilateral commerce and stemming espionage losses. Furthermore, the United States and the Soviet Union now face a rising need for global interdependence and trade deficit management that has been impaired by unilateral trade controls imposed from each side. Throughout both alliance systems, superpower economic policy in 1986–87 was judged ineffective and inappropriate.

Given these developments, a new, more stable basis for West-West and East-West commerce may be attainable. The central ingredients for a common Western alliance policy would include the following:

1. Agreed multilateral controls in CoCom, OECD, and among Asian NICs in place of unilateral controls by the United States.
2. Focus on security controls related to specific weapons systems and critical components with greater intelligence exchange among Western industrial economies.
3. Increased discipline and indigenous penalty procedures in each Western industrial country related to unintended supply of militarily relevant technology. The Toshiba-Kongsberg case is accelerating this consideration.[23]
4. Multilateral Western policy to discourage effective use of Eastern espionage by whatever means may be required.
5. More selective and effective use of controls, such as embargoes and sanctions, for foreign policy purposes.

Development and implementation of a CoCom consensus policy along these lines will be an essential precondition to significant changes in East-West commercial relations. Given the fact that joint ventures between Soviet and Western firms, if they materialize, will likely be highly computer-assisted, agreed multilateral and manageable export control policy will be necessary to establish reasonable parameters for interaction and exchange. Such an approach would build on the lessons of Toshiba and ensure more effective control of these technologies with direct military significance.

With a CoCom consensus established, the United States approach to new forms of economic relations with the Soviet Union, including joint ventures, would be influenced by trade legislation and summitry. The USSR emphasis on the Third Industrial Revolution and the U.S. interest in both effective and technological competitiveness suggest that there may be negotiable issues for both countries.

Conclusion

The Soviet Union and the United States, spurred by the implications of the Third Industrial Revolution, may find themselves increasingly drawn into greater interdependence within the world economy. The Soviet need of expanded interaction with the West, both for the stimulation of scientific innovation and the effective transfer of advanced technology required by industrial modernization, has led to some new initiatives in foreign economic policy that may be expanded upon over time, and may be best fulfilled through direct relations with the United States. The U.S. interest in reducing the barriers to greater West-West trade and American global competitiveness is leading to reforms in the export control system that could affect a consensual policy in West-East trade as well. With these changes in approach by each country and in the context of a summit process, the United States may find it has both better leverage and greater incentive to gain Soviet agreement on the parameters of East-West exchange. The United States may lead a focused, multilateral Western control policy as no other Western country could. Only such a policy could promise effective control of militarily relevant exports and assume a stable commercial environment for long-term economic exchange in manufacturing sectors.

U.S.-USSR agreement on several primary issues would be necessary elements in any broader negotiated agreement.

1. The negotiation of comprehensive joint ventures and long-term agreements that assure conditions of mutual benefit in commerce and broad exchanges.
2. Limitations on the use of Soviet espionage to obtain technology out-

side the core military programs. Such agreement would be consistent with a U.S./CoCom effort to focus and concentrate resources on controlling transfers directly related to core military programs of the USSR, and with the latter's interest in improving the effectiveness of technology transfer for industrial modernization.

3. Joint participation in global and multilateral institutions to enhance global economic health and improve bilateral economic interests.

As global balance of payments and competitiveness issues and alliance cohesion have become increasingly important, the cost of continued use by the United States and Soviet Union of economic interchange as a primarily bilateral political instrument has steadily risen. Whereas political pressures may persist in both countries to continue to link economic interchange to Great Power political cycles, the broader trends of globalism and interdependence in the world economy may make the economic price of the old politico-security superpower policy ever higher.

Notes

1. Gorbachev's Modernization Program: A Status Report. Joint Testimony of the Central Intelligence Agency and Defense Intelligence Agency before the Joint Economic Committee of the U.S. Congress (Washington, DC: March 19, 1987), pp. 26–27.

2. For more detailed discussion of Gorbachev's economic reform strategies, see John P. Hardt and Jean F. Boone, "Gorbachev's Economic Prescriptions," in Arthur Gunlicks (ed.), *Gorbachev's First Year* (New York: Praeger, 1987).

3. See the report "On the Party's Tasks in Fundamentally Restructuring Management of the Economy," speech by General Secretary Mikhail Gorbachev at the plenary meeting of the CPSU Central Committee, *Pravda* (June 26, 1987), pp. 1–5; and "Law on State Enterprise," *Izvestiia* (July 1, 1987), pp. 1–4.

4. Nikolai Ryzhkov, "On the Basic Guidelines for the Economic and Social Development of the U.S.S.R. for 1986–1990 and the Period Through the Year 2000," report to the 27th CPSU Congress, *Pravda* (March 4, 1986), pp. 2–5.

5. Heinrich Vogal and Hans-Henning Schroder, "Security Aspects of Science and Technology in the U.S.S.R.," Murray Feshbach (ed.), *National Security Issues of the U.S.S.R.* (Boston: Martinus Nijhoff, 1987), p. 112.

6. Ryzhkov, "Basic Guidelines."

7. William K. McHenry, "The Integration of Management Information Systems in Soviet Enterprises," *Gorbachev's Economic Plans*. U.S. Congress, Joint Economic Committee, 100th Congress, 1st session (Washington, DC: U.S. GPO,

1987). Hereafter, noted as *Gorbachev's Economic Plans.*

8. Peter B. Nyren, "The Computer Literacy Program: Problems and Prospects," *Gorbachev's Economic Plans.*

9. Richard W. Judy, "The Soviet Information Revolution: Some Prospects and Comparisons," *Gorbachev's Economic Plans.*

10. Paul Cocks, "Soviet Science and Technology Strategy: Borrowing From the Defense Sector," *Gorbachev's Economic Plans.*

11. National Academy of Sciences, *Scientific Communication and National Security* (Washington, DC: National Academy Press, 1982.)

12. Seymour Goodman, in Chapter 2, describes a model of a Soviet-style information society that differs from the Western approach in its goals, driving forces, systemic conditions, and progress in development and application of information technologies. He suggests that the USSR to date is pursuing the information revolution within a much more narrowly defined and institutionally constrained manner than has occurred in the West, and with more modest goals. The question remains whether this kind of development will be sufficient to allow the Soviet Union to compete as an international economic and military power.

13. See Iu. Shiriaiev, in Oleg Bogomolov (ed.), *The World Socialist Economy* (Moscow: USSR Academy of Sciences, 1986).

14. Kazimierz Poznanski, "Opportunity Cost in the Soviet Trade with East Europe: Discussion of Methodology and New Evidence," *Soviet Studies* (forthcoming).

15. See paper presented to the Workshop on East-West European Economic Interaction by Bela Cikos-Nagy, at the Vienna Institute for Comparative Economic Studies in December 1985.

16. National Academy of Sciences, *Balancing the National Interest* (Washington, DC: National Academy Press, 1987), p. 155.

17. See Leonard G. Kruger and Richard B. Rowberg, "Superconductivity," *Congressional Research Service Review,* 8, no. 7. (July 1987), pp. 24–26.

18. Lionel H. Olmer, "Export Control Policy: The Need for Fundamental Reform," in John P. Hardt and Jean F. Boone (eds.), *Proceedings of the CRS Symposium on U.S. Export Control Policy and Competitiveness* (Washington, DC: CRS Report 87-388S, April 30, 1987).

19. *Balancing the National Interest,* p. 264.

20. "President's Competitiveness Initiative," *White House Press Release* (January 27, 1987), p. 8.

21. Paul Freedenberg, Assistant Secretary of Commerce for Trade Administration, *Testimony* before the House Foreign Affairs Committee, Subcommittee on International Economic Policy and Trade (March 11, 1987), pp. 1–2.

22. Paul Betts and Louise Kehoe, "Curbs Eased on Sale of Personal Computers to the Eastern Bloc," *The Financial Times* (August 12, 1987), p. 1.

23. In reaction to the illegal sale of equipment to the Soviet Union, purportedly permitting Soviet submarines to operate silently enough to avoid detection, both the House and Senate have passed legislation that would impose bans on imports to the United States of Toshiba and Kongsberg products. Penalties have been imposed on the companies by the Japanese and Norwegian governments as well in an attempt to demonstrate their desire to prevent future diversions.

Bibliography

Alekseev, A. S., ed. *Perspektivy razvitiia avtomatizirovannykh sistem upravleniia, proektirovaniia i informatsii.* Novosibirsk: Nauka, 1986.

Amann, Ronald, and Julian Cooper. *Technical Progress and Soviet Economic Development.* New York: Basil Blackwell, 1986.

Azbel, V. O., et al. *Gibkye avtomatizirovannye sistemy.* Leningrad: Izdatel'stvo mashinostroenie, 1985, 2nd ed.

Baranson, Jack, ed. *Soviet Automation: Perspectives and Prospects.* Mt. Airy, Md.: Lomond Publications, Inc., 1987.

Bogomolov, Oleg, ed. *The World Socialist Economy.* Moscow: USSR Academy of Sciences, 1986.

Campbell, R. W., et al. *Soviet Science and Technology (S&T) Education.* McLean, VA.: Science Applications International Corporation, October 15, 1985, FASAC-TAR-3050.

Cherkasov, Iu. M., et al. *Avtomatizatsiia proektirovaniia ASU s ispol'zovaniem paketov prikladnykh programm.* Moscow: Energoatomizdat, 1987.

Critchlow, Arthur J. *Introduction to Robotics.* New York: Macmillan, 1985.

Dobson, Richard B. "Communications and Control in the USSR," *Research Memorandum.* Washington, D.C.: USIA Office of Research, November 24, 1986.

Eremin, S. N., and E. V. Semenov. *Nauka i obrazovanie v strukture NTR.* Novosibirsk: Nauka, 1986.

Ershov, A. P., and V. M. Monakhov, eds. *Osnovy informatiki i vychislitel'noi tekhniki.* Moscow: Prosveshchenie, 1985 and 1986, 2 vols.

Feshbach, Murray, ed. *National Security Issues of the U.S.S.R.* Boston, Mass.: Martinus Nijhoff, 1987.

Forester, Tom, ed. *The Information Technology Revolution.* Cambridge, Mass.: MIT Press, 1985.

Gamdlishvili, V. N. *Vychislitel'nye seti.* Tbilisi: Sabchota Sakartvelo, 1987.

Goldman, Marshall I. *Gorbachev's Challenge: Economic Reform in the Age of High Technology.* New York: W.W. Norton, 1987. 2nd ed.

Gorbachev, M. S. *Perestroika i novoe myshleniie.* Moscow: Politizdat, 1987.

Govorun, N. N., ed. *Problemy povysheniia effektivnosti ispol'zovaniia EVM bolshoi proizvoditel'nosti.* Moscow: VTs AN SSSR, 1987.

Gunlicks, Arthur, and John D. Treadway, eds. *The Soviet Union Under Gorbachev.* New York: Praeger, 1987.

195

Hardt, John P., and Jean F. Boone, eds. *Proceedings of the CRS Symposium on U.S. Export Control Policy and Competitiveness*. Washington, D.C., April 30, 1987. CRS Report 87-388S.

Hoffman, Erik P., and Robbin F. Laird. *Technocratic Socialism: The Soviet Union in the Advanced Industrial Era*. Durham, N.C.: Duke University Press, 1985.

Kanaev, E. M., et al. *Promyshlennye raboty dlia obsluzhivaniia oborudovaniia razlichnogo tekhnologicheskogo naznacheniia*. Moscow: Vysshaia shkola, 1987.

Kassel, Simon. *A New Force in the Soviet Computer Industry*. Santa Monica, CA: RAND, 1987.

Makarov, I. M., ed. *Robototekhnika i gibkie avtomatizirovannye proizvodstva*. Moscow: Vysshaia shkola, 1986, 9 vols.

Maslov, V. A., and Sh. S. Muladzhanov. *Roboto-tekhnika beret start*. Moscow: Politizdat, 1986.

Molodchik, A. V., and V. N. Kobelev. *EVM na stole: Personal'nyi kompiuter*. Perm': Knizhnoe izdatel'stvo, 1987.

Naumov, B. N., ed. *EVM massovogo primeneniia*. Moscow: Nauka, 1987.

Naylor, Thomas H. *The Gorbachev Strategy: Opening the Closed Society*. Lexington, Mass.: Lexington Books, 1988.

Nazarov, A. P., comp. *Komp'iuternyi vseobuch i povyshenie kvalifikatsii spetsialistov*. Moscow: Znanie, 1987.

Otani, Tadao. *Komp'iutery*. Baku: Azerneshr, 1987.

Pavlishchev, K. S., ed. *Narodnoe obrazovanie v SSSR: Sbornik normativnykh aktov*. Moscow: Iuridicheskaia literatura, 1987.

Perry, Charles M., and Robert L. Pfaltzgraf, Jr., eds. *Selling the Rope to Hang Capitalism? The Debate on West-East Trade and Technology Transfer*. Elmsford, New York: Pergamon Brassey's International Defense Publishers, 1987.

Przhiialkovskii, V. V., ed. *EVT: Elektronnaia vychislitel'naia tekhnika*. Moscow: Radio i sviaz', 1987.

Riccobono, John. *Instructional Technology in Higher Education*. Washington, D.C.: Corporation for Public Broadcasting, 1986.

Rodionov, V. V., ed. *Tekhnicheskie i programmnye sredstva vysokoproizvoditel'nykh kompleksov SM EVM*. Moscow: INZUM, 1987.

Sinclair, Craig, ed. *Status of Soviet Civil Science*. Dordrecht, Netherlands: Martinus Nijhoff, 1987.

Sitniakovskii, I. V., et al. *Tsifrovye sistemy peredachi abonentskikh linii*. Moscow: Radio i sviaz', 1987.

Smirnitskii, E. K. *Dvenadtsataia piatiletka, 1986–1990*. Moscow: Politizdat, 1986.

Traub, J. F., ed. *Cohabiting with Computers*. Los Altos, Calif.: William Kaufmann, 1985.

Tverdov, B. I., et al. *Telegrafnaia i faksimil'naia apparatura: spravochnik*. Moscow: Radio i sviaz', 1986.

Ulanov, G. M., et al. *Metody razrabotki integrirovannykh ASU promyshlennymi predpriiatiiami*. Moscow: Energoatomizdat, 1983.

U.S.S.R. [Union of Soviet Socialist Republics]. *Narodnoe khoziaistvo SSSR v 1987 g.* Moscow: Finansy i statistika, 1988.

———. *Narodnoe khoziaistvo SSSR za 70 let.* Moscow: Finansy i statistika, 1987.

[United States]. Central Intelligence Agency. *Enterprise-Level Computing in the Soviet Economy.* Washington, D.C.: Directorate of Intelligence, August 1987. SOV C 87-10043.

———. *Soviet Acquisition of Military Significant Western Technology: An Update.* Washington, D.C., Directorate of Intelligence, September 1985.

———. *The Soviet Weapons Industry: An Overview.* Washington, D.C., Directorate of Intelligence, September 1986. DI 86-10016.

———. *The USSR Confronts the Information Revolution.* Washington, D.C.: Directorate of Intelligence, May 1987. SOV 87-10029.

———. Congress, Joint Economic Committee. *East European Economies: Slow Growth in the 1980's.* Washington, D.C.: U.S. Government Printing Office, 1986. 2 vols.

———. *Gorbachev's Economic Plans.* Washington, D.C.: U.S. Government Printing Office, 1987. 2 vols.

———. Department of Defense. *Assessing the Effect of Technology Transfer on U.S./Western Security.* Washington, D.C.: Office of the Undersecretary of Defense for Policy, February 1985.

———. National Academy of Sciences. *Balancing the National Interest.* Washington, D.C.: National Academy Press, 1987.

Vasenkov, A. A., and Ia. A. Fedotov, eds. *Mikroelektronika i poluprovodnikovye pribory.* Moscow: Radio i sviaz', 1984.

Vpichinskii, A. M., et al. *Gibkie avtomatizirovannye proizvodstva.* Leningrad: Izdatel'stvo mashinostroenie, 1987.

Index

Academy for the National Economy
executive training program in, 121
Academy of Pedagogical Sciences, 23
Academy of Sciences, 23, 46, 69, 94
collaboration with West by, 161–62
funding of, 163
heritage of, 157–58
and GKNT, 156–57
and production ministries, 157
role of, 160–61
Academy of Sciences, politization of
erosion of independence, 160–61
long-range effects, 161–62
militarization, 162–63
Academy of Sciences, research
applied vs. basic, 157–58
leadership in, 160, 162
pressures on, 162
shift in emphasis of, 161
Afghanistan, 123, 125
Aganbegian, Abel G., 120
computer-based experiments of, 119
reform strategies of, 121
Agat PC, 2, 27, 30, 69
and Apple II, 20
characteristics of, 20
and education, 20, 21
Ailamazian, A. K., 29
Akademset' (at the Academy of Sciences), 104, 105
Aleksandrov, A. P., 165, 166
Algorithmic approach, 31
All-Union Correspondence Machine-
Building Institute, micro-com-
puter training at, 50
All-Union Institute of Scientific and
Technical Information (VINITI),
104
All-Union Scientific Research Institute
for Applied Automated Systems.
See VNIIPAS
All-Union State Committee on Com-

puter Technology and Informatics, establishment of, 47, 181
All-Union State Network of Com-
puters. *See* GSVTs
All-Union System for the Collection and
Processing of Information for Ac-
counting, Planning and Manage-
ment of the National Economy.
See OGAS
All-Union System of Data Transmission (OGSPD), 88
Andropov, Iuri V., 123, 125
economic experiments of, 117, 119,
120
Angola, 123
Apple Computer Corporation, 62, 73
Macintosh shipment, 27, 63
and pirating, 71
risks in design, 66, 67
Apple II, 24, 30
cloning of, 69
software availability, 20
Applicon, 135
Argentina, 123
ARM-PLAT, 136
ASPR (Automated System of Planning
Calculations of the State Planning
Committee, 96 (Table 6.2)
delayed completion, 100
difficulties of, 98–99, 100
equipment for, 98–99
and integration with ASUs, 99
norms for, 99
plan of, 98
update designs for, 99
ASU (Automated Management Systems), 95, 99
envisioned plans for, 97
functions of, 97
ASUP (Enterprise Automated Management Systems), 96, 97
industrial use of, 3

199

definition of, 128–29
and flexible systems, 91–92
goals of, 7, 140, 150–51
integration of, 93
and robots, 91
CIM, USA, 91
products, 93–94
Classroom computers, 25, 26, 27
generations, 27
production outlook for, 27
Western supply of, 27
CMEA, 79
economic effectiveness of, 72, 186
Fifteen Year Plan of, 177
Gorbachev's policy toward, 176–77
PC technology of, 3–4, 62
and the socialist alternative, 186
Soviet trade, 119, 120
and Western contacts, 186
and Warsaw Pact defense burden, 186
CNC (Computer Numerically Controlled machine tools), 128
Cocks, Paul, 182
CoCom (Coordinating Committee on Multilateral Export Controls)
agreements with, 190
export control role of, 71, 177, 189, 193
Collective Use Computer Centers. *See* VTsKP
Commodore, 20, 24, 64
Communist Party of the Soviet Union. *See* CPSU
Complex Program of Scientific-Technological Development, 185
Computer
"heart" of Third Industrial Revolution, 179
Computer-aided Design. *See* CAD
Computer-aided Manufacturing. *See* CAM
Computer-aided Process Planning. *See* CAPP
Computer education, USSR, 36, 38–39
assessment of, 31–32
beginnings of, 4, 6, 19–20
in contrast to USA, 30
goals of, 26, 27, 35
and ready-made software, 31
Computer education, instruction
ideals of, 23

levels of, 48–49
local variation of, 21
methods for, 21–22
Computer education, problems of, 20, 22–23, 75–76
condition for success in, 32
narrowness of, 30–31
and obsolete equipment, 49
pressure for reform in, 31–32, 35
Computer experiments, USSR, 119
Computer forecasts, USSR, 121
Computer languages, 28
compatibility of, 24
Soviet versions of, 24
Computer network, 7
and architecture, 90
conditions for, 89
and hardware availability, 89–90
and users' role, 90
Computer research, USSR
agenda, 116–17
analytic tools, 117
effects, 117
problem-specific models of, 118
simulation experience of, 117
Computer simulation analysis
as economic assessment, 115–16
major role, 126
Computer technology, USSR, 26
compared to USA, 179–80
Gorbachev's plan, 179–80
need for improvement, 93
Computer use, USSR
goals, 90
Computer-integrated manufacturing. *See* CIM
Computer-simulated analysis
as basis for reform, 107. 122
Computer-simulated experiments, 120
Computing and communications. *See* C&C
Cooper, J., 145
Coordinating Committee on Multilateral Export Controls. *See* CoCom
Corson Report, 184
Council for Ministers,
new superagencies for, 183
Council for Mutual Economic Assistance (CMEA)
computer development coordination with, 47

About the Authors

JEAN F. BOONE is senior research assistant in Soviet economics at the Congressional Research Service, Library of Congress. She has contributed to a variety of studies prepared for the U.S. Congress on the economies of communist-ruled countries.

RICHARD B. DOBSON is analyst for Soviet affairs, Office of Research, United States Information Agency. He did his undergraduate work in history at Stanford University, earned an M.A. in Soviet regional studies and a Ph.D. in sociology from Harvard University. Dr. Dobson taught at the University of Colorado at Colorado Springs and was a national fellow at the Hoover Institution. He has published numerous articles on society, sociology, and education in the USSR.

SEYMOUR E. GOODMAN is professor of management information systems and policy at the University of Arizona. He has held academic positions at Virginia, Princeton, and Chicago. Dr. Goodman's current research involves the international development of computing technology, technology transfer, computer-related public policy issues, and the design and implementation of computerized information systems for long-term trend and policy analysis.

JOHN P. HARDT is associate director for research coordination and senior specialist in Soviet economics at the Congressional Research Service, as well as adjunct professor of economics at the George Washington and Georgetown universities. He frequently accompanies congressional trade delegations to Eastern Europe and the People's Republic of China, and has edited and contributed to many volumes on the communist economies for the U.S. Congress.

RICHARD W. JUDY is senior research fellow at the Hudson Institute in Indianapolis and director of its Center for Soviet and East European Research. Formerly a professor of economics and computer science at the University of Toronto, he founded the Systems Research Group Inc. and the International Software Development Company in Toronto. His recent publications have appeared in *Soviet Economy* and *Gorbachev's Economic Plans,* published by the Joint Economic Committee of the U.S. Congress. His research interests encompass socioeconomic reform in the Eastern bloc, educational computing, and the application of expert systems to decision making in the public sector.

JANE M. LOMMEL is director of educational computing for the Indianapolis Public Schools. She received her Ph.D. from Kansas State University in educational technology. Her dissertation dealt with personal computer authorizing systems.

WILLIAM K. McHENRY received his Ph.D. in management information systems from the University of Arizona in 1985. He is an assistant professor at the School of Business Administration, Georgetown University. Professor McHenry's publications include articles about Soviet computing in *Communications of the ACM* and *Soviet Economy*. His current research interests include Soviet and Eastern European computing, the social impact of computing, data base management and information retrieval systems, group decision support systems, computer technology transfer, and organizational issues in the introduction of computing.

THOMAS H. NAYLOR is professor of economics and business administration at Duke University and managing director of The Naylor Group, an international management consulting firm specializing in strategic management. He had been founder and president for nine years of SIMPLAN Systems, Inc., a computer-based software firm. The author of 22 books, Dr. Naylor's two most recent ones are *The Corporate Strategy Matrix* (New York: Basic Books, 1986) and *The Gorbachev Strategy: Opening the Closed Society* (Lexington, MA: Lexington Books, 1988).

RICHARD F. STAAR is coordinator of the international studies program at the Hoover Institution, Stanford University. His most recent books include *USSR Foreign Policies After Detente,* revised edition (1987), and *Soviet Military Policy Since World War II* (1986), which he coauthored with William T. Lee.

ROSS A. STAPLETON, a doctoral candidate at the University of Arizona in Tucson, has been an exchange student in the USSR and a Fulbright fellow in Bulgaria. His research interests include small computer systems, applications and supporting industries with emphasis on the USSR and Eastern Europe, and research automation systems.

JOHN R. THOMAS is currently special assistant for Soviet science and technology in the Office of the Secretary of Defense. During 1984–87 he served in the science bureau of the U.S. Department of State as the American coordinator of U.S.-USSR science and technology programs. Prior to that, he worked for other government agencies analyzing USSR developments and implementing the 1972 U.S.-Soviet Science and Technology Agreement.

Other Books by Richard F. Staar

Arms Control: Myth Versus Reality (editor)
Aspects of Modern Communism (editor)
Communist Regimes in Eastern Europe
Long-Range Environmental Study of the Northern Tier of Eastern Europe in 1990–2000
Poland, 1944–1962: Sovietization of a Captive People
Public Diplomacy: USA Versus USSR (editor)
Soviet Military Policies Since World War Two (coauthor)
USSR Foreign Policies After Detente
Yearbook on International Communist Affairs (editor)